Barrie Thorne

Gender and Ethnicity in Schools

Gender and Ethnicity in Schools

This reader is one part of the MA in Education, Classroom Studies Module and the selection is therefore related to other material available to students. It is designed to evoke the critical understanding of students. Opinions expressed in it are not necessarily those of the course team or of the University.

If you would like to study this course, please write to the Central Enquiry Service, The Open University, Walton Hall, Milton Keynes MK7 6YZ, for a prospectus and application form. For more specific information write to The Higher Degrees Office at the same address.

Gender and Ethnicity in Schools

Ethnographic Accounts

Edited by Peter Woods and Martyn Hammersley

London and New York
in association with
The Open University

First published 1993
by Routledge
11 New Fetter Lane, London EC4P 4EE

Simultaneously published in the USA and Canada
by Routledge
29 West 35th Street, New York, NY 10001

© 1993 Selection and editorial material copyright The Open University

Phototypeset in Palatino by Intype, London
Printed and bound in Great Britain by Richard Clay Ltd, Bungay, Suffolk

British Library Cataloguing-in-Publication Data
A catalogue record for this book is available from the British Library

ISBN 0–415–08967–0
ISBN 0–415–08968–9 (pbk)

Library of Congress Cataloging in Publication Data
has been applied for.

Contents

List of figures and tables   vii
Acknowledgements   viii
Introduction   1

Part I Gender

1 Gender implications of children's playground culture   11
  Elizabeth Grugeon

2 Sex and the quiet schoolgirl   34
  Julia Stanley

3 We're back with Gobbo: the re-establishment of gender
  relations following a school merger   49
  Joan Draper

4 Humour as resistance   75
  W. S. Dubberley

5 Gender imbalances in the primary classroom: an interactional
  account   95
  Jane French and Peter French

6 An evaluation of a study of gender imbalance in primary
  classrooms   113
  Martyn Hammersley

Part II Ethnicity

7 Ethnicity and friendship: the contrast between sociometric
  research and fieldwork observation in primary school
  classrooms   127
  Martyn Denscombe, Halina Szulc, Caroline Patrick and Ann Wood

8 Beyond the white norm: the use of qualitative methods in the study of black youths' schooling in England   145
   Máirtin Mac an Ghaill

9 Genre, ethnocentricity and bilingualism in the English classroom   166
   A. Moore

10 School processes – an ethnographic study   191
   Cecile Wright

11 Case not proven: an evaluation of a study of teacher racism   216
   Peter Foster

Index   224

Figures and tables

FIGURES

6.1 Distribution of turns at talk for boys and girls   116
7.1 Sociomatrix I: Class A October 1983   133
7.2 Sociomatrix II: Class A April 1984   133
7.3 Sociomatrix III: Class B October 1983   134
7.4 Sociomatrix IV: Class B April 1984   134

TABLES

5,1 Interaction turns during the lesson   96
5.2 Detailed breakdown of interaction turns   97
6.1 The ranking of pupils in terms of percentage of turns at talk 116
7.1 Description of the two classes (October 1983)   129
7.2 Criswell Index: Classes A and B   132
7.3 Friendship choice by ethnic group   132

Acknowledgements

Chapters 1, 3 and 9 were specially commissioned for this volume. For permission to reproduce other material, acknowledgements are due to the following: Chapter 2, 'Sex and the quiet schoolgirl', reproduced from the *British Journal of Sociology of Education* with the kind permission of Carfax Publishing Company; Chapter 4, 'Humor as resistance', reproduced from the *International Journal of Qualitative Studies in Education* with the kind permission of Taylor & Francis; Chapter 6 'An evaluation of a study of gender imbalance in primary classrooms', reproduced from the *British Educational Research Journal* with the kind permission of Carfax Publishing Company; Chapter 7, 'Ethnicity and friendship: the contrast between sociometric research and fieldwork observation in primary school classrooms', reproduced from the *British Educational Research Journal* with the kind permission of Carfax Publishing Company; Chapter 8, 'Beyond the white norm: the use of qualitative methods in the study of black youths' schooling in England', reproduced from the *International Journal of Qualitative Studies in Education* with the kind permission of Taylor & Francis; Chapter 10, 'School processes – an ethnographic study' previously published in *Education for Some* by Trentham Books; Chapter 11, 'Case not proven: an evaluation of a study of teacher racism', reproduced from the *British Educational Research Journal* with the kind permission of Carfax Publishing Company.

Introduction

Over the years we have become ever more aware that children's experience of school life is very diverse, and a growing body of educational research has been concerned with exploring that experience. Ethnography has been the main research approach employed for this. It is well-suited to the task, as a result of its open-ended orientation and concern with detailed investigation of diverse perspectives and of the complexities of human social interaction.

Yet, in retrospect, it is disquieting to recognize how far the focus of ethnographic research has been influenced by prevailing educational and social concerns. Despite its much-quoted capacity to treat the familiar as strange, and (along with the 'new sociology of education' generally) to 'make' rather than 'take' problems for investigation (Hammersley and Atkinson 1983; Young 1971), the ethnography of the 1960s and 1970s inherited the primary emphasis given to social class characteristic of earlier quantitative work in the sociology of education. Other forms of social inequality were largely neglected, and there was a disproportionate amount of research on boys. Only more recently have researchers given serious attention to the experience of girls in schools and to the role of gender and of ethnic differences (and the interconnections among these and social class) in shaping children's experience of school. And in large part this has been stimulated by the influence of feminism and of arguments for multicultural and anti-racist education.

In this book we collect together some typical recent examples of ethnographic work which highlight gender and ethnicity and illustrate key features of ethnographic methodology. Some of these are new (chapters 1, 3 and 9); others are influential articles drawn from the journals. Discrimination and injustice, not all of it intended, is a common theme. So, too, is resistance, achievement in adversity, and the preservation of dignity. Most chapters concentrate on the pupils' perspectives, showing how qualitative methods can be used to explore their meanings and understandings, and to reveal worlds far different from those of many adults' assumptions.

We also examine some of the controversies to which this work has given rise. It is not surprising that disputes have arisen, given the current political significance of gender and ethnicity. Another source of controversy is the growing diversity of view among ethnographers about the form that their research should take, evidenced in debates about, for example, the extent to which ethnographers' accounts can represent reality, and the relationship between research and political and educational practice.

The book is in two parts. The first focuses on gender, the second on ethnicity and 'race'. In each part the final chapter is a methodological critique of one of the previous chapters. Some of the criticisms made of these chapters, and no doubt additional ones, could be applied to the other chapters as well. We hope, therefore, that taken together the papers and the critiques will show some of the strengths and weaknesses of the ethnographic approach. Some advances in balance and rigour may have been made since the 1970s. However, as Hammersley and Foster show, there is a constant need for vigilance and self-reflectiveness in qualitative, as in all, research; and this would appear to be especially important in the sensitive areas under review here.

In chapter 1, Grugeon considers the oral culture of the playground, and particularly the games that girls play. She argues that this is a subversive culture, opposed to the dominant culture and challenging the girls' powerlessness in the classroom. It both provides information about the social order, especially gender, and a means to challenge it. It presents opportunities to explore girls' roles, relationships and expectations. This culture is child initiated and mediated, and largely untouched by adults. Many of the games have a long history, surviving by being handed down from older to younger girls within the 5–9-years-old range. But it is not just sentiment that keeps them alive. Grugeon argues that the preservation of this culture has much to do with children's receptivity at that age to this kind of oral activity, the highly textured nature of the language form, and prevailing structures within the social order. The article is notable for the rich detail of young children's activity, much of it conducted in secret, and for the discovery of new formulations.

Grugeon refers to the boys' dominance in the playground with their main activity of football, and the girls being forced into more reclusive pastimes. This dominance operates more generally, and the girls' strategy of apparent retreat is reflected also in their demeanour in mixed-sex situations, giving rise to a prominent characteristic of many schoolgirls – their 'quietness'. Stanley argues, in chapter 2, that this has contributed to a stereotype of female passivity and weakness. She was concerned to discover pupils' own understandings and spent over a year in a West Midlands comprehensive school, using ethnographic techniques. Both pupils and teachers had stereotypical images of boys' and girls' capabilities at school subjects, and of their future destinations. One of the factors behind girls' traditional choice of subjects seemed to be their 'quietness', and a failure to communicate with teachers, which reinforces conventional teacher attitudes. However, 'quietness' is not an inherent female attribute, as is clear from the girls' own views and their variable behaviour (this challenge to the stereotype puzzled the boys); nor is it a product of differential growth rates during puberty and adolescence. It is an adaptation to social circumstances, a highly successful one, argues Stanley, since it deals with the stressful demands imposed on them at school, and symbolizes resistance to any assumptions of their inferiority. It is not so much 'quiet and weak', therefore, as 'silent and strong'.

Draper, in chapter 3, provides further commentary on the theme of male dominance–female resistance in a study of the amalgamation of three secondary schools (two of them single-sex) into one comprehensive. Institutional change, especially non-regularized change, is one of those 'natural experiments' beloved of qualitative researchers. It disrupts established routines and throws into relief the main structures upon which social order rests. One of these structures is gender relations, and Draper shows how these were highlighted during the transition. Many boys and girls were brought together after years apart. There followed a 'process of re-establishment' (Ball 1980), wherein boys sought to secure what they saw as their traditional male superiority. Draper examines the strategies used by the boys and the responses of the girls in such areas as general behaviour, the curriculum, academic achievement and appearance. Overall, the article highlights several ways in which gender issues are brought, or re-brought, to prominence during non-regularized status passage (Glaser and Strauss 1968), and how it is perceived and managed by the various participants. It also illustrates the work of a 'teacher-researcher', as Draper herself was involved in the transition and carried out the work while a full-time teacher in the school.

In chapter 4, Dubberley shows one approach to the complexities of the interrelationship between gender and social class. He argues that, at least in the school he studied, social class is the predominant factor, though sexism abounded in teacher–teacher, pupil–pupil and teacher–pupil relationships. Teacher–pupil interaction has often been represented in terms of culture conflict. Dubberley traces the origins of this conflict in his research school, and finds it to be in the imported middle-class culture of the teachers impacting against the home-grown local pit community of which the school and pupils are a part. The culture of this community is centred around the digging of coal. Humour is a prominent feature of this culture. It fortifies the self against hardship, and tests for membership. The teachers, no less, are tested through typically rough-edged humour. If they showed weakness or misunderstanding they invited attack, since that indicated that they were unworthy of being a teacher. The 'lads' tested them on the basis of the rules of acceptable behaviour from the perspective of a working-class male of the community. Women teachers who were not 'hard' enough, and male teachers who adopted bogus images, were particularly badly treated. The 'lasses' were even more unrelenting, and teachers were easily outmanoeuvred and outwitted, male teachers especially feeling the weight of the lasses' sexual power. This was not simply anarchic behaviour from low ability children. They wanted a good education, and showed high levels of wit, vitality and creativity in their resistance. They responded well to some teachers, those who could have, and take, a laugh; who showed a 'tough love and wry humour' with pupils, and had the knack of accommodating to the contradictions between school and the culture of the community. Unsuccessful teachers asserted their own culture as dominant, and gave offence with sarcasm and insults. Dubberley argues that the exploitation of women, through the rampant sexism in the school, is not a matter of patriarchy, but is linked to the socio-economic structure, and in particular in this instance to the social relations surrounding the production of coal. A solution to this kind of counter-productive culture clash, he argues, is more community control over educational processes.

One of the most common concerns in research dealing with gender difference in orientation to school, as we saw with Stanley's chapter, is the 'quietness' of girls. Of course, this quietness is relative to the 'noisiness' of boys. A growing body of research has been concerned with the differential participation of boys and girls in lessons, and the extent to which teachers' attention is concentrated on the former at the expense of the latter. Much research on this topic has been quantitative, focusing exclusively on differences in the amount of attention of various types received by boys and girls. What has been neglected in this work is study of the patterns of classroom interaction that generate these differences and the reasons for the differential participation of girls and boys. In chapter 5, French and French examine the distribution of teachers' attention between girls and boys in a primary school lesson. They begin from quantitative differences in participation, but go on to provide a qualitative analysis of classroom processes designed to show how, by attention-seeking strategies, a small number of boys monopolize the teacher's attention. As a result of such strategies, they suggest, teachers are manipulated into giving more attention to boys than to girls.

We noted earlier how important it is that ethnographic work be subjected to detailed methodological assessment. In the final chapter of this first part of the book, Hammersley provides a critical assessment of French and French's principle. He argues that they make implicit assumptions about the importance of differential participation by boys and girls in lessons, and suggests that these are not entirely convincing. He also explores the quantitative data that they supply, looking at alternative interpretations of them. In particular, he questions whether turns-at-talk is an adequate measure of teacher attention, and he points to the danger of basing generalizations about differential patterns of classroom participation by girls and boys on the study of a single lesson.

The first four chapters in part II illustrate aspects of the qualitative method in the study of 'race' and ethnicity in schools. In chapter 7, Denscombe and his colleagues challenge the findings of previous work that children in primary schools belong to discrete ethnic friendship groups. This conclusion had been indicated by the results of sociometric tests with pupils in a wide range of schools. But it did not accord with the observations of teachers in the schools of Denscombe's research. The researchers used sociometric tests of nominated contacts *and* long-term fieldwork observation of actual contacts between pupils during free association in both class and playground. The sociometry seemed to indicate the usual pattern of ethnic grouping, but the fieldwork showed a high degree of racial integration, thus supporting the teachers' observations. Quantitative measures select from the range of interaction, and may be misleading if taken as indicative of the whole range. They also are not designed to penetrate pupils' understandings of 'friendship'. This raised the question of the validity of sociometric tests and quantitative surveys used on their own as methods of investigating pupils' relationships. The combination of quantitative and qualitative, it would seem, provides a much sounder basis for drawing conclusions (see, for example, Hargreaves 1967; Lacey 1970, 1976).

In chapter 8, Mac an Ghaill shows how the use of qualitative method can change the initial conceptualization of a problem, and thus how theory becomes 'grounded' in data (Glaser and Strauss 1967). When he began his research on Asian and Afro-Caribbean students, his research design 'implicitly shared the white norm of classifying black students as a "problem" '. As the work progressed, however, and he talked more and more with the students, he came to a new perspective. Placing the students at the centre of the enquiry enabled the researcher to build up a graphic picture of alienated black youth, operating in a society structured by 'race' and gender at several levels.

He began to see them, therefore, as the victims, rather than the perpetrators. They have developed a 'different reality' from the white population, which continues to see them in deviant terms, contesting the system, and thus, for the Afro-Caribbeans, contributing to their 'educational underachievement'.

What they are contesting, argues Mac an Ghaill, is racism, and the legitimation of a system based on racism. He sees their behaviour as 'coping strategies', as 'resistance within accommodation', and the subculture that they developed as a legitimate response to discriminatory and unjust pressures. His discussions with pupils led him also to reformulate his approach to their parents, placing his questions in a wider context embracing their experiences of immigration, housing and work. This enabled him to identify a connection between the formation of pupil groups and subcultures and the 'parent' culture, suggesting a commonality of experience among this particular sector of the working class, who are 'creating their own history within their community'.

Moore, in chapter 9, shows that even where teachers are adopting a declared multicultural policy, their view of reality can still be rooted in their own culture. This ethnocentricism prevents their appreciating what a minority ethnic bilingual pupil has to offer, and leads them to challenge not only surface features of writing such as grammar and punctuation, but substantive content and style. They treat their own approach as the only 'correct' one. In the first example he discusses, Moore considers why an unconscious and unintended attempt to enculturate did not succeed and may have helped alienate the pupil from his work. School policy in general was informed by Cummins's theory of 'common underlying proficiency'. While helpful to some degree, its major drawback of ignoring the differences between languages was not recognized. Moore contrasts the experience of another Bangladeshi pupil whose work was treated in a more appropriate way. The teacher here was more reflective and multi-ethnic oriented, could distance herself from her own cultural forms, and situated the style and content of the pupil's writing within his own culture. She made surface-feature corrections, but built on the pupil's reality and encouraged emergent skills. The pupil responded with improvements in his writing, some totally unexpected. This coincided with some remarkable developments in his work elsewhere. While there might have been a range of factors influencing these outcomes, it would seem that the contrasting pedagogies figured prominently among them.

In a widely cited article (chapter 10), Cecile Wright examines social processes in two comprehensive schools that she believes led to the underachievement of Afro-Caribbean children in these schools. In many respects her concerns parallel those of Mac an Ghaill and Moore.

She reports differential treatment of black pupils in lessons and in allocation to remedial groups and to sets, and claims that this led Afro-Caribbean pupils to develop a negative attitude towards school and that this in turn served to reinforce stereotypes of them and their underachievement. Her work represents one of the most influential accounts of the process by which the English education system is believed to disadvantage Afro-Caribbean pupils.

The final chapter of the book provides a critical assessment of Wright's article. Peter Foster argues that the evidence on which she bases her claims does not supply convincing support for them. In documenting the existence of differential treatment of the Afro-Caribbean pupils by teachers, she relies primarily on reports from a small number of teachers and on the accounts of some of the pupils, elicited in group interviews; rather than on direct observational evidence. And she takes little account of possible sources of error in these reports. Furthermore, she fails to establish the causal relationship between the differential treatment she claims to have documented and the attitudes and underachievement of Afro-Caribbean pupils. Foster points out that the teachers could simply have been responding to the behaviour of the pupils. His critique highlights the difficulties that ethnographic research sometimes has in establishing policy-relevant claims, especially in controversial areas. (For further discussion between Wright and Foster about these issues, see Wright 1990 and Foster 1991).

CONCLUSION

There is now a wide range of ethnographic research looking at the role of gender and ethnicity in school processes. It is a growing field, adding considerably to our understanding of the process of schooling and its role in the wider society. This book provides a sample of work in the area, indicating many of the approaches to be found in the literature and some of the controversial issues raised. We hope that it will stimulate further studies, studies that build on this work both substantively and methodologically.

REFERENCES

Ball, S. J. (1980) 'Initial encounters in the classroom and the process of establishment', in P. Woods (ed.) *Pupil Strategies*, London: Croom Helm.

Foster, P. (1991) 'Cases still not proven: a reply to Cecile Wright', *British Educational Research Journal* 17(2): 165–70.

Glaser, B. G. and Strauss, A. L. (1967) *The Discovery of Grounded Theory*, London: Weidenfeld & Nicolson.

Glaser, B. and Strauss, A. (1968) *Time for Dying*, Chicago, Illinois: Aldine.

Hammersley, M. and Atkinson, P. (1983) *Ethnography: Principles in Practice*, London: Tavistock.

Hargreaves, D. H. (1967) *Social Relations in a Secondary School*, London: Routledge & Kegan Paul.

Lacey, C. (1970) *Hightown Grammar*, Manchester: Manchester University Press.

—— (1976) 'Problems of sociological fieldwork: a review of the methodology of *Hightown Grammar*', in M. Hammersley and P. Woods (eds) *The Process of Schooling*, London: Routledge & Kegan Paul.

Wright, C. (1990) 'Comments on a reply to the article by P. Foster', *British Educational Research Journal* 16(4): 351–5.

Young, M. F. D. (1971) *Knowledge and Control: New Directions for the Sociology of Education*, London: Collier-Macmillan.

Part I

Gender

Chapter 1

Gender implications of children's playground culture

Elizabeth Grugeon

INTRODUCTION

Starting school at the age of 5 is daunting. Whatever their previous pre-school experience – nursery, playgroup, four-plus unit – for most children the move into statutory schooling requires the most formidable readjustment. It is a time of considerable stress which parents and teachers attempt to buffer in a variety of thoughtful ways. Becoming a pupil, entering the new culture of the school, means learning new patterns of behaviour, developing new expectations and relationships (Willes 1983). Adult intervention in this process tends to focus on the child's role as a member of a new community which is predominantly concerned with the child's development as a learner. The demands are predictable, the process well-structured. Parents and teachers consciously mediate this process, ensuring as easy a transition into the new culture as possible. In this brief study, I want to explore the possibility that the children themselves have a means of negotiating this particular status passage that is often overlooked.

On the school playground there is also a culture to be negotiated and it is every bit as complex, structured and rule-bound as anything that goes on in the classroom. Entering this culture requires learning sets of rules and rituals which are quite as arbitrary as those produced by the education system. While the culture of childhood is contextualized by the adult world, it is also the context within which children socialize one another as well as with each other (Geertz 1975: 12). The playground is the site for the rehearsal and exploration of adult roles.

Observation on playgrounds also suggests that the process of entering the culture may be different for girls and boys. A brief glance at any infant or lower school playground will usually reveal that boys and girls are not playing together and may also show different kinds of grouping, the girls in small inward-looking groups often sitting down, the boys running about.

A recent study in Norwich (Stutz 1992) involving over 500 pupils aged from 7 to 14 observed that, on the playground, boys and girls tended to play separately.

Certain patterns of behaviour emerged which were repeated with slight variations in each of the playgrounds visited. These patterns clearly showed in the differences discernible between the girls' and boys' play.

Girls' play seemed to be characterized by a physical closeness and intimacy. They played in 'little or big circles or knots, always facing into the centre'. Sometimes sitting in small groups, at other times in large circles, they were observed playing 'complicated, and energetic games' where it appeared that

they all know exactly what they are doing although one cannot see them discussing any plans or rules, and it is difficult to understand from the outside what the rules are. These games may come into being quite suddenly and then, just as quickly, come to an abrupt but happy end. Or they go on for quite a long time. In all these games the girls are completely absorbed. It is clear that they have a well developed communication system.

Another characteristic of the girls' play that was observed

was the universality of their sociability and friendliness. They all seemed happy and well integrated with their friends and I was never aware of any disharmony, quarrelling or competitiveness between them.

It seemed that boys would often stand on the edge watching these games with evident interest and respect.

On a number of occasions they joined in and the girls showed no sign of either pleasure or displeasure at this; they just accepted them as a matter of course. And I never saw a boy spoiling such a game. On a number of occasions I noticed girls teaching boys how to skip and do hand clapping or dipping games, the boys happily following instructions.

The Norwich research provides further evidence of the co-operative nature of girls' play in the large variety of singing, rhyming, hand-clapping and dipping games that were observed. In contrast, a dominant feature of the boys' play was its competitiveness and 'a combative or confrontational tendency which can easily flare up into a fight'. Boys' play seemed to lack 'the sociability which was such a marked feature with the girls' (Stutz 1992: 26).

There is evidently a fairly rigid gender separation in children's play at school and in the culture of childhood itself. Looking more closely at some of the cultural practices involved in this process of socialization in the playground, it is possible to isolate some of the ways in which girls acquire a social identity, largely in the company of other girls.

I first became aware of this phenomenon – an informal status passage – when my daughter Jessica started school. She was just 5 and playing with Sarah, nearly 7, in the back garden. I could see that Sarah was teaching her an elaborate hand-clapping routine. They were deeply engrossed in getting the movements right. Jessica was concentrating ferociously; I was witnessing an example of the process of apprenticeship by which older girls pass on to younger girls the traditional games of an oral culture which seems to be their exclusive property (Opie and Opie 1985). Later, I asked Jessica to show me what she and Sarah had been doing and was amazed to discover that in her first six weeks at school she had acquired a repertoire of songs and games that were certainly not part of the mainstream curriculum. I had to admit that I was surprised by the number of rhymes she had learnt in such a short time; even more by their subject matter. The oral culture of the playground engaged with issues of birth, death, courtship and marriage, using a dynamic, dramatic vocabulary (Ashton-Warner 1980): 'supersonic', 'dynamite', 'fart', 'willy', and played with nonsense, rhyme and rhythm: 'rom pom pooli', 'elli elli chickali, chickali', 'ticker tacker tooey'. The narrative structures 'and this is how my story goes', 'one day when I was walking', 'and this is what she said' – were a far cry from the adult-mediated text of her first reading schemes (see Appendix). I made a recording and put it in a drawer.

It was some years later that I became interested again. I had returned to school playgrounds as a lecturer in education and the Opies' book *The Singing Game* had just been published. All Jessica's songs were there, some were very old, others from far away. I started to observe and talk to children as I crossed their playgrounds and soon had an increasing collection of examples.

COLLECTING AND ANALYSING THE EVIDENCE

To begin with, I did not have a particular methodology: the process of collecting examples continued over a period of years in a random way. However, I did develop certain procedural rules. It was important to respect the players' privacy. These games are not intended for public performance or adult ears. Permission to observe, record and photograph had to be obtained, not only from the schools but from the players.

Whenever possible, I taped the songs in the playground and occasionally obtained permission to photograph the action. It is helpful to record these games as they are being played in a naturalistic setting.

It is essential to hear them, as each one has a different tune and the mode of delivery, speed, intonation and emphasis tells the listener a great deal about the players' attitudes. Versions collected indoors, in more formal interview situations, lack dynamic and dramatic immediacy; often the players forget what comes next or feel constrained about the appropriate actions and accompanying movements. Written versions recorded in notebooks give no sense of the urgency of the players nor of the particular effects they are trying to create. The games are essentially unselfconscious existential events, no two are ever the same in performance.

As my collection grew, so did the need for some explanation of the phenomena. I began to talk to older girls, 11- and 12-year-olds, to see what light they could throw on a process which they had only recently outgrown. A series of interviews conducted at home and in school provided interesting insights. I would play a sample recording of the games I had collected and ask them to tell me what games they remembered playing, who had played them, where and when they had played them, how they had learned to play them and whether boys had joined in. I also asked them about playing generally, what other games they had played at school and after school. At the same time, I continued to talk to younger children and recorded their perceptions of the process as they were involved in it. Their responses gradually began to provide a context for the examples I had been collecting. They reinforced my impression of the gender specificity of particular games and raised questions about their role in the players' acquisition of their social identity.

Thus, I became engaged in looking for a theoretical explanation for the continued existence of an oral tradition that is historically constructed and socially maintained by very young children. In this study I want to focus on the way gender identity may have a powerful structuring role in the development of social relationships. Concentrating on those games which are the exclusive property of girls, I want to consider how far they enable the players to confront and experiment with gender stereotypes and how far they may reinforce those stereotypes.

THE GIRLS' PERSPECTIVE

Once I had started listening to the texts of their games, I became aware that when the bell rings for playtime, schoolchildren move into a different domain; the playground is the site of a thriving oral culture, a subversive counter-culture to the official school culture. Listening carefully to the rhymes and songs which accompany their games reveals the extent to which their interests and concerns are at variance with the dominant culture of the classroom they have just left. These concerns reflect and challenge their powerlessness in the school system.

Teachers are in the front line of attack:

On top of a mountain
all covered in sand,
I once shot my teacher
with an elastic band.

I shot him with pleasure, I shot him with pride,
I shot my poor teacher right on his backside.
He fell down the mountain, he fell on his head,
And then my poor teacher,
He dropped right down dead.

I went to the funeral,
I went to his grave,
I didn't throw flowers,
I threw a grenade.

Many rhymes like this, often sung to familiar tunes, deal with aspects of their lives that are beyond their control:

School dinners, school dinners,
Burnt baked beans, burnt baked beans.
Soggy semolina, soggy semolina,
I feel sick
Toilet quick
It's too late
I've done it on the plate.

The issues they touch extend beyond the playground:

Margaret Thatcher stick her in a bin
Put the lid on, sellotape her in.
If she gets out, hit her on the head,
Glory, glory Maggie Thatcher's dead.

They deal with the taboos of sex and death, drawing on the culture that they are exposed to both inside and outside school:

Jesus Christ super star,
Went round the corner on a Yamaha.
Did a skid, killed a kid,
Caught his balls on a dustbin lid.

Nursery rhymes, traditional and popular songs are subverted to explore taboos on safe territory:

Jack and Jill went up the hill
To fetch a pail of water,
I don't know what they did up there
But now they've got a daughter.

Oh you'll never get to heaven
On a piece of glass
'cos a piece of glass
Will cut your arse.

All this has been documented and explored in Iona and Peter Opie's scholarly and exhaustive studies of children's lore and language which, as they are able to demonstrate, seems scarcely to alter from generation to generation. The Opies' collections are a unique source for locating and identifying the origins of the rhymes and games being played on school playgrounds today: they are my own first point of reference.

Playground culture involves a unique kind of play which has received very little attention, and that chiefly from folklorists and anthropologists; linguists and psychologists have rarely considered ethnographic studies of speech play as a social phenomenon; the ludic aspects of language have been generally ignored (Kirshenblatt-Gimblett 1976: 2). In addition, female peer group interaction has received little attention (Romaine 1984: 185). While boys and girls undoubtedly share in the language and lore of the playground – the ritual insults, the flaunting of taboos, parodies of the adult world – there are games which are solely played by girls. Looking at the themes and issues they explore it becomes obvious why. Talking to girls gives an idea of the overlap and exclusivity of certain kinds of games, including clapping, which are almost the exclusive preserve of young girls. Clapping is often the non-verbal signal for the start of an intensive and meticulous exchange of bodily movements, accompanied by ritualistic chants. An 8-year-old explained 'There's three sorts of clapping, one where you just go plain and then there's one where you've got to do it in angles, then there's the fancy ones . . . and I don't know any more of clapping things'. She demonstrated the way fancy clapping would accompany one of their most popular games at the moment. It has a very complex syncopated rhythm which cannot be transcribed and was delivered at high speed.

Apples on sticks
They make me sick,
They make my heart go two, four, six.

Not because you're dirty,
Not because you're clean,
Because you kissed the boy behind the magazine.
Come on girls let's have some fun,
Because here comes Lee Pu [or any other boy's name] with his pants
    undone.
He can wibble, he can wobble,
He can do the splits,
But I bet you ten quid he can't do this.
Count to fifteen with his eyes shut
One, two, three, four, five . . . fifteen.
Eeny, meeny, dessameeny,
You are the one ameeny.
Education liberation, I like you.
Town, town baby, down by the riverside.
Sweet, sweet baby, no place to go,
Caught you with your boyfriend.
Naughty, naughty,
Stole a bit of candy?
Greedy pig.
Wouldn't do the dishes,
Lazy, lazy,
Jumped out of the window,
Flipping crazy.

'Fancy claps' and the accompanying words have evidently been picked
up in apprenticeship with older girls. 'We heard some girls on the
playground and then we asked them, me and a friend, we went
together and asked two people to help us and then we gradually got
it right'. It is demanding, 'you first put your hands together and
there's another person, you sort of knock them between and lift them
up and hold them back and then you've got to go by side to side,
click your fingers . . . when I said count to fifteen, you've got to do
it with your eyes shut, the fancy claps, which is quite hard.'

One of the features of two girls' talk, looking back at their first
school, is their surprise and pleasure that things had been like that:

Jess: The thing about lower school was that the whole school did
        everything together.
Lucy: We were all so friendly, weren't we?
Jess: I mean, whereas in this school you wouldn't shout to every-
        one 'Anybody for Rover!' or anything.
Lucy: No, we used to go round with our arms over each other.
Jess: There'd be about a row of twelve.

Lucy: Who wants to play?

Jess: Who wants to play? Yeah I can remember that and the whole school would be playing one game and you wouldn't think anything of it.

Jess: It was so much more friendly. I suppose it's probably because we were younger but there were so many games we thought up but nowadays, you just wouldn't do that.

This part of the discussion referred to games played by boys and girls together. However, they remind each other that the boys did not join in their singing games and Jess remarks, 'I reckon in a way most of the things that girls did were just far more imaginative to what the boys were doing but they joined in with a few of the things we were doing and it was a load more friendly than it is at a middle school but . . . when you look back and see all the things you've, sort of, done, it was really pretty amazing.'

They suggest that the boys did join in the less elaborate games, particularly the rude ones, but more often they comment on the absence of the boys. Their explanation is the gender specificity of the songs:

Lucy: Because no, most of them were about girls though, weren't they?

Jess: Yeah, I mean.

Lucy: I mean it was, I mean you'd never catch the boys singing the one about, um, 'please will you marry me'.

Jess: No.

Lucy: It's too . . .

Jess: I mean that was just sissy, wasn't it?

Lucy: Yeah, the boys would never have been seen dead doing that.

Jess: I reckon, I think, um Robert sang the one about the ten foot willy.

Lucy: Oh yes the boys sang *that* one, because that was the rude one and they sang 'Batman and Robin in the batmobile'.

Jess: Yeah they sang all the Batman ones and that.

Lucy: But they didn't sing things like, 'When Suzie was a baby' and things like that.

Jess: I don't, I can't think where the boys must have been . . . I didn't even notice what the boys were doing when we were playing our games.

Their emphasis suggests a flourishing girls' culture on the playground and agrees with the Opies' observation that 'the games are now under the haphazard guardianship of girls about seven to nine years' (Opie and Opie 1985: 2). It seems to be a child-mediated culture, a kind of socialization which is very different from the adult-mediated construct that attempts to constitute them as social beings in their homes and the classroom. *Centuries of Childhood* (Aries 1973) shows how very recently children have been established as identifiable social beings; the concept of childhood is a relatively recent phenomenon. With it has come the social construction of children and a developmental model that marks out stages, like rungs on a ladder: teething, talking, walking, reading, all have their appointed times; parents and professionals can refer to norms which have come to seem so natural that they are taken for granted. Becoming socialized is a carefully monitored process.

However, the playground is a place where children have sway and can maintain an alternative culture, largely unobserved. This includes naughty and exciting language which is learnt, recited and performed to, with vitality. *The Singing Game* includes two examples which the Opies feel are 'more daring than most' in that they include explicit sexual reference such as 'I slept with me granny, And tickled 'er fanny'. Jessica admitted to knowing a version where the caravan had 'a hole in the middle/where I did my piddle'.

GAMES FOR GIRLS ONLY

Songs like 'I'm a little Dutch girl', 'When Suzie was a baby', 'My Mummy is a baker' and 'My boyfriend's name is Tony' seem, on the face of it, to prefigure and reflect their future as women in terms of the discourse of romantic love. In these games we see the other side of the coin: far from being the means of challenging the world around them, they seem to accede to the stereotypes, to accept and explore them. In playing these games they are like the little girls Carolyn Steedman writes about in *The Tidy House* (Steedman 1982: 25) taking part in the process of their own socialization, using these games to help them to understand the social beliefs that have brought them into being. These games are concerned with marriage, motherhood, family relationships, birth and death.

These are all the themes which they also explore in what Lucy and Jessica refer to as their 'plays'. These took place alongside the singing games, and gradually, as they moved up the school, began to take over. When a young neighbour arrived in school, Jessica was in the fourth year and preparing to move on to middle school. Looking back she was interested in the speed with which the younger girl had picked up the traditional lore, but felt that she herself was now growing out of it.

When Kristy came three years later, she picked them up and did them as well, you know, she was going along 'I've lost my bra in my boyfriend's car', all the time and it really got up my nose because you know, you sort of think you were too 'hard' to do that right then and we were just all too busy with the plays we were doing.

They refer to their plays several times during their discussion,

Jess: After we stopped sort of doing those singing things, we always used to do plays, didn't we? We had a little secret place we'd go in, somewhere round the corner.
Lucy: Oh yeah and we used to make up plays.
Jess: And everybody got kidnapped and things.

They talk about how they went down behind the swimming pool in winter, out of bounds, to make up plays. Their talk about the singing games is frequently diverted as they remember these games.

Jess: And we always used to play mums and dads.
Lucy: And you were always the mum.
Jess: I was always the mum.
Lucy: Or the dad
Jess: It was so unfair, they would say I want to be baby so I used to lug these people the same size as me around.
Lucy: It was Lyn and Rhiannon were always the babies, weren't they?
Jess: Yeah, I know.
Lucy: Or the big sisters.
Jess: Something like that.
Lucy: And you were always the mother. I remember that.

Clearly Jessica did not relish this role. What seems to have been happening in these plays is much more than an enactment of their future roles; it sounds more like a tough negotiation and exploration of their present roles and relationships. However, it is significant that being mother seems to have been the least desirable role. Perhaps, like the little girls in *The Tidy House*, they are also aware that being mother rarely appears to be particularly rewarding or enjoyable in real life.

Carolyn Steedman (1982: 94) suggests that it is not surprising that girls think, write, talk and play with the ideas of motherhood; in contemporary society, nearly all children have experienced being mothered by women and the mother's role is particularly comprehensible, 'because it is visible and produces concrete results'. The singing games often clearly represent this, 'When Suzie was a mummy, she went cook, cook, cook, cook, cook/When Suzie was a granny she went, knit, knit, knit, knit, knit'.

'I'm a little Dutch girl' is the oldest game in Jessica's repertoire. It appears in a section of *The Singing Game* which the Opies' call 'Mimicry'; these are games in which the players depict, with appropriate actions, a succession of states of life. Robert Louis Stevenson referred to them as 'juvenile lyrical drama' but the Opies feel that there is nothing creative about them: 'The activities they mimic, or the people they characterize under the guidance of tradition are painfully humdrum . . . what we are seeing is ourselves through their eyes' (Opie and Opie 1985: 285).

In the case of the little Dutch girl, the drama is extraordinarily protracted: eighteen verses of skipping back and forth. It is a simple story of courtship, marriage, married life: 'Now we've got a baby', old age, and death. In Jessica's version both courtship and death take a very long time.

Looking back, they are surprised that they had apparently enjoyed such a protracted ritual.

Jess: I can remember I always used to be the little Dutch boy.

Lucy: I can remember that.

Jess: And you were always the girl and I used to think cor that's really unfair. I want to be the Dutch girl because she does all the . . . I just say no you can't marry me.

Lucy: I remember I was always glad that I was the smallest then.

Jess: But we used to do a sort of dance, didn't we?

Lucy: Yeah.

Jess: We sort of, we used to sort of . . .

Lucy: Just kept sort of prancing forwards.

Jess: And when you're witches 'now we're witches, witches', sort of prancing about like witches.

Lucy: We used to float around for ghosts and . . .

Jess: God! I used to really sort of enjoy doing that one apart from the fact that. . .

Lucy: It's boring isn't it?

Jess: Yeah, I don't know how I could have liked it, I mean it sort of goes on and on and on.

Lucy: I quite like the bit after you were dead because then it just sort of hurried up but once you were sort of 'now will you marry me marry me', that was really boring.

It is interesting to note here that it is the Dutch girl in this game who takes all the initiatives and controls the drama; the game does not represent the standard stereotype of romantic courtship.

The ritualistic drama of 'I'm a little Dutch girl' is repeated in 'When Suzie was a baby' which also mimics and rehearses a girl's expectation of life. The Opies trace it to a popular song of the eighteenth and nineteenth centuries, 'When I was a Lady', a song 'characterized by a devil-may-care attitude to life's responsibilities', which has re-appeared as a clapping game on the twentieth-century playground. In the late 1960s it apparently became very popular and additional stages and descriptions of Suzie's life were added. The two girls remember this as a particularly popular game.

Jess: Oh gosh, we did that all the time practically.
Lucy: Except, you know, the one where Suzie was a schoolgirl and it goes Miss, Miss, I can't do this – do you remember what we used to say?
Jess: Oh yes we used to say.
Lucy: Miss Miss I need a piss.
Jess: I used to think cor that's rude. I remember doing that all the time.

The daring rudeness of the teenage Suzie losing her knickers and leaving her bra in the boyfriend's car was also a major attraction.

These games would seem to be a creative exploration of the gender stereotypes which young girls are encountering. Playing them undoubtedly contributes to their knowledge about what it means to be female (James 1990), but they are by no means innocent or passive in the reception and processing of this information. They have arrived at school with preconceived ideas about their sex roles (Oakley 1972; Maccoby and Jacklin 1975) and may well be aware of the requirement to conform to certain expectations in the culture of the school (Clarri-coates 1978) or their homes. When I asked one of my informants why she thought boys did not play the singing games, she replied, 'I suppose it's tradition, I mean, a girl grows up and gets shoved a load of toys and dolls and a boy gets shoved an action man.' Talking about the 'rudeness' of many of the rhymes, another admitted to a double standard, 'We'd never sort of do that when our mums and dads were around . . . such a goody-goody'.

Even before they go to school, playing at mummies and daddies, children are forming generalizable rules with which they can explore the complexities of gender relationships in the future (James 1990). By the time they reach the gender segregation of the playground during the first year at school it may be argued that these meanings are no longer in the future but embedded in the cultural practices of child-hood itself and it is these that they are passing on to one another.

But what exactly are girls passing on when they play these games? Not the versions of true love of the popular culture that surrounds them nor versions that entirely reflect the stereotypes. Listening to the words of the songs which accompany these games and watching the actions involved, a robust and challenging tone is apparent – parodying and ridiculing. Men and boys are mocked, 'He bent down to kiss her/but WOW did he miss her', 'Come on girls, let's have some fun/Here comes Andrew with his pants undone', 'He jumped in the lake and he swallowed a snake/And came up with a belly ache', 'I gave my love an apple/I gave my love a pear/I gave my love a kiss on the lips/And threw him down the stair'. In many versions the boyfriend is thrown around until he loses his underpants. Boyfriends have 'pickles' on their nose and are in danger of having willies drasti-cally shortened and balls caught in barbed wire.

However, the girls are undoubtedly provoked and the language of their games provides a peaceful means of retaliation. A conversation with 9-year-old girls who had just transferred to middle school illus-trates a real problem for girls: the boys' domination of the physical space on the playground.

The girls suggest that games like football may well be the reason why they are unable to play some of the games they enjoyed on their lower school playground.

Ann: Sometimes in the playground it's really horrible because the boys, um, won't let you play, you have to be stuck in the corner.

Maria: And they catch your balls sometimes and throw them.

Charnjit: And then you walk over there and another boy picks it up and throws it and you have to walk back again.

Emma: See what the girls do, 'cos boys take up a lot of room playing football, is sit in little corners.

Kate: The boys take up most of the playground, so we sit in the little corners.

(Grugeon and Woods 1990)

Clearly, there was no room for group skipping activities or hand-clapping and dancing games on this playground, even if the girls had still felt these were appropriate. As recent research has observed

it is plain that football, when played in the same area with other games, causes a number of problems and sometimes leads to unpleasantness and possible rowdiness. If left unchecked it can dominate the whole playground area and those not playing i.e. the quieter boys, as well as girls, are pushed to the periphery and made to feel they are in the way.

(Stutz 1992: 25)

SOCIALIZATION AND CHALLENGE

There is no doubt that clapping games help little girls in their first weeks at school; they are able to participate in non-threatening group interaction, to play with language, to rehearse adult roles, to investigate and challenge social and sexual aspects of the world and to become involved in peer group relationships; the gender specificity of the games introduces them to a girls' culture. The playground is indeed a site for cultural transmission and socialization where girls may work out rules of behaviour and ways of accepting or resisting these rules.

Socialization

For many little girls, the rhyming game may be an important means of socialization. As Bronwyn Davies (1982) in her carefully documented accounts of primary school children has observed:

When children first arrive at school they may be traumatized at the situation they find themselves in if they have no contacts among their peers . . . Once they have made friends and gained access to childhood culture, they must be careful not to annoy or offend their friends, or they may find themselves alone again. The fearfulness of this aloneness, the possibility of being outside children's culture should not be under-estimated when seeking to comprehend the children's understanding of the world of friendship.

Her interviews with children show how this uncertainty about how to behave competently in a new situation is alleviated by finding a friend with whom it is possible to build a system of shared meanings and understanding, so that the world becomes a more predictable place. Her conversations with the children reveal how much of this building of shared meanings takes place through play and how this allows them to take a greater degree of control over their lives. She describes how a particular game, involving an exchange of insults, looks random and chaotic but has a degree of structure and a complex purpose in enabling children to make contact with each other.

In her chapter, 'Friends and fights' she shows how a child's view of friendship may be very different from that of adults. Opie and Opie (1959) observe that 'children's friendships are far from placid . . . they make and break friends with a rapidity disconcerting to the adult spectator.' Bronwyn Davies suggests that this is because adults construe friendship differently; for adults, liking a person comes first; for children this is not important: proximity, being with someone, is. Making and breaking friends serves a purpose as a way of exploring the dynamics of interpersonal relationships. When children first arrive at school they have to make sense of a strange new world and Davies (1982: 70) has observed ways in which they do this with each other:

> Friends are a source of meaning-making in this new situation . . . they can by their presence and shared meaning, render the world a sensible and manageable place. Their particular mode of viewing the world with its accompanying language, taboos, rituals and sanctions which function to maintain this meaning world, are developed in interaction with each other.

Challenge

Susan Stewart (1978) describes how children from a very early age have access to the means to challenge particular forms of discourse; Valerie Walkerdine (1981) describes how children are able to seize power through language. To use a Hallidayan metaphor (Halliday 1978: 186) the playground can be seen as the environmental determinant of the texts which have taken place on it and these texts or linguistic structures are a realization of the social structure, capable not only of transmitting the social order but also of maintaining and even modifying it. I want to discuss some of the ways in which the singing games contribute to this process and in particular the ways in which children can become powerful.

It can be argued that rhymes like 'My friend Billy' are examples of girls' resistance to the relations of power in the playground. The 5-year-old girl on the playground is particularly aware of her physical weakness and powerlessness in the face of the older children and boys, in particular. Chanting this rhyme, along with other girls, may provide the ammunition for little girls' resistance, and the means by which they may seize power in discourse. As Walkerdine argues, when she comments on little girls' play in the wendy house, they may, 'despite their institutional positions, achieve power'.

Older girls seem to enjoy rhymes like

When I was young
I had no sense
Caught my balls
On a barbed wire fence.
Off to the hospital

I did go,
Both my balls
I did show.
Nurse came in
With a red hot lance,
Stuck it up my arse
And made me dance.
I daren't go near
That fence no more.

In rhymes like this, girls' discourse renders boys powerless and vulnerable as possessors of willies, balls and arses; it is a *nurse* who wields the 'red hot lance' and the *girl* next door with the rake. Little girls may be understood as powerless children, 'oppressed both by the power of an oppressive educational system' as well as by a patriarchal society but, as Walkerdine argues, individuals are not produced as unitary subjects but are 'a nexus of contradictory subjectivities', with the potential to be both subject and object of a variety of discourses, to be powerful or powerless.

Since individuals are powerful or powerless depending on which discursive practice they enter as subject, Walkerdine argues that

> girls are not always passive and dependent . . . but are constantly struggling with the boys to define their play and to redefine it into discursive practices in which they can be powerful. To understand the power and resistance in the play of children we have to understand those practices that they are recreating in their play.
>
> (Walkerdine 1981)

In my collection of singing games, there are many examples of games in which the girls could be said to be imaginatively, if not actually, seizing power by making boys, teachers and the school the objects of their discourse.

Teacher, teacher, we don't care,
We can see your underwear . . .

If your teacher interferes,
Turn her up and box her ears.
If that does not serve her right,
Blow her up with dynamite.

Outside the classroom and among their peers girls quickly drop the lady-like behaviour which is often expected of them in school (Clarricoates 1978). In their peer group on the playground, they develop a complex culture which has little to do with the adult world

(Davies 1982). They will discover the taboo rhymes are not merely the 'childish acts of rebellion' that Ian Turner (1978) suggests, but also as Stewart (1978) and Walkerdine (1981) argue, tools for resistance and criticism.

PLAY AS RULE-GOVERNED BEHAVIOUR

Bruner (1975) suggests that children develop their own templates for viewing the world and that, far from being arbitrary and chaotic, these are detailed rules for appropriate behaviour. He also suggests that play among humans inevitably reflects the culture in which it occurs (Bruner *et al.* 1976). Davies (1982) proposes that children's culture is centred around friendship and it is with friends that the rules of this culture are learned, how to predict what is acceptable and appropriate behaviour in the different situations of home, school and playground. In a detailed ethnographic study she asked children to talk about the social world as they perceived it. She tests out her theory that children have a culture of their own, that they have their own perspective of the social world and strategies for dealing with it, by talking and listening to children's accounts of their relationships in school. Her account helps to place girls' early games, not only in the corpus of an existing and well-documented oral tradition and as important preliterate linguistic activity, but as a contribution to their entry into the world of schoolchildren where cultural meanings, rules and beliefs have to be learned and maintained.

LEARNING ABOUT THE CULTURE OF THE PLAYGROUND

One of the purposes of the games children play is that they provide access to the culture of the playground and, in particular, the language of that culture. The language of children's games has a vital role in the organization of their experience and behaviour: for Bernstein 'it continuously signals the normative arrangements of the group rather than the individual experiences of its members.' Its use reinforces solidarity with the group. Traditional speech play, he asserts, influences the organization of the child's experience and behaviour, making her 'sensitive to the role and status and also to the customary relationships connecting and legitimizing the social positions with the peer group' (Bernstein 1960: 178–81).

But how do girls get into this kind of game in the first place, particularly if they have arrived on the playground without a friend?

Jane: Ah, I came at half-past eight 'n nobody was in the office, and um, I was sittin' there 'n' I was real shaky and started

> to cry a bit, and some of the teachers said 'ullo, then Mr Bell
> got me an enrolment form and took me around there and I
> got in friends with Betty and Vanessa came along.
>
> (Davies 1982)

The uncertainty is alleviated by finding a friend, and Jane has taken
the first step towards being a competent person in the new social
setting of the school. The next step, the building of shared meanings,
will probably take place through play. This step may take place
through participation in clapping games. The clapping game is essentially social and because it only involves one other person, not very
threatening, as Ian Turner (1978) illustrates

> The movements of the hand-clapping game are fairly standardised.
> The two clappers stand face to face, about two feet apart. In
> sequence they clap the palms of their hands on their own knees,
> together, two hands to two hands, together, right hand to right
> hand together, left hand to left hand together, two hands to two
> hands together . . . and so on, until the end of the rhyme is
> reached . . . in a whirl of breathless exhaustion.

The sequence may change, the movements and rhythms may vary but
'it is common to find the clappers going faster and faster as they move
through the rhyme, vying with one another to see who can last the
longest without breaking the sequence'. The rhyme, in fact, may seem
a secondary feature, its function only to accompany and structure the
game.

> Girls clapping a long game have no time to think whether the words
> they are chanting are sense or nonsense. They are concentrating all
> their energies on saying them in the right order and remembering
> the actions that go with them driven by the need to keep in time
> with their partner.
>
> (Opie and Opie 1985: 445)

Starting a clapping game would seem to need no elaborate preliminar-
ies; it can be initiated simply by a child raising her hands and beginning to clap, a gesture signalling 'This is play!' (Bateson 1955). But
Sutton-Smith (1968: 103) sounds a note of caution: getting into and
out of games may not be as easy as it seems; there are codes that
govern entries and exits, differences in the ease with which individuals
can initiate and integrate such play encounters. Some children can
cross the boundaries since they involve fairly brief periods of co-
operation. None of the games I recorded last for more than 2 minutes;
they average about 30 seconds and are tightly structured by the rhyme,
which prevents the boundaries of the play encounter breaking down.

BECOMING APPRENTICED

Just how complex the physical aspect of these games can be and how much concentrated co-ordination is required emerges when children attempt to explain the actions that accompany deceptively simple rhymes. 'Hands together' has no other function than to describe and accompany specific movements. At 5 years old Jessica was not sure how it went. I asked her to show me and I couldn't do it either but as she showed me I got a useful clue about the way she had learned these games. 'Who do you do it with?' I asked, 'Janine, of course' she replied. Jess had become Janine's apprentice and was clearly receiving expert tuition in the slick movements that the clapping games required.

She had found the fast routine difficult, but in working at it with Janine she was being initiated into the culture of the playground and learning a role which she was later to take on herself with younger girls. Ervin-Tripp and Mitchell-Kernan (1977: 17) describe the way that children frequently undertake this kind of teaching of other children both by word and example, 'when they have a younger or novice participant in play'. Brice-Heath (1983: 99) enlarges this observation in her account of the way pre-school girls in Tracton participated in the older girls' playsong games where the major purpose of the games seemed to be the involvement of young children:

> The preschool girls are given part of the public stage in their partici-pation in older girls' playsong games . . . jump-rope songs, hand-clap songs. . . . They have a repertoire which they use on these occasions, as well as another repertoire used at recess and before and after school.

Thus little girls become apprentices and are drawn into a co-operative girls' culture, one which Romaine (1984: 185) identifies as a gender-specific culture learned from peers. She argues that sex-specific pat-terns of behaviour may emerge as a result of the social organization and types of activity which girls engage in. Romaine regrets that sociologists and linguists have paid less attention to female peer groups than male ones which makes it difficult to be sure that girls do, in fact, have a distinct subculture. But she refers to research which suggests that

> girls learn to accomplish 3 things with language (1) to create and maintain relationships of closeness and equality; (2) to criticize others in acceptable ways; (3) to interpret accurately the speech of other girls. These ways are connected with ways of behaving and playing in groups. Girls' activities are generally co-operative and non-com-petitive.
>
> (Maltz and Borker 1982)

The singing games are essentially co-operative: rule-governed, ritualistic but not hierarchical or competitive.

Clapping games may have a unique function in enabling girls, in their first weeks at school, to participate in non-threatening group interaction with other girls. Participation in this playground culture also enables girls to manipulate language, to rehearse adult roles, to investigate and challenge social and sexual aspects of the world and to become involved in peer group relationships. Thus the playground is an important context for the acquisition of social identity.

While I have suggested that girls gain substantially from the essential features of the playground culture – co-operative apprenticeship to older girls, shared community rules and structures – and that this makes for a positive contribution to their gender identity, others have argued that games can be seen as a conservative force that perpetuates gender stereotypes (James 1990). The group of girls singing

> My name is Dorothy,
> I am a movie star,
> I've got a cute cute figure
> and a lovely guitar.

and wiggling their hips seductively may be contributing to their marginalization in the playground. But perhaps the games are an ambivalent force, both conservative and challenging?

REFERENCES

Aries, P. (1973) *Centuries of Childhood*, London: Jonathan Cape.

Ashton-Warner, S. (1980) *Teacher*, London: Virago.

Bateson, G. (1985) 'A theory of play and fantasy', in J. S. Bruner, A. Jolly and K. Sylva (eds) *Play*, Harmondsworth: Penguin.

Bernstein, B. (1960) Review of *The Lore and Language of Schoolchildren*, by P. Opie and I. Opie, *British Journal of Sociology* 11: 178–81.

Brice-Heath, S. (1983) *Ways with Words: Language, Life and Work in Communities and Classrooms*, Cambridge: Cambridge University Press.

Bruner, J. S. (1975) 'The ontogenesis of speech acts', *Journal of Child Language* 2: 1–19.

Bruner, J. S., Jolly, A. and Sylva, K. (eds) (1976) *Play*, Harmondsworth: Penguin.

Clarricoates, K. (1978) 'Dinosaurs in the classroom – a re-examination of some aspects of the hidden curriculum in primary schools', *Women's Studies International Quarterly* 1: 353–64.

Davies, B. (1982) *Life in the Classroom and Playground. The Accounts of Primary School Children*, London: Routledge & Kegan Paul.

Ervin-Tripp, S. and Mitchell-Kernan, C. (1977) *Child Discourse*, London: Academic Press.

Garvey, C. (1977) *Play*, London: Fontana.

Geertz, C. (1975) *The Interpretation of Culture*, London: Hutchinson.

Grugeon, E. (1988a) 'Children's oral culture: a transitional experience', in M. MacLure, T. Phillips and A. Wilkinson (eds) *Oracy Matters*, Milton Keynes: The Open University Press.
—— (1988b) 'The singing game: an untapped competence', in M. Meek and C. Mills (eds) *Language and Literacy in the Primary School*, Brighton: The Falmer Press.
Grugeon, E. and Woods, P. E. (1990) *Educating All: Multicultural Perspectives in the Primary School*, London: Routledge.
Halliday, M. A. K. (1978) *Language as a Social Semiotic*, London: Edward Arnold.
James, A. (1990) ' "Cub scout, you're out"; games of identity in childhood', paper presented to Department of Anthropology, University of Manchester.
Kirshenblatt-Gimblett, B. (ed.) (1976) *Speech Play: Research and Resources for the Study of Linguistic Creativity*, University of Pennsylvania Press.
Kirshenblatt-Gimblett, B. and Sanches, M. (1976) 'Children's traditional speech play and child language', in B. Kirshenblatt-Gimblett (ed.) *Speech Play: Research and Resources for the Study of Linguistic Creativity*, University of Pennsylvania Press.
Maccoby, E. E. and Jacklin, C. N. (1976) *The Psychology of Sex Difference*, London: Oxford University Press.
Maltz, D. and Borker, R. (1982) 'A cultural approach to male–female miscommunication', in J. Gumperz (ed.) *Language and Social Identity*, Cambridge: Cambridge University Press, pp. 195–217.
Oakley, A. (1972) *Sex, Gender and Society*, London: Temple Scott.
Opie, I. and Opie, P. (1959) *The Lore and Language of Schoolchildren*, London: Oxford University Press.
Opie, I. and Opie, P. (1985) *The Singing Game*, Oxford: Oxford University Press.
Romaine, S. (1984) *The Language of Children and Adolescents*, Oxford: Blackwell.
Steedman, C. (1982) *The Tidy House*, London: Virago.
Stewart, S. (1978) *Nonsense. Aspects of Intertextuality in Folklore and Literature*, New York: Johns Hopkins University Press.
Stutz, E. (1992) *What are They Doing Now? A Study of Children Aged 7–14*, Norwich: Play for Life.
Sutton-Smith, B. (1968) *Boundaries, The Games of New Zealand Children*, Houston: The American Folklore Society, University of Texas Press in B. Sutton-Smith and R. E. Herron (eds) (1971) *Childsplay*, John Wiley.
Turner, I. (1978) *Cinderella Dressed in Yella*, Melbourne: Heinemann.
Walkerdine, V. (1981) 'Sex, power and pedagogy', *Screen Education*, No. 38.
Willes, M. (1983) *Children into Pupils*, London: Routledge & Kegan Paul.

APPENDIX

1 My friend Billy had a ten foot willy,
  Show it to the girl next door.
  Thought it was a snake
  and hit it with a rake
  And now it's only four foot four.

2 Batman and Robin in the batmobile,
  Batman did a fart and paralysed the wheel.
  The wheel wouldn't go,
  The engine wouldn't start,
  All because of Batman and his supersonic fart.

3   I went to the Chinese restaurant
    To buy a loaf of bread, bread, bread.
    I saw a Chinese lady
    And this is what she said, said, said.
    My name is elli elli
    Chickali chickali
    Chinese chopsticks
    Willy willa whisky
    Pow Pow Pow.

4   We break up, we break down,
    We don't care if the school falls down.
    No more English, no more French,
    No more sitting on the old school bench.
    If your teacher interferes,
    Turn her up and box her ears.
    If that does not serve her right,
    Blow her up with dynamite.

    Teacher, teacher, we don't care,
    We can see your underwear.
    Is it black or is it white,
    Oh my god it's dynamite.

5   My mummy is a baker,
    My daddy is a dustman,
    Yum yummy pooey, ticker tacker tooey.

    My sister is a show off,
    My brother is a cowboy,
    Yum yummy pooey, ticker tacker tooey,
    Turn around and pow.

6   I'm a little Dutch girl, Dutch girl, Dutch girl,
    I'm a little Dutch girl, from over the sea.
    Please will you marry me, marry me, marry me,
    Please will you marry me, from over the sea?
    No I won't marry you, marry you, marry you,
    No I won't marry you, from over the sea.
    Why won't you marry me, marry me, marry me,
    Why won't you marry me, from over the sea?
    Because you stole my necklace, necklace, necklace,
    Because you stole my necklace, from over the sea.
    [Repeat verse for bracelet and ring]

    Now we've got a baby, from over the sea,
    Now we're getting older,
    Now we're dying,
    Now we're dead,
    Now we're witches,
    Now we're ghosts,
    Now we're dust,
    Now we're nothing.

[All these are accompanied by dramatic representations]
Now we're in heaven, heaven, heaven.

7   1 2 3 together,
     Up together,
     Down together,
     Backs together,
     Fronts together,
     Up, down, in, out,
     Sides together,
     Bums together.

8   My boyfriend's name is Tony,
     He comes from Macaroni,
     With a pickle on his nose
     and ten fat toes
     and this is how my story goes.
     One day as I went walking,
     I heard my boyfriend talking,
     with two little girls and two black curls
     and this is what she said.
     She said I L/O/V/E love you,
     I K/I/S/S kiss you,
     I jumped in the lake and I swallowed a snake
     and came up with a belly ache.

9   I'm Popeye the sailor man,
     Full stop,
     I live in a caravan,
     Full stop,
     When I go swimming
     I kiss all the women,
     I'm Popeye the sailor man,
     Full stop,
     Comma, comma dash dash.

10   When Suzie was a baby
     She went goo, goo, goo, goo, goo.

     When Suzie was a sister
     She went scribble, scribble, scribble, scribble, scribble.

     When Suzie was a school girl
     She went Miss, Miss, I can't do this.

     When Suzie was a teenager
     She went help, help, I lost my bra in my boyfriend's car.

     When Suzie was a mummy
     She went cook, cook, cook, cook, cook.

     When Suzie was a granny
     She went knit, knit, knit, knit, knit,
     I've lost my stitch.

Chapter 2

Sex and the quiet schoolgirl

Julia Stanley

Source: Stanley, J. (1986) 'Sex and the quiet schoolgirl', *British Journal of Sociology of Education* 7(3): 275–86.

The trouble with girls, especially quite a large proportion of secondary schoolgirls, is that they are so quiet. Of course they can make enough noise with their screaming and giggling in groups, but sit them down on the back row of a classroom, and they seem to have nothing to say for themselves at all, at any rate in comparison to the sort of rebellious lads who interested Willis.

Most educationalists are familiar with Paul Willis's pioneering piece of school ethnography, misleadingly entitled, *Learning to Labour: How Working Class Kids Get Working Class Jobs* (1977). Women have not been backward in pointing out that the book deals only with 'the lads' and how they came to fit themselves for factory life, but it is understandable that at the time the book was written ethnographers preferred the somewhat easier task of researching their own sex. Moreover, many teachers would privately have agreed with Willis's decision to tackle the boys first because on the face of it they are so much more interesting than girls.

Later writers such as Carol Buswell (1984) have shown that girls are not necessarily quieter, or better behaved than boys, but the case study I am working on suggests that the myth, if not the reality, of the quiet schoolgirl is still very much alive and shaping pupils' adaptations to school life. The quietness of the girls at Cator Park School is a response to school itself, rather than a natural aspect of their personalities, and serves the useful purpose of allowing them to shrug off inappropriate bits of themselves, rather as one might leave an overcoat at the classroom door, and put it on again on the way home.

CATOR PARK SCHOOL

In September 1984, I started a two-year case study of one class of pupils at Cator Park School in the West Midlands. The school is almost entirely white, a mixed 11–16 comprehensive in Morriston, an affluent suburban borough which owes its prosperity to car factories and allied services. The catchment area of Cator Park is mixed, consisting mostly of good-quality owner-occupied housing, mostly owned by skilled or lower grade professional workers, and some areas of council housing. The school reflects the conservative values of the area, which is relatively prosperous in spite of the recession in the region.

Class 4T is a fourth-year mixed-ability tutor group, established at the behest of a new headmaster, who arrived two terms before I did and immediately began to break down the rigid banding which had previously prevailed. I spent much of the first few weeks trying to get to know the group as a whole, just as they were exploring contacts with other fourth years who were in different teaching sets and had not formerly been mixed in at tutor time. It was not always easy to find groups who would be at ease together when I made my first round of interviews with the whole class.

During these early group interviews pupils talked fairly freely about their view of school, and I let the conversation take its own path in the hopes of getting a theoretical direction from the children's own concerns. They did raise a number of subjects which I had not been especially interested in before I met 4T, among them the role of the head, school uniform, and 'boys' and girls' subjects'. All of these 'grounded' topics subsequently proved invaluable in learning to see through the pupils' eyes.

I also followed the usual practice of going to lots of lessons, especially in the company of boys and girls who particularly interested me and had consented to be 'victims' of the research; I hung around the playing fields and halls during break times, and generally hoped to get the feel of the school during the first few weeks. My initial impression was that Cator Park was a happy and smoothly run establishment, with traditional but warm and friendly relationships between staff and pupils, and an equally traditional tendency towards gender stereotyping which was not especially surprising in view of the nature of the catchment area. A further reason to expect some degree of male dominance in the school was that it had started life as boys' secondary modern school and had retained its original headmaster and deputy for the best part of twenty years.

During the preliminary interviews, I asked the children to say what they thought their reputation was in school. Out of a total of thirteen girls, all but two said that among other things they were often described as 'quiet'. Of the fourteen boys in the tutor group, only five believed that they were regarded as 'quiet' in school.

SHEEP AND GOATS

There are several ways in which Cator Park unintentionally conveys
the message that girls are not only fundamentally different from, but
also inferior to boys. These hidden messages have been documented
elsewhere: by Sandra Acker (1983, 1984), Michael Apple (1983) and
others with respect to women's 'semi-detached' status in teaching; by
Lynn Davies (1984), Madeleine Arnot (1983) and others interested in
co-education and gender in schools; and by many writers from various
parts of the world who have considered the problems of women's
access to high status work (see, for example, Cunningham 1984;
Dupont 1981; Gaskell 1985).

Despite a growing body of feminist literature on the subject, most
teachers at Cator Park, as elsewhere, simply do not see gender as
being a cause of concern. In common with many educational writers,
past and present, they regard minor matters such as school uniform
and seating arrangements as trivial administrative details, rather than
as part of a pattern of constant unnecessary discrimination between
the sexes which contributes to the genderizing of relationships in
school. Conversation with pupils at the school highlighted the voluntary segregation of the sexes within what was ostensibly a co-educational school, a fact reported, but then allowed to drop, by Monk
in a thesis on pupil identities in secondary school (1981).

Here is part of a taped conversation between three quiet, diligent,
popular upper band girls:

Me:	Who do you usually go around with in school?
Samantha:	Upper band girls and some lower band boys who are friends with my brother.
Barbara:	Boys tend to be more brainier in science subjects! [She means that this explains why they don't go around with upper band boys.]
Me:	What other subjects are boys good at?
Samantha:	Art.
Carol:	Games [murmurs of agreement].
Samantha:	They seem to be more creative at art than the girls do.
Barbara:	Maths [she had previously told me that a lady maths teacher had told her mother that girls were generally OK at maths until they reached the stage where they had to solve problems].
Me:	What are girls good at?
Anne::	Spelling.
Samantha:	I'm terrible at spelling! They are said to be good at

	cookery, aren't they, I suppose? They are sort of put into that category. It's all the girls taking HE, they say. And yet in the Food Technology, TVEI thing, there's more boys taking it than girls. I took Physics for my space on the timetable [laughs].
Me:	How are you coping?
Samantha:	Not too badly.
Anne:	[Talking about computer studies]. . . . There's five girls in our group and we all seem to have the same problem that we don't understand it. I mean – I think we show it more than the boys do, if they don't understand it. 'Cos they don't want to appear that they don't.

The most striking thing about this extract is that three able and likeable girls agreed amongst themselves that boys seemed better at practically every subject, including their own traditional spheres of art, cookery and spelling (in one case). Nearly all the early interviews produced the familiar categorization, whether the groups were boys or girls, mostly pointing out that girls are 'good at languages'. Only one of the groups interviewed was mixed, because the pupils chose their own friends to come along with, and in the end we were left with one pair of boys and one pair of girls, all four upper band 'swots', who consented to be interviewed together.

The near silent Carol later became the subject of an individual case study because she was a most interesting example of a quiet upper band girl. In spite of being one of the most tongue-tied interviewees at first, she is studying French and German, both of which are largely taught orally at Cator Park. She is near the top in both subjects, but I did not find this out for some time, because I made the same mistake as some of the pupils reported by Monk (1981). I fell into the trap of thinking that because Carol said very little in lessons, it meant she did not know the answers, which was not the case.

An able and extrovert upper band boy who was also one of my 'victims' confided to me that he had been amazed when Carol got consistently high marks in language tests, because like all the more able girls in his sets, she 'took a back seat'. Dominant upper band boys are hogging the limelight, not only in the science lessons described by Alison Kelly (1985), but also in subjects which have a 'more feminine image'. According to my interviewees, languages were, in fact, the *only* area of the curriculum where girls were considered to be best, which makes it all the more surprising that my informant Gregory should have been taken by surprise by Carol's excellence, and that the (female) French teacher should have confided to Carol's parents that her 'extreme quietness' was worrying.

Anne gave a rather different picture of computer studies lessons, where far from working hard at 'impression management' – not asking enough questions to find out what they needed to know – the pioneering group of upper band girls not only 'showed themselves up' by pestering the teacher, but helped out two of the less able lower band boys in my presence. The girls who braved convention by taking this 'masculine' subject were all ebullient extroverts outside the classroom, and this may explain their willingness to 'put themselves forward'. For complementary reasons, the normally talkative upper band boys may have been unwilling to jeopardize their image as Men of Technology.

WHAT DIFFERENCE BETWEEN THEM?

All 4T and most of the teaching staff at Cator Park subscribed in varying degrees to the conventional gender stereotyping of secondary pupils' abilities. Two questions arise from this finding: first, how had the conventional attitudes to boys and girls rooted themselves so firmly in the Cator Park soil, and second, had the established view that girls and boys succeed in different subjects any basis in real educational needs?

One reason why differences between the sexes come to be spotlighted in secondary school is that the different rate of puberty is especially noticeable in the middle years. 4T were very concerned about real or supposed differences arising from the girls' more rapid development: both sexes believed that girls were 'moodier' than boys, pointing out that this could be put down to the effect of hormones being felt earlier in girls, while the full onslaught of adolescence does not hit boys until they are at least halfway through secondary school.

Some such female 'problems' seemed to be in one boy's mind when he told me that Mandy, daughter of a feminist lady member of staff and the only girl in the school to be studying engineering drawing for O level, had abruptly left the room at the start of a lesson and had not returned that day. Dave did not know what had caused this sudden 'moodiness', but rather than wondering about the difficulties the girl must have been facing in this man's world, he felt that she was probably 'feeling ill, or something'. In spite of her strong and controlled personality, Mandy looked thoroughly unhappy whenever I saw her in ED, as did the only boy to be taking O level religious knowledge.

Neither the different rate of growth, nor the alleged peculiarities of temperament which are linked to it in the children's minds would seem to justify different educational provision. Even if it is true that teenage girls are moodier than boys (and as a parent of both, I doubt it), this ought not to be elevated to the status of a guiding principle. Nobody has ever seriously suggested that normally shy children, for example, should be given permanent special treatment because they are fundamentally different from less inhibited types. The preferred tactic is to teach them to get along together.

Most parents would probably have doubts about distinguishing between children on the basis of temperamental characteristics, real or imagined, but because the majority of Morriston families feel that secondary schooling should be geared to the need to find work, it could be argued that gender has a direct bearing on the vocational needs of older pupils.

In the second round of group interviews at the end of their fourth year, 4T talked to me about their hopes for the future, and it was clear that most girls expected to work for most of their lives. Like the adolescents studied by Jane Gaskell (1983, 1985), they based their expectations on the way their own families lived, and did not expect to be the main breadwinner, taking it for granted that problems of child-rearing and a lower earning capacity would combine to force them to give up work while their children were young, even though this was not necessarily what they wanted. Most of the girls also thought they would have to work part-time for many years for the same reasons, while the boys looked forward with some trepidation to the time when they would have to 'lose their freedom' and take on the main responsibility for keeping the family.

The traditional belief that girls can find emotional and financial security through the marriage market, as an alternative to a career, conditions what many families see as their educational needs. Although modern divorce statistics throw doubt on the view of marriage as a safe haven for women, and many educationalists would dispute that schools should be concerning themselves primarily with the vocational needs of either sex, the case study indicates that these twin assumptions are influencing Morriston people when they make decisions about exam courses at the end of the pupils' third year. Moreover, traditional assumptions about future lifestyles are influencing pupils not only through the medium of the home, but also through the implicit values of teachers (Smail 1985), and colleges of further education (Blunden 1984; Hargreaves 1985).

Traditional employment patterns in the West Midlands are so much a part of local people's ideas that they have been fed back into the gender-stereotyping in schools in an interesting way. Some girls assume that boys are naturally gifted in those subjects in which they have traditionally dominated:

Me:	What other subjects are boys good at?
Caroline:	Woodwork.
Brenda:	And TD (Technical Drawing).
Diane:	We're not allowed to do them, are we?
Annette:	You are – they've got Mandy in TD.
Diane:	I wanted to do woodwork.
Me:	Why didn't you?
Diane:	'Cos they didn't know I wanted to do it.
Brenda:	It wouldn't get you anywhere, anyway. . . . We just messed about in that and didn't bother revising.
?:	Art is a kind of mixed subject, really.

This snippet connects with several points which have been raised by writers considering the importance of gender in schools. On the face of it, poor Diane is a good example of a girl who has allowed herself to be pushed into a traditional choice of subjects because she 'lacks confidence' to tell the teachers otherwise. But anyone who met Diane would see that she is not an unconfident girl: her problem has been caused by her failure to communicate with teachers – by her quietness. It so happens that Diane was the first pupil to tell me categorically that this quietness was an intentional adaptation to school (see below). Martin Monk (1981) pointed out that quiet children were at risk of being underestimated by others in the class, and Michelle Stanworth (1981) reported that able and ambitious girls were consistently under-estimated because they were quieter than dominant boys, but Diane seems to have been conveyed down the school's gender-tracking system because of a simple failure of communication.

On the other hand, the teachers may be encouraged to assume that 'most girls don't want to do woodwork' since Brenda says they messed about in woodwork – they 'did not think it would get them anywhere'. In other words, as Lynda Measor found (1984), many children have a very poor opinion of subjects which do not seem to them to be market-able, and 'marketable' skills are still gender-specific to some extent.

The self-imposed silence of girls reinforces the conventional teacher attitudes reported by Davies (1984), Stanworth (1981) and others: that many able girls 'lack confidence' or 'lack ambition'. And the girls do sometimes seem to be in a position where everything they do reinforces somebody's negative attitudes towards them. The traditional belief that girls should do well at languages does not seem to dominate teachers' thinking to anything like the same extent as the idea that boys will do well in technical subjects, as I found when I went to French and German classes with Carol.

WHAT IS QUIETNESS FOR?

> Accommodation and resistance, even when it takes the form of turn-
> ing away or withdrawal, is an active process. The analysis above
> suggests that most girls are not passive victims of sex-role stereotypes
> and expectations, but are active participants in their own develop-
> ment.
>
> (Anyon 1983)

The quiet girls in 4T could be described both as accommodating to the
stressful demands of school and as silently resisting its assumption of
superior knowledge, but this is not a sufficient explanation of why so
many girls, of widely differing characters, should adapt to school in
the same way.

A reason they gave themselves was the commonsense one that this
is what teachers require of them: they are constantly asked to 'be
quiet', and girls who wish to get on in school do often take the advice
of teachers very literally. As well as trying to 'turn over a new leaf
and quieten down', Samantha also began her fourth year with a
serious attempt to revise every lesson in every subject at home each
night, in the belief that it was essential to pass O level.

In contrast, boys do not always take teacher's advice so literally.
Although they had no doubt been exhorted to silence just as often as
the girls, the two upper band boys in 4T who described themselves
as 'quiet' stressed that they did not allow this to hold them back. They
would choose a tactful moment to go out to the teacher for a whispered
consultation because they saw 'excessive quietness' as an educational
handicap. Contrast this with the view of Diane, newly promoted from
the lower to the upper band:

Diane: I've got a big – everybody tells me I've got a big gob. Like
with the teachers, everybody puts on a false opinion, like.
But when you're out of school you're not. . . . You're completely different.

Me: Why are you quiet in school?

Diane: 'Cos I want to do well. . . . Get me O's and everything.

Me: You think if you make a lot of noise, that's going to affect
you doing well? [I meant that it would PREVENT her doing
well, but this was not clear, so Diane restated her position.]

Diane: No. Being quiet like. Because I'm quiet like when I'm with
the teachers, but when they're not there, I'm noisy.

Like Carol, Samantha, and many others, Diane firmly believed that
keeping her mouth shut was the way to 'get me O's'. But she used

this strategy selectively: she had been abandoned by her lower friends when she joined the swots, and had tried to regain her lost popularity by breaking every school rule she could think of – outside the classroom. On the playing fields and in the evenings she was far from 'quiet', or conforming.

Diane also made the point, common to many of the girls, that she had been *incorrectly* labelled, while accepting that she herself 'put on a false opinion'. Out of a total of five boys who described themselves as having a quiet reputation in school, four also said that this description was consistent with their behaviour at home – they were quiet there, too. Many of the girls said that the comments on their reports about quietness merely proved how little the teachers knew them, and Barbara acknowledged the effect their attitude had on boys.

Barbara: I don't know why exactly, but I saw this magazine article that said girls do more homework and smoke more.

Me: Any idea why?

Barbara: Because they're trying to show that they're not so good. Because they're meant to be good at lessons, and the band. . . . They're meant to be practically brains, and they don't want to be labelled as a sort of goodie-goodie because they're meant to be brainy.

'I'LL NEVER UNDERSTAND GIRLS'

Barbara was one of a group of four able, articulate and funny upper band girls who were interviewed together. An exactly parallel group of upper band boys spontaneously made the same point about able girls smoking, and also drew some conclusions from it:

Gregory: You find most of the upper don't usually get into trouble. You find some [who do].

Me: What about lower band?

Gregory: They smoke – well, and the upper band girls. It's not usually upper band boys who smoke.

[They say they know several band boys who have recently given up, and I ask if this is because they want to get fit?]

Gregory: I don't think so. I reckon it's – with groups – they will go off in their group and smoke, but others just don't want to. It's more anti-social than bad for you. It's a social gathering. They just don't want to smoke.

Carl: I think the reason a lot of girls do it is to try and rebel, like.

Gregory: Girls try to copy, in tight skirts and all earrings and things like that.

Carl: I don't know why they want to try and get out the uniform.

Me: Why ? Don't you?

All: It's not worth it!!

Carl: I've no idea. I'll never understand girls! It's to rebel, I suppose.

Me: Why them and not you?

Gregory: Some do . . . They don't seem able, don't seem to express themselves, possibly. They can't develop their own personality by speaking out so they do it by show. . . . Strange clothes, and a fag in their hand.

Some upper band girls, like most lower band boys, appear to smoke as a form of resistance to school, as Carl said. The keenest sportsmen do not smoke, nor do any upper band boys in 4T, and Gregory gave an interesting account of how group pressure had brought the lads into line in this respect, although this did not prevent him from going on in the next breath to condemn girls for doing the same thing. In one sentence he damned girls doubly for being passive copycats and at the same time unsuitably sexy, ignoring Carl's perceptive comment that this is a form of resistance too.

The comments of these bright boys were typical of many and suggest that the girls' selective adaptation to the conflicting demands of social and academic life in school confuses boys. As a result, they take refuge in stereotypes which do less than justice to their intelligence and attitudes. Carl's claim that he would never understand the opposite sex cannot be taken seriously – he has lived for years with only his mother for company and gets on well with most of his girl classmates and women teachers. Gregory, too, is popular with the ladies, and in fact explained very well how they are forced into tacit rebellion against the school by their inability (in his view) to 'develop their own personality by speaking out'.

This puzzling, chameleon-like behaviour of girls in school, coupled with the quietness which Gregory evidently thinks of as an inherent deficiency, may be reinforcing these typical Morriston men in an easy and unfounded arrogance. Here is some more of their homespun wisdom:

Me: What are the girls' subjects?

Andrew: Cookery!
Gregory: Not really, we're better at cookery.
Andrew: Languages! There seem to be more girls –
Carl: Yeh. They're better at languages.
Me: What things do you do better?
Andrew: Everything else! [Laughter].
Carl: Things like logic – like maths – there are probably more boys in top sets.
Gregory: Science.
Andrew: Physics, yeh –
?:   – Physics is a boys' subject, biology's a girls' subject, and chemistry is a mixture . . . everyone likes it.
Gregory: I think the teachers have something to do with it. I like old Mr Brown.

Greg may well be correct in attributing the girls' success in chemistry in part to the teaching of the popular head of faculty. If so, he offers hope that the right sort of teaching can help to undermine some of the sexist views which he has illustrated. In recent papers, both Alison Kelly (1985) and Kessler *et al.* (1985) have shown how aspects of the school curriculum can interact with latent sexism in the community to confirm stereotypes. Maybe these boys are being encouraged to believe in 'the little woman' in the classroom because of the seeming lack of opposition from silently studying ambitious girls.

IN CONCLUSION: FALSE OPINIONS

Everybody in the area agrees that the people of Morriston are a conservative lot, and the young people and some of their parents who took part in the ethnography described here conformed to that image in many ways: there was a commitment to the old Protestant values of hard work and honest dealing; a distrust of foreigners and of unfamiliar ways of doing things; a respect for the established order, even amongst those parents and children who confessed to having kicked against the system at some time or another.

But in some significant ways, the parents and pupils in 4T seemed to be less conservative than some of their teachers. Five children had embarked on the new TVEI courses which had been regarded with deep suspicion by many teachers because of the way they ran counter to established ideas about 'academic' and 'vocational' education; four of the boys stated their intention to do catering, although only one of them went on to take the subject after the counselling process in the third year had run its course; one of the girls had a secret wish to study woodwork, four went in for computer studies; quite a few girls took several sciences, and four of the most able boys took some drama or languages; most of the children envisaged their future life as a marriage in which both partners would be doing paid work for most of the time.

The Cator Park case study therefore seems to bear out Sara Delamont's (1983) contention that secondary schools are conservative, not only in the sense of reflecting the prejudices of an essentially conservative society, but in the more specific sense of 'treating males and females as much more different than the outside world does'. Conversation with some of the girls, and above all the impression left by meeting eleven parents in their own homes suggests that the working mums of Morriston are actively engaged in what Kessler *et al.* (1985) call 'feminism without banners'. The boys who wanted to do catering were supported by their parents, if only for the commonsense reason that 'everybody needs food, but not everyone want chunks of metal', as a lower band boy explained.

Despite the willingness of many of 4T to experiment with new courses and to 'opt' for subjects which did not fit the conventional gender role, the school appeared to be sorting them out on the basis of traditional assumptions which have little to do with the commitment to equal opportunities which is implied in a system of comprehensive, co-educational schooling. Rather, many of the teachers seemed to be unconsciously driven by notions of men's and women's spheres which are based on the realities of a previous generation and are fast becoming out-dated in modern day Morriston. As Robert Everhart (1983) asked in a study of a similar junior high school in middle America: 'What is the conception of adulthood for which they are being prepared?'

The 'conception of adulthood' which informs the attitudes and actions of teachers is not limited to traditional notions about men's and women's work: it also colours their views of what constitutes suitable behaviour for girls and boys. In spite of being willing to try 'boys' subjects', and even though they were all assuming that they would take a place in the public domain of paid work, all but two of the girls in 4T believed that they were labelled 'quiet' in school, and took this as a compliment. The girls are actively working towards acquiring a public persona which stresses quietness in the public forum of the classroom, never mind what they get up to behind the smoking tree.

The girls themselves are fairly clear that this is a good thing – several of them told me that this is the 'way to get me O's', and their dread of 'being shown up' has been widely reported. Detailed case studies of two upper band girls also suggested that they and their teachers viewed their commitment to silent study in a thoroughly positive light, even though the dominant upper band boys in the same teaching groups had successfully used wit and badinage as a way of securing an unfair share of teacher attention. The children themselves made it clear that in their view, quietness was a successful adaptation to the academic and social requirements of school, even though it appeared to be one less commonly employed by upper band boys.

Many of the phrases used by teachers and pupils to describe quiet girls are highly perjorative: Michelle Stanworth (1981) found a girl who described herself as a 'wallpaper person', and a charming young man who spoke of the 'faceless bunch'; teachers at Cator Park and elsewhere have spoken to me of 'mouses', 'puddings' and 'boringly well-behaved girls', even contrasting them unfavourably with the 'more rewarding' tough lads who dominate classes by their bad behaviour and constant attention seeking. Girls' behaviour has been defined as a problem by reference to the masculine 'norm', even though in the case of the quiet schoolgirls it is they who are performing in exactly the way required of them by parents and teachers, and the boys who are out of step.

As well as conforming to the expected pattern of behaviour for the academic child, quiet schoolgirls are also adopting a line which they see as appropriate to formal education. They adapt selectively to the circumstances of school 'putting on false opinions' in front of teachers; trying to live down this 'goodie-goodie' image in the more relaxed setting at the bottom of the playing field and elsewhere in social gatherings; sharing confidences with the cosy female circle in 'girls' lessons' like child care.

Girls who fail to adapt to the various demands of school life in this way feel that they should try to. One of the two able girls who did not describe herself as 'quiet' in school said that she was making every effort to 'turn over a new leaf' and quieten down, as her previous report had been very bad. When I asked her how she thought it would improve matters to be quiet, she said: 'I suppose you think there's a time and a place for everything . . . if you want to act the loudmouth and be a bit of a yob – out of school!'

Many of the girls report themselves, and are described by others, as being 'far from quiet' out of school. A more extrovert persona presumably has its own uses in the outside world, as the pattern of life which most girls envisaged for themselves called for well-developed social skills in adapting to confusing and conflicting demands. Housework and paid work; child care and attracting the opposite sex; female solidarity and getting a man require kaleidoscopic role changes in which a self-confident extroversion could be helpful at times. Certainly, a talent for 'putting on false opinions' seems called for.

The quiet role which most 4T girls adopt when in school happens to chime in well with conventional expectations of the woman's role in a patriarchy. It could even be argued that it is directly helpful in establishing what Kessler *et al.* (1985) have identified as the 'perspective of the dominant group in the dominant sex' – perhaps the loud-mouthed young wits of the upper sets will metamorphose into over-bearing husbands. The case study at Cator Park was not directly concerned with the social and sexual relationships of young people outside school, but Carol supplied a hint that some quiet girls are far from subservient, and make their own terms in dealing with the same boys who are so dominant in the classroom:

> I dunno why, but I do feel sort of – ashamed that I know them, if you know what I mean. There's Bret Fuller's sort of reputation, if you know what I mean. He's sort of bad, 'cos he's fooling along with the teachers, and things like that. I'm just, sort of ashamed that I'm friends with him. . . . He's fine out of school – he's a really nice person. You can talk to him! I actually talk to him out of school! . . . He lives just up the road. I've known him since junior school.

The title of this paper is a deliberate reference to the image of the sexy schoolgirl which lurks in the pornography of our society. Here, the gym-slipped schoolgirl symbolizes immaturity and submission – she is the classic victim. But the quiet girls of 4T were not victims: their quietness was a response to a model of the 'successful upper band pupil' which had become interlocked with conventional ideas about gender imported from the conservative community outside. Far from being weak and immature, Carol and her friends are mature and highly adaptable – perhaps another stereotyped image fits them better: that of the 'strong, silent type'.

ACKNOWLEDGEMENT

Thanks to Bill Reid and Lynn Davies, of Birmingham University, for talking me through innumerable drafts of this paper. The end result is my own responsibility, of course.

REFERENCES

Acker, Sandra (1983) 'Women in teaching: a semi-detached sociology of a semi-profession', in Len Barton and Stephen Walker (eds) *Gender, Class and Education*, Lewes: Falmer Press, pp. 123–39.
—— (1984) 'Sociology, gender and education', in Sandra Acker, Jacquetta Megarry, Stanley Nisbet and Eric Hoyle (eds), *World Yearbook of Education: Women in Education*, London: Kogan Page; New York: Nichols, pp. 64–78.

Apple, Michael (1983) 'Work, class and teaching', in Len Barton and Stephen Walker (eds) *Gender, Class and Education*, Lewes: Falmer Press, pp. 53–67.

Arnot, Madeleine (1983) 'A cloud over co-education: an analysis of the forms of transmission of class and gender relations', in Len Barton and Stephen Walker (eds) *Gender, Class and Education*, Lewes: Falmer Press, pp. 69–91.

Anyon, Jean (1983) 'Intersection of gender and class: accommodation and resistance by working class and affluent females to contradictory sex-role ideologies', in Len Barton and Stephen Walker (eds) *Gender, Class and Education*, Lewes: Falmer Press, pp. 19–37.

Blunden, Gillian (1984) 'Vocational education for women's work in England and Wales', in Sandra Acker, Jacquetta Megarry, Stanley Nisbet and Eric Hoyle (eds), *World Yearbook of Education: Women in Education*, London: Kogan Page; New York: Nichols, pp. 153–62.

Buswell, Carol (1984) 'Sponsoring and stereotyping in a working class English secondary school', in Sandra Acker, Jacquetta Megarry, Stanley Nisbet and Eric Hoyle (eds), *World Yearbook of Education: Women in Education*, London: Kogan Page; New York: Nichols, pp. 100–9.

Connell, R. W., Ashenden, D. J., Kessler, J. and Dowsett, G. W. (1982) *Making the Difference*, Sydney: Allen & Unwin.

Cunningham, Shirley (1984) 'Women's access to higher education in Scotland', in Sandra Acker, Jacquetta Megarry, Stanley Nisbet and Eric Hoyle (eds), *World Yearbook of Education: Women in Education*, London: Kogan Page; New York: Nichols, pp. 173–87.

Davies, Lynn (1984) *Pupil Power: Deviance and Gender in School*, Lewes: Falmer Press.

Delamont, Sarah (1983) 'The conservative school? Sex roles at home, at work and at school', in Len Barton and Stephen Walker (eds) *Gender, Class and Education*, Lewes: Falmer Press, pp. 93–105.

Dupont, Beatrice (1981) *Unequal Education*, Paris: UNESCO.

Everhart, Robert B. (1983) *Reading, Writing and Resistance*, London: Routledge & Kegan Paul.

Gaskell, Jane (1983) 'The reproduction of family life: perspectives of male and female adolescents', *British Journal of Sociology of Education* 4: 19–38.

—— (1985) 'Course enrollment in the high school: the perspective of working class females', *Sociology of Education* 58: 48–59.

Hargreaves, David (1985) Chief Education Officer of Inner London Education Authority, quoted in *The Times Educational Supplement*, 1 November.

Kelly, Alison (1985) 'The construction of masculine science', *British Journal of Sociology of Education* 6: 133–54.

Kessler, S., Ashenden, D. J., Connell, R. W. and Dowsett, G. W. (1985) 'Gender relations in secondary schooling', *Sociology of Education* 58: 34–48.

Measor, Lynda (1984) 'Pupil perception of subject status', in Ivor F. Goodson and Stephen J. Ball (eds) *Defining the Curriculum: Histories and Ethnographies*, Lewes: Falmer Press, pp. 201–17.

Monk, Martin J. (1981) 'The class nexus: description of pupils' identities as capable school learners', unpublished PhD thesis, Chelsea College, London.

Smail, Barbara (1985) 'An attempt to move mountains: the "Girls into Science and Technology" Project', *Journal of Curriculum Studies* 17: 351–4.

Stanworth, Michelle (1981) 'Gender and schooling: a study of sexual divisions in the classroom' (London, Hutchinson, this edition, 1983).

Willis, Paul (1977) *Learning to Labour: How Working Class Kids Get Working Class Jobs*, Farnborough: Saxon House.

Chapter 3

We're back with Gobbo
The re-establishment of gender relations following a school merger

Joan Draper

For all those involved in a school merger the concept of 'status passage' (Van Gennep 1960; Turner 1969; Glaser and Strauss 1971; Measor and Woods 1984) is relevant. In a status passage there are several phases: a separation from the old order, a period of transition and then a phase of incorporation into the new order. With each stage of the passage there is some change in status, which will require a reappraisal of 'self' in the Meadian (1934) sense of the term. This study is concerned with the status passages of fourth year pupils during the transitional phase of the merger of three schools, and the way in which they adapted to the amalgamation.

The mixed school, which I shall call 'Lymescroft', was the result of the merger of two single-sex, 12–18, bilateral schools, 'Mordaunt School for Boys' and 'Mordaunt School for Girls', and one smaller, 12–16, secondary modern school, 'Homefield'. The majority of the pupils could be termed 'middle class', based on the Registrar-General's groupings of parental occupations. I was a full-time teacher at Lymescroft after having taught for many years at the Mordaunt Girls' School, so my role was that of teacher-researcher.

Although they were built on the same campus, there had been virtually no communication between the two single-sex schools over the years before the merger. The ethos of each school was very different. Mordaunt Boys' School was traditional and authoritarian; in the words of a male teacher 'A fine school, the best disciplined of the three schools, run on strict lines, with a strong value system and a smart uniform'. Mordaunt Girls' School was the antithesis of this, with an emphasis on the development of the whole pupil and few imposed rules. Homefield School was run on paternalistic lines being described as 'small and comfortable' by a female teacher, where every pupil and member of staff knew everyone else.

Each school had a core of loyal teaching staff who had absorbed the essential character of their school and had passed it on to their pupils. Pupils had therefore adapted to the behaviour patterns that were accepted in the culture of the institutions to which they belonged. They had learned to recognize the signals that indicated what attitudes they were required to hold in order to have a high self-value, and what were the acceptable social parameters of behaviour that would maintain their self-esteem and the esteem of others. In the creation of Lymescroft, however, since the three constituent schools had each presented a different set of signals, the pupils from each school each saw 'self' from a different viewpoint, which in some cases caused conflict.

At the beginning of my research the pupils whom I was studying were 14 years old, and entering the fourth year of secondary schooling. Those who had been in the single-sex schools had experienced two years of segregated education since they had left their middle schools. All had to go through several formal status passages – they were moving from one school, territorially and dimensionally to another; from one school ethos to another; from third year into fourth year external examination courses; and some were going from a single-sex to a mixed school. The interaction of the pupils who moved from single-sex to mixed education had a noticeable influence on their gender identities which in turn had a strong impact on their sense of 'self'. This was, for me and a number of my colleagues, somewhat unexpected. In this study, therefore, I propose to explore their informal status passages – the processes of interaction with one another and the re-establishment of their informal gender relationships within the new school. First, however, I shall say a few words about my role as teacher-researcher and how I gathered my material.

MY ROLE AS TEACHER-RESEARCHER

There were a number of advantages to being a full-time practising teacher at the school compared to the situation of an outside researcher. I had no problem about access since my Head gave me permission to do my research. I was a 'complete participant' (Hammersley and Atkinson 1983) in the school, and so therefore did not have to 'pass as a member' (Patrick 1973; Jules-Rosette 1978). I had somewhere (my own teaching classroom) to interview the pupils where I was unlikely to be interrupted, and it was sufficiently out-of-the-way (at the top of forty stairs) for me to be reassured that the pupils would not have come had they not wanted to. I did not have to 'act a part' (Goffman 1971) in order to be accepted, since I understood the processes and subtleties of the life of the school from the beginning – in fact, as a founding member I helped to shape them.

There were, however, a number of difficulties. The greatest of them was lack of time, which is felt by all researchers, and even more

acutely by teacher-researchers (Peake 1984; Pollard 1985). I was a head
of department and a school counsellor, and had a full teaching time-
table, so any free periods had to be filled with departmental, pastoral
and other duties. This meant that, although I was a participant, it was
very difficult for me to occupy the role of 'observer' in other teachers'
classrooms, although I was welcome to do so. I had, therefore, to use
my own classroom experience as observation in the class setting, and
rely on interviews with other teachers to get their classroom experience
secondhand. I had to squeeze interviews in during lunch hours or
after school, and I was unable to interview some colleagues at all
because we could never find a moment that was mutually available.

To get the information that I needed from the pupils I used questionnaires combined with interviews in addition to my observations. I
also developed a research diary (Burgess 1981; Forward 1989) which
contained records of conversations, incidents and my own and other
people's opinions. Sometimes I used a notebook, and other times I
jotted down notes on odd pieces of paper and put them in my 'diary
file'.

The questionnaires were given to the pupils during lesson time in
PD (personal development), which I did not teach, and I was grateful
to have the co-operation of my colleagues who did. The only condition
made was that the questionnaires should be anonymous, which was
perfectly acceptable to me since I did not know most of the pupils
anyway. The completed questionnaires were thus only differentiated
by gender and the school that the pupils had come from. Three questionnaires were given to the fourth year pupils: one at the beginning
and one at the end of their first year of the new school, and then one
just before they completed their compulsory schooling, when they
were in fifth year.

I interviewed a number of fourth year pupils. Like Woods (1979),
Burgess (1983) and Pollard (1985), I found that it was more acceptable
to them to be interviewed in groups rather than singly. In my study
I used groups of two to five boys or girls. Woods (1979: 265) found
that 'the company of like-minded fellows helped to put the children
at their ease'. The girls were friendly and informal with me and it was
easy to chat with them. They bounced ideas off one another, they
'acted as checks, balances and prompts to one another' and incidents
and their reactions to them were 'recalled and analysed' (Woods 1979:
265). However, the interviews with some of the boys did not conform
to the same pattern. Since I interviewed volunteers in *their* free time
and guaranteed confidentiality, they felt that they had complete autonomy to say what they liked. They filled the interviews with expletive-
laden conversation, which I thought was full of lies. Later, however,
when I came to analyse their tapes, I found that I could use a lot of

what they said, and I wondered whether what I considered to be 'lies' was my own 'self' intruding and refusing to accept that they could be telling me the truth as they saw it, because my own experience in the girls' school had been so different – for example in some of their attitudes towards females. It was also possible that filling the conversation with expletives was their way of showing me that they did not consider me to be a teacher of the 'old school', before whom it would have been culturally impossible for them to swear. However, there was no way that I could confirm my suspicions because by the time of the analysis of the data the boys had left school and were dispersed in the outside world. This problem cropped up again and again throughout my analysis. Questions that I could have asked frequently arose when I no longer had access to the respondents. My other great difficulty was in getting beyond my own subjectivity in order to achieve an academically acceptable analysis, since I was sometimes unable to see that other pedagogies could also be valid. This remains a problem, although as time went on I came to respect the integrity of colleagues with other ideologies even when I could not agree with them.

THE 'PROCESS OF ESTABLISHMENT'

In any educational situation involving change, particularly of the order of a merger, a 'process of establishment' (Woods 1979, 1983; Ball 1984; Measor and Woods 1984) must occur, in which 'strategies are tested and rules established' (Ball 1984: 108). Part of the process involves teacher–pupil relationships, but also in this case pupil–pupil relationships, and in the establishment of Lymescroft School gender was a prominent issue.

As in their relationships with teachers, with pupils there was an initial 'honeymoon period' (Ball 1984; Measor and Woods 1984). Before the merger, pupils had expressed anxiety about getting to know one another, but this proved groundless since many boys and girls were meeting up again with pupils whom they had known at middle school. There was at first a kind of euphoria about the atmosphere of friendliness in the school.

> I like being with my old mates. The school is more friendly now it has girls in it.
>
> (ex-Mordaunt Boys' pupil)

> I like the friendly atmosphere and also the way everyone gets on. It is nicer to be in a mixed school as you find it easier to get on with boys out of school and don't feel embarrassed.
>
> (ex-Mordaunt Girls' pupil)

I like the friendship between the schools.

(ex-Homefield pupil)

However, this initial period of euphoria began to come to a close when it became apparent that some of the boys were setting out to establish their male dominance over the girls, making a bid for 'power' in the Weberian sense of 'carrying out [their] own will in the pursuit of goals of action, regardless of resistance' (Abercrombie *et al*. 1984)

MALE STRATEGIES FOR ESTABLISHING DOMINANCE

The culture of the boys' school had been strongly patriarchal in the sense that there was a general (rather than explicit) acceptance that in society males were dominant and females subordinate.

I suppose we were rather old-fashioned in some of our ideas. We believed in loyalty and honour in manhood, and the protection of women and children.

(ex-Mordaunt Boys' male teacher)

A man should be responsible for his family. I'd never let my wife go out to work.

(ex-Mordaunt Boys' pupil)

The boys tend to think that they're the only ones that matter because the girls will stay at home, girls will get married and everything so they think it's not so important for them.

(ex-Mordaunt Girls' pupil)

With the presence of girls in the new school, some of the ex-Mordaunt boys tried to establish their male superiority in similar ways to those described by Griffin (1985), Mahoney (1985) and Riddell (1989), and some of the methods that they used could hardly be said to be 'honourable'. The ex-Homefield boys did not figure so largely in these interactions, although they were by no means silent, perhaps because they had not experienced the split at secondary level into single-sex education, and so had never stopped exercising their male gender dominance in their school.

The first indication of some of the boys' attempts at dominance came when they began to remember incidents that had occurred at first and middle school, which were unfavourable to the girls. Some of the boys seemed to forget that during the two years of their separation they had all moved on, and looked upon the girls as they had last seen them, as if they had been 'frozen in time' (Woods 1985) over the intervening years. Nicknames that the girls thought they had long outgrown were disinterred ('Bummy', 'Gobbo', 'Buster', etc).

Everybody had forgotten about me being called 'Gobbo' until those little prats started it all up again. I can't help having a loud voice.
(ex-Mordaunt Girls' pupil)

Such pejorative treatment caused loss of self-esteem among the girls concerned, and indicated to all the girls the social role that the boys were endeavouring to impose upon them (Morgan *et al*, 1979; Woods 1990). Although events still occurred which caused nicknames to be acquired, in most cases the derogatory implications in the boys' nick-names for each other ('Fatso', 'Brains' – for a boy of low ability – or corruptions of their surnames such as 'Horseface' for Horsefield) had long been assimilated, and often appeared to be used affectionately in the context of peer solidarity (James 1979; Morgan *et al*. 1979; Woods 1990). Indeed, some girls, too, still retained such names ('Lofty' – for a particularly short girl – and 'Baldy' for a girl named Baldwin), but these were not considered to be offensive.

Embarrassing moments, many of them involving girls' trans-gressions or accidents to their body functions were disinterred and retold by boys as if they had only just occurred.

[He] had to tell everyone about the time that Gemma was sick down [the Head Teacher's] trousers didn't he? He did it with noises and gestures and everything. Gemma went all red and called him a shit.
(ex-Mordaunt Girls' pupil)

They can only remember the stupid things that happened.
(ex-Mordaunt Girls' pupil)

Girls were barked at in corridors, and received verbal abuse (Griffin 1985, Jones 1985, Lees 1986, Kelly 1988, Halson 1989). They were jeered and taunted by boys if they spoke up in class, with sighs and groans and such phrases as 'Shut up'. 'Turn it off' and 'Oh God not again'; and called 'stiffs', or 'squares', or 'boffins' (Mahoney 1985). This may have been the reaction of some boys who felt academically threatened by girls, but was seen by girls as a personal insult. Two of my ex-Mordaunt Girls' informants, both of high ability, discussed this in an interview:

Helen: I hate the way the boys put people down, and they get personal and call people names.
Claire: Oh shut up, you stiff, you square.
Helen: You boff [laughter].
Claire: They're always playing us up and being nasty. Those few boys have ruined the whole class.

Girls across the whole ability range had to put up with verbal abuse containing direct anatomical references, particularly to 'tits' and 'bums', and were constantly humiliated (Wood 1984; Riddell 1989) through sexual taunts and insults. Some of the most commonly used words were 'slag' and 'dog'. The majority of girls in the upper band did not respond to the treatment, tending to 'retreat into passivity' in the face of the boys' name-calling, referring to the boys as 'stupid' (Mahoney 1985).

Helen: It just gets really stupid when they come out with really bad comments. You've only just got to walk down the corridor and you get called 'slags' and 'dogs'.

Claire: And there's no name like 'slag' or 'dog' that you can call a boy.

Helen: And if you insult him by calling him 'cissie' it's only like insulting ourselves.

Claire: We can't win.

Helen: I mean it's pathetic. They just don't care. They just make crude comments about the size of something they haven't got.

Claire: They're not a bit sensitive are they. That certain person, Craig Addie, he's so crude he makes me sick.

Helen: And then when he said 'I'd never let my wife go out to work', I felt like saying 'You'll be lucky to find someone to marry you'. I mean I'm not moaning, well I am.

What makes this piece of conversation especially interesting to me is that in the girls' school the girls had been particularly reactive to insults. Elsewhere (Draper 1985: 99) I have written about the attitudes of the girls' school pupils:

[The girls] were deeply insulted if a teacher implied that they were sexually promiscuous. If one girl called another a 'slag' or a 'tart' it was an invitation to physical violence, but if a teacher did so it implied a stigma that could mean an angry parent coming to the school to demand an apology.

Now, however, girls were frequently receiving these very insults, and were responding passively, not actively. It seemed that their 'definition of the situation' depended upon who was giving the insult, and therefore it had not been the insult that they were responding to but the giver of the insult. If the boys did the insulting, girls responded in a gender stereotypical manner by ignoring it. At no time did I see or hear of girls confronting the boys and directly challenging their verbal assaults. This has also been pointed out by other researchers (Lees 1986; Halson 1989). Furthermore, when the boys gave them verbal abuse, the girls' lack of response may have been interpreted as permission to continue with the abuse. Most of the girls whom I consulted had not been prepared for the boys' behaviour, and when I asked them what they thought was the reason for it, they said that the boys were just being stupid and immature, or wanted to show off. Typical girls' replies to my question were:

> They're so stupid and immature. They are pathetic. They are not worth bothering with. They get on my nerves.
>
> (ex-girls' school pupil)

> The boys just want to show off, they are stupid. I don't want to have anything to do with them when they behave like that.
>
> (ex-girls' school pupil)

> They are immature. They try to embarrass people to make themselves look big.
>
> (ex-Secondary Modern girl)

To some of the girls from the girls' school, these boys were only the boys they had known at middle school, who were continuing to reinforce the gender stances that they had taken two years previously. Their dismissal of the boys as 'stupid and immature' could also be interpreted as the coping strategy of 'accommodation and resistance' (Anyon 1983), since they did not know how otherwise to respond to the situation. Also, they did not know what might have happened if they had retaliated, they might have received worse treatment. One upper band girl said:

> You know I used to speak up and that. But now I won't say anything because they will only turn round to me and start getting personal and calling me names and it'll last for how long I don't know. Well I'm not going to suffer that just for the sake of saying it.
>
> (ex-girls' school pupil)

Not all the boys were sexually aggressive towards the girls, however. A number of them simply ignored the girls and stayed together in their all-male friendship groups as if the girls did not exist. This meant that they also ignored the sexist behaviour that was going on around them. They seemed mentally to shrug their shoulders and let their peers get on with it. They did not see it as any business of theirs; they were in school to learn, not to interfere with the other boys' behaviour. 'It's nothing to do with me. I don't take any notice of the girls', one ex-boys' school pupil remarked.

It seemed that these boys had allowed the other boys to carry out this behaviour pattern in middle school, and perhaps they too were afraid of retaliation if they tried to prevent it, by being called names and labelled as 'cissies'. I suggest also that by ignoring females altogether they were able to maintain their own feeling of status, in the same way that some of the girls were coping with the situation. 'I just go my way and [the girls] can go theirs. I'm not going to contaminate myself with them' (ex-Mordaunt Boys' pupil).

This 'turning a blind eye' behaviour was not confined to upper band boys. It went on right across the ability range, and across the social scale. However, some of the boys in the lower band, particularly those who had been at the secondary modern school, were also brutally sexist (McRobbie 1978; Wood 1984) and forthright in their language towards the girls. They made loud remarks about girls' clothes, especially their blouses and jumpers or skirts if the girls' contours were obvious. They would lean across girls to pass pens or rulers, brushing against them as they did so, or try to touch their breasts or buttocks whenever possible. Insulting remarks in the classroom included: 'She must be a lezzy, she ain't got nothing there'; 'Great tits – I'm only a bird watcher'; 'Titty titty bum bum', and some of the boys kept up a constant barrage of innuendo.

In the lower ability band, the girls from the secondary modern school showed that they had learned to cope with this behaviour in several ways. One of these was to stay in their own all-female peer groups and ignore the boys' abuse (McRobbie 1978). Others were to return the verbal abuse or to take on the boys and fight them. At second and third year level in the school many of the girls had been physically bigger than the boys, and in the fourth year some still were. They tended to choose boys who were smaller than themselves (the 'weeds') and would clout with great force, using as weapons anything that came to hand – schoolbags, rulers, books or trainers. This behaviour was considered to be 'unfeminine', in the sense that it had crossed the divide into what was widely judged to be 'masculine' behaviour (Wood 1984). It provoked one of my 'conformist' informants to remark: 'Some of the girls – blooming heck!' (ex-boys' school pupil).

A small number of girls flaunted their sexuality before the boys, getting attention from them by being sexually provocative, and some of the boys responded to this. An ex-girls' school teacher reported an incident in her class:

They are much more aware of their sexuality than they were last year, because they are mixed with the boys. 'Miss, he's looking in my bag, there's a tampax in there', in a very loud voice, so the rest of the class can hear. . . . And [one girl] tends to flaunt herself which gets the boys looking, and then when they go anywhere near her she sort of pushes them away and there's a mini scrap. I wouldn't have expected that sort of thing if they'd been in a fourth year just girls group last year.

(ex-Mordaunt Girls' female teacher)

Another teacher reported how a girl provoked one of the boys by her sexual behaviour, and yet when the boy turned the tables and won the contest, she got very upset.

[One girl] painting her lips and saying 'Come and kiss me Darren'. you know, and Darren one lesson walking around the room thrusting his loins forward and teasing, you know. Then he called her 'Zit-face' and she immediately burst into floods of tears and rushed out of the door.

(ex-Mordaunt Girls' female teacher)

The overt sexual behaviour on the part of the boys seemed to be taken for granted as 'normal' by some of the men, particularly teachers from the boys' school.

You've got to understand that our boys can be a bit boisterous. They've been in an all-male environment for a couple of years, and it's their way of breaking out of it. After all it's quite normal behaviour in healthy young males.

(ex-Mordaunt Boys' male teacher)

However, the same teacher echoed the consensus of ex-boys' school teachers that some of the responsibility for the boys' behaviour should devolve upon the girls by saying: 'What else can you expect when you've got that type of girl in the school.' In this he was supported by at least one of the ex-girls' school female teachers who remarked that she wouldn't have expected that sort of behaviour from 'our girls'. It seemed, therefore, that girls who flaunted their sexuality soon got a reputation from all quarters – boys, other girls and teachers. Their behaviour was 'unfeminine', and tended to justify the truth of the insults ('slag', 'dog', etc), that were being made. But if the boys flaunted their sexuality at the girls in the same way, it was felt that they were 'just being normal' when they were provoked into it by girls, and they did not get the same reputation. Thus some of the generally held beliefs about gender stereotypes (Delamont 1980; Mahoney 1985; Weiner 1985; Riddell 1989) were reinforced. One of the ex-boys' school teachers was convinced that much of the boys' aggression towards the girls in low ability groups originated with the girls themselves:

Lots of girls have said, well mainly this [low ability] group, that 'We can't get on because the boys are so silly'. But I think that a lot of it has been provoked, yes I'm sure a lot of it has. That they will sit behind the boys and kick, you know. And once the lad's had enough of that he turns round and retaliates. And it's the thump that you see, not the kicking under the chair.

(ex-Mordaunt Boys' female teacher)

Again, this viewpoint strengthened the feeling held by a number of boys and teachers that girls were less straightforward and more devious and difficult than boys (Humphries 1981; Davies 1984; Stanley 1989; Riddell 1989).

What was gradually becoming clear to me, however, was that boys and girls each had totally different perceptions of their own and each other's sexuality, and that neither sex seemed to be aware of the difference, or what that implied. I now propose to look briefly at this lack of understanding.

PERCEPTIONS OF SEXUALITY

Although the female teachers from the girls' school, who had little experience of teaching boys, had accepted the sexist stereotype that males were probably preoccupied with their own genitalia, what had not been appreciated was the status given to penis size (Menell 1990). Within the first two or three weeks of Lymescroft it was generally made known to me that Andy Moss [one of my informants] had the largest penis in his peer group, and was very proud of the fact. The message was conveyed in multiple ways. It was written on desks, tables and other school furniture. It was scrawled on the fly leaf of his textbook with a crude illustration. It was shouted out in class.

Pupil: He's got a big penis, Miss.
Andy: I've got a big penis. I mean a big mouth.

I was told several times during my interview with Andy and his mates. The other boys, who presumably had witnessed the phenomenon for themselves, indicated that they were highly impressed, as they were convinced that a larger penis enhanced sexual proclivity, which they considered to be highly desirable. They were puzzled by the lack of reaction from the female population of the school.

Many girls had not even been aware of the fact that penis size could differ. Unlike the female breast with its blatant sexual symbolism, the penis is hidden from view in mixed company, and male clothes are cut to make it indiscernible. Girls only saw male attributes above the navel, and to them the size of the penis was totally unimportant. Most of them had a much more romantic conception of 'boys', despite the examples that they were seeing all around them. They were looking for a loving and trusting relationship which was not exclusively physical. They had been conditioned to envisage the role model of a 'perfect mate' (McRobbie and McCabe 1981; Walkerdine 1984; Hudson 1984) who would be as caring to them as they were prepared to be in return, with whom they could sustain a long and stable partnership, although to many of them this was pure fantasy, and they were realistic enough to know that it was probably unachievable (McRobbie 1978). Also, girls' magazines do air many 'real' teenage problems in their pages in addition to their romantic fiction (Hudson 1984).

Julie: [My perfect boyfriend] would be older than me, about two years, and really mature. You know, good looking, but caring.
Denise: You must be joking. Do you think any of this lot could possibly be like that in only two years?

One of the teachers of PD (personal development) illustrated how she had tried to open the lines of communication between the boys and the girls:

T: We had this lesson on what do boys want from girls and what do girls want from boys. The girls were so scathing about what the boys wanted and the boys were quite flabbergasted about some of the things the girls were saying.
JD: Tell me what they were.
T: Oh the boys, what they wanted from the girls was all physical you know – big boobs and things, as crude as they could get because it was all done for effect. And the girls were saying 'Someone you could talk to'. And then the boys said that they just didn't believe what the girls had said. They said 'The girls are interested in other things', so I said 'What other things?'. So they said 'You know, I mean, you know'. So I said 'No, I don't know. What?' And they said 'A boy's thing, you know, Miss'. So I said 'You mean a penis?' 'Yeah.' So I said 'Well, girls, are you?' And the girls went 'Ugh-ugh' and the scorn that was coming from them, it was fascinating. . . . And the girls were making comments about what the boys had said, you know, about big boobs and so on. I said 'Girls, have you got any comments about what the boys want?' and they said 'Well it just goes to show how immature they are doesn't it'. . . . One of [the boys] said 'Well, why doesn't it matter to girls what size it is?' So I thought, now how am I going to handle this one. So I said 'Well it's technique, not size that counts'. You should have seen his face though, it was so amusing.

Despite the efforts of the PD department, through which sex education was taught within the general context of 'caring relationships', some boys continued to harass girls right up to the end of their compulsory education. If they achieved intimate sexual access to a girl and publicized the fact, it humiliated the girl and made her more liable to being insulted. Although pupils were given careful instruction regarding pregnancy and birth, contraception, VD and AIDS, the personal sexuality of pupils, or sexual experience, particularly of girls, was not discussed. Measor (1989) has commented on the enormity of the gap between sex lessons and the adolescent's sexual world. In PD at Lymescroft the emphasis too was not on present adolescent sexuality but on sexual fulfilment as part of a heterosexual future (Rocheron 1983), in keeping with the 'middle class ethic of deferred gratification' (Jackson 1980). The manner in which sexuality manifested itself in school, for instance 'as an axis of power relations' (Wood 1984), was never explored. Girls were never informed that they could gain sexual pleasure without sexual intercourse, and any underlying male dominance (Rocheron 1983) within the arena of practical sexual union was therefore never challenged.

However, there were other direct challenges made by the boys over the girls which involved gender but were not sexual in an overt way.

THE ESTABLISHMENT OF GENDER RELATIONS IN SCIENCE

A very interesting example of a masculine challenge occurred in science. Although this was traditionally a 'boys' subject' (Measor 1983; Kelly 1985; Whyte *et al.* 1985; Woods 1990), the girls' school had been interested in promoting science education among girls. When the schools got together, it became clear that, in their previous school, the girls had been more participatory that the boys in this subject. One of the ex-girls' school female science teachers soon found that in the laboratory, whereas girls had been accustomed to using equipment, boys had not been given the same practical responsibilities and had been accustomed to watching demonstrations.

T: The girls have been used to using all this equipment, whereas the boys, I've since found out, had a lot of demonstrations.

JD: You mean they didn't use the equipment?

T: They didn't use the equipment because they couldn't behave if they used it. A lot of members of staff were scared to let them use it. I've since learned this you know. When I started teaching this year I treated the boys and girls exactly the same. So we had a lot of experiments and I spent more time starting and stopping them, and going back to theory work, because I wasn't going to have the responsibility of something burning, eh? You know, I'd find the boys doing silly things like, if they had a bunsen burner, burning paper or burning pens, like the second years. I mean the girls are out of that habit by the time they're in fourth year. So that's what happened. And gradually I would say that the skills that the girls had have taken a step backwards by watching the boys and seeing what they get up to.

JD: What about the theory.

T: I've had to feed it into them. They haven't been able to find it out for themselves.

This accords with observed practices in mergers of other schools. Mahoney (1985) quotes the male head of science at a newly amalgamated school:

Before we went mixed the girls used to be really interested in science, they used to love doing the experiments and working out why things happened. Now they can't get a look in, the boys rush in and collar all the equipment, I waste hours hauling them off. Now the girls just hang around, I just don't understand it.

(Mahoney 1985: 35)

It is significant that here, as at Lymescroft, when girls were on their own, they had shown themselves to be capable of using equipment and understanding the theory – as they continued to do in home economics, and business subjects such as typewriting (Measor and Woods 1984; Kelly 1985). Yet, when they got together in a mixed class, instead of taking advantage of their prior progress to remain ahead of the boys, they responded to the masculine signals they were receiving, and permitted the boys to dominate the lessons.

Kelly (1985) argues that science is male-orientated through textbook coverage – all about 'things not people', including guns, cars, football, etc. (p. 137) – and the emphasis on science as 'power' (p. 146). Boys, who are 'participatory and enthusiastic' (p. 139), and bring into lessons 'a conception of masculinity which includes toughness, aggression, activity and disdain for girls' (p. 145), therefore tend to prefer science. Girls, on the other hand are socially conditioned into 'timidity, conscientiousness, deference, personal orientation and a concern for appearance' (p. 145) and therefore tend to be 'less interested' in science (p. 138).

Mahoney's and my findings conflict with Kelly's. The Lymescroft girls had previously proved themselves perfectly capable of handling apparatus and scientific theory at this level, as their examination results had shown. I would argue that at Lymescroft science was 'taken over' by the boys because they wanted to use (and often abuse) the equipment themselves – as was discovered by my informant and is also reported elsewhere (Measor and Woods 1984; Woods 1990), and at the same time they intimidated the girls. The girls themselves certainly felt that this was so:

> Well at first we started to do things for ourselves, but the boys made such crude comments all the time. They just made comments and took the mickey, and wouldn't let us get on because they mucked about all the time so we just gave up.
>
> (ex-girls' school pupil)

This remark reinforces the view that some of the passive behaviour of the girls was a deliberate measure that they used to retain their integrity and avoid being victimized by the boys (Stanley 1989). Only a few, high ability, motivated girls stayed ahead.

THE SPIRIT OF COMPETITION

There had been a spirit of competition at the boys' school which had not existed at the girls' school. This was pointed out by a number of teachers:

> I think probably, I would guess that perhaps in the boys-only situation that a sort of competitiveness would have been allowed to flourish, more than I wanted it to, because I wanted to make sure that the girls didn't allow themselves to be shrinking violets and totally overwhelmed and let the boys dominate everything.
>
> (Head of Maths, ex-Mordaunt Girls' male teacher)

Rank order was very important to the boys and a number of them aimed at 'position rather than performance' (Woods 1983). For some, competitive behaviour was endemic, manifested as 'continuous power play' (Askew and Ross 1988), and now that they were in mixed classes, they wanted to get better marks than the girls.

> I like to beat the girls.
>
> (ex-Mordaunt Boys' pupil)

> If I feel that any of those keeno girls are going to do better than me I get a sudden surge of stiffiness [sic].
>
> (ex-Mordaunt Boys' pupil)

Several teachers also commented on this:

> They don't really care what their marks are so long as they have done better than the girls.
>
> (ex-Mordaunt Girls' female teacher)

I suppose you've got to expect the lads to want to do better than the girls. After all it's been a boys' subject longer.

(Head of CDT, ex-Mordaunt Boys' male teacher)

I told them that the pass mark was 50 per cent, and the highest mark was 49, so none of them passed. But the boys didn't care. [One of them] only got 36 per cent, but he got one more mark than Tina and two more marks than Jane, both of whom usually beat him, so he said 'Oh that's all right then', and I said 'No it damn well isn't'.

(ex-Mordaunt Girls' female teacher)

The introduction of girls into a classroom in which a boy's position had previously been acknowledged, particularly girls who were bright, some possibly even brighter than himself, recruited a grave threat to the situation. In the girls' school the girls had not been encouraged to be competitive, although there was a hidden covert element of competition among some of the higher ability girls, who all knew where they stood in relation to the other girls. Now, however, when some of them experienced direct competition they accepted the challenge:

Helen: Lots of girls think they've got to be better than the boys. They think 'Oh I've got to beat him in this test'.
Claire: But if you get a really low mark the boys really laugh at you.
Helen: Like if I'm in a lesson with a certain fascist who shall remain nameless, in other words he's really pig-headed and we all know who we mean.
Claire: i.e. Craig Addie.
Helen: If he's really mouthing off, in an examination I think 'I'm going to do bloody better than him. If I don't do better I'm going to get really mad'.

These were two girls who had become very quiet in class since they were mixed with the boys. They had not been so quiet in the girls' school. But they had hit upon a way of getting back at the boys without opening their mouths – to get higher marks than them, and the boys did not like this at all. The only thing they could do in response to this strategy was to make a greater effort to beat the girls next time, and they did not always do that.

THE ESTABLISHMENT OF FEMALE GENDER ROLES IN THE CLASSROOM

Some boys felt that they were receiving different treatment from the teachers, and complained about what they saw as teachers' 'unfairness'.

No matter how hard they tried to establish themselves in the classroom, many boys felt that the girls were allowed to get away with more than they were. Girls, they felt, were permitted to 'go beyond normally accepted bounds of behaviour' (Woods 1977; Denscombe, 1980), and they did not understand why.

> The girls are a bunch of creeps and the teachers are more lenient to them.
>
> (ex-Mordaunt Boys' pupil)

> Some teachers favour the girls more than the boys.
>
> (ex-Homefield boy)

> The teachers don't give a toss about the girls messing about or bunking off but the boys get it in the neck.
>
> (ex-Mordaunt Boys' pupil)

This feeling among the boys again suggests that they were beginning to realize that some of the girls were a lot more devious than they first seemed to be. When the boys stereotypically monopolized the teachers' attention (Delamont 1980; Stanworth 1981; Burgess 1983; Deem and Weiner 1984; Mahoney 1985; Woods 1979, 1983), as long as the other pupils were quiet the teacher had no time to see what they were doing, and so girls were able to take advantage of the situation by doing very little work, and filling their time in other ways. Two of my high ability male informants resented the fact that they were being discriminated against in some lessons. They felt that some girls' behaviour was being ignored, while the boys' behaviour was being picked up every time.

> Kevin: The girls get away with more than us. They're not naughty in front of the teacher's face, do you see what I mean, but they still get away with more.
>
> Fin: Yeah, I do find that a lot. There's a lot of subjects where teachers are anti boys. Like when we first had Mrs Johnson, and she rounded off her view of boys – they were all immature.
>
> Kevin: Everybody had to prove that, you know. I mean Rachel mucks about like anything but she doesn't round off girls as immature does she, because Rachel and Becky sit at the

back and muck about. And Gemma and that lot they sit and muck about. That covers half the girls in the class who muck about but she still rounded it up.

It seemed to the boys that they had to make greater efforts to gain status in lessons where they saw teachers positively discriminating in favour of the girls, and they were perplexed to find that they were at a disadvantage. They were receiving signals that at a deeper level girls could be gaining advantages over them. With the boys' employment of traditional gender strategies the girls had modified their behaviour, and the boys were perhaps beginning to realize that this modification was an accommodation to the situation (Anyon 1983) and that the girls were using covert resistances in order to retain their self-esteem. Perhaps the boys had not re-established themselves after all. However, it has been pointed out in feminist literature (Spender and Sarah 1980; Stanworth 1983; Deem and Weiner 1984) that the girls, too, were disadvantaged when teachers had to direct their time and energy to the boys.

As the school entered its second year, new influences were beginning to take effect, and some of these were to do with the appearance of the pupils.

SCHOOL UNIFORM AND PERSONAL APPEARANCE

School uniform

The two single-sex schools had used a similar colour scheme for their school uniform, and yet the approaches to its use by the pupils differed considerably. The boys' school had established the fact that appearance was 'important for the maintenance of self' (Stone 1962), and the teachers went to great lengths to maintain the level of uniform conformity. The teachers, as well as the majority of boys, felt that uniform was the non-verbal signal that carried with it the symbolism of manliness, militaristic efficiency and good attendance, and they knew that they had full parental approval of a 'smart turnout'. Yet it is interesting to note that many of these parents were the very same people who had simultaneously supported their daughters in the girls' school who wanted to get away from the 'traditional depersonalised' uniform and the 'old school tie look-alike image' (Davies 1978). The girls themselves had very strong views on fashion trends. They studied style very carefully, but liked to be individual in their appearance, so they 'adapted' the uniform to what they felt suited them.

The colour of the new uniform (black) was considered to be 'very trendy' by the girls, and the boys welcomed it because prefects at the boys' school had had the privilege of wearing black blazers. When the new school opened, the boys all wore smart black blazers, 'white-white' shirts, regulation ties and knife-pleated trousers. No girl wore a blazer, but although they had argued and won the case for having an option of trousers, most wore long black skirts with baggy black sweaters and 'hipster' belts over their white-white school blouses. The subtleties of the girls' approach to school uniform, however, were not appreciated by some of the ex-boys' school teachers, who could not understand the girls' desire to interpret school uniform and adjust it in line with current fashion.

The girls are letting the school down by their sloppy appearance.

(ex-Mordaunt Boys' male teacher)

I think we're going to have trouble in this direction.

(ex-Mordaunt Boys' male teacher)

Some of the boys, too, echoed these sentiments. Many of them had come to Lymescroft with the internalized views of their previous school:

Fin: Can I say something about uniform. Well the girls are a disgrace. You look around in general – overall the boys are a lot smarter.

Jason: The boys are a lot smarter. The boys get away with a lot less than the girls can. I think they might as well just not bother with uniform at all if that is how it is going to be.

Fin: You can always spot the [boys' school] boys.

The 'militaristic turnout' of the ex-boys' school boys, however, was sending out two different sets of signals within the school. To the staff of the old boys' school, the boys' smart appearance projected self-values and conduct that were upright, manly and honourable and of higher status than the girls. To some of the girls and women teachers, this uniform signified authoritarianism and gender dominance, and was manifested in the boys' strategies designed to lower the status of females.

It's the jackboot image.

(ex-Mordaunt Girls' female teacher)

I mean with the teachers from the boys' school they stand to attention all smart and smarmy and say 'Yes Sir' and 'No Sir' and the teachers don't realize that the boys can be right bastards.

(ex-Mordaunt Girls' pupil)

The boys' appearance was thus seen positively and negatively at the same time (Hebdige 1976), yet both perceptions echoed the dialectic processes that were going on in the re-establishment of gender identities in the new school.

Gradually, however, over the first year, as the boys outgrew their expensive blazers they were not renewed, and they began coming to school in regulation black V-necked sweaters. Then, when these wore out, as they came into their fifth year, some of the boys, like the girls, started to 'interpret' the school uniform. The sweaters became more individualized, some in two tones of black and grey, in the height of the trendiest fashion. This was a concrete sign that the gap between the boys' and the girls' 'definition of the situation' was beginning to close. Without their smart blazers it was no longer possible for the boys to present themselves with the same strength of macho imagery as before. This was non-verbal evidence of a change in their validation of 'self'.

> The development of self requires costume. . . . Players leave themselves behind . . . they doff ordinary dress and don extraordinary dress so that the play may proceed.
>
> (Stone 1962: 109)

Jewellery, make-up and hair-styles

The new school rules stipulated that no decorative jewellery could be worn, and nothing was mentioned about make-up, although it was tacitly accepted that the old girls' school rules of 'Only clear nail varnish' and 'Discreet make-up in Upper School only' was held. Girls with pierced ears wore sleepers or studs in their ears, as did a number of ex-secondary modern boys. During the first two terms, however, some of the ex-boys' school boys started to wear a single earring, and, when they were not pulled up about it, went on to have the other ear pierced. Again, this was presenting to the school a different image of their perception of 'self', which was allowed to stand. Mostly nothing was said, although there were mutterings in the staffroom:

> I suppose we have to expect this sort of thing.
>
> (ex-Mordaunt Boys' male teacher)

> It's the writing on the wall!
>
> (ex-Mordaunt Boys' male teacher)

Many of the girls wore some make-up as they felt it 'boosted their self-confidence' (Draper 1985), although those who 'plastered themselves to the tips of their eyelashes' (ex-girls' school pupil) were made to remove the excess. However, no-one had bargained for boys wearing make-up or nail varnish, and when, for a short period of time, a small minority of boys started to appear wearing eye shadow, lipstick and painted nails, the ex-boys' school teachers did not know how to handle the situation:

> Mr West, he was shouting 'Get it off, get it off' and [the wearer] was shouting 'Why should I? It don't say anywhere that I can't wear it. I'm not breaking the school rules'. I thought Mr West was going to have a heart attack.
>
> (ex-boys' school pupil)

Even the ex-girls' school teachers found it 'a bit odd':

> There was this lad with bright red fingernails. I said to him 'I think you will find that the rules say "colourless nail varnish only" '.
>
> (ex-girls' school female teacher)

Some boys were heavily involved in a rock group and it is possible that they allowed the contextual fantasy of flamboyant self-presentation to spill over into their school life. But also, by this cultural behaviour they were making a non-verbal statement about their own previously suppressed identity, and at the same time were testing out the teachers once more, particularly those from the boys' school, since teachers from the girls' school did not react so strongly.

More pervading, however, as the first year wore on, were the new hairstyles. A proportion of both girls and boys started to have parts of their heads shaved, mostly in a semi-circle around their ears, with the rest of their hair in various degrees of length, or spiked up on top of their heads. More changed the colour of their hair, even my 'conformist' informant Jason:

Fin:	Look at the girls. Look at the girls' hair. Think, if a boy dyed his hair like a. . . .
Jason:	What's wrong with the boys changing the colour of their hair?
Kevin [to me]:	He has highlights, Miss, he lights it.
Jason:	The girls dyed my hair for me.
Fin:	But the girls sort of have different, they sort of have purple and blue and stuff.
Jason:	I don't see what's wrong with that. I'm going to have more next time.
Fin:	Well I can't see me. But I suppose if you can't beat 'em you join 'em [laughter].

By casting off the militarist look-alike image of their previous uniform, by adopting individual hairstyles and by wearing jewellery, some boys were leaving behind the social terms that they had previously accepted – the image of patriarchy, machismo and dominant masculinity. They were beginning to move away from their superior male perception of 'self' and take on another identity within the informal culture of the school.

At the same time, too, many pupils were meeting one another socially outside the school. At the end of their fifth year, in our last interview Helen and Claire discussed this, and showed that despite the boys' attempts at gender domination, they preferred to be mixed with the boys:

Helen: We think this school has sort of got us used to being with boys, so it's prepared us for when we leave.

Claire: We enjoyed it while we were in the girls' school, but we're glad that we had the chance to see what it's like here.

Helen: We like the boys socially because we get invited to more parties.

Claire: And we meet more people and we're all friends.

Helen: Yeah but we get fed up.

Claire: We sometimes get fed up with the way that we're treated, and we always compare it with the old school.

Helen: And we think that if we hadn't been single-sexed out we'd have appreciated this school more, because we wouldn't have known any different, but if we had the chance to go back to the girls' school now we don't think we would.

Claire: And what we're going to miss mostly is the people, not the lessons, not the layout of the school or anything, just the people.

Helen: Because people really matter.

CONCLUSION

In their old schools, before the merger, the pupils had felt secure because they were given acknowledged status. This gave them confidence, an acceptable level of self-esteem, and room for manoeuvre within well-defined parameters. The changes caused by the merger meant that they had to go through status passages (Van Gennep 1960; Glawer and Strauss 1971; Measor and Woods 1984) which contained a number of stages of transition. The informal passages examined in this study were concerned with the processes of establishment of gender identities and relations.

When the new school opened many of the pupils experienced a short-lived phase when reality was suspended, and there was a general sense of euphoria. It soon became apparent, however, that pupils had different perceptions of 'school', based on the concepts that they had internalized in their previous schools. Some of the boys, particularly from the boys' school, saw that these differences were posing a threat to their sense of 'self' in the new school. They promptly set out to protect their status and retain their self-value by establishing their traditional male dominance over the girls. In this next transitional phase they used various strategies to insult and humiliate the girls and make them look small, thereby endeavouring to lower the girls' status and raise their own.

Some of the girls tacitly accepted this situation even though those from the girls' school had experienced two years of single-sex education in which for the most part they had been free of any male threat of dominance. They apparently assumed their own socially determined gender roles of social subordination to the boys, and through this experienced a lowered perception of 'self'. It also meant that they tended to become covert and manipulative rather than docile or passive. By making it clear to me that this was a deliberate coping strategy, they showed that they had not lost all their self-esteem or personal feeling of status, but had changed their behaviour in order to avoid unpleasantness. A few girls actively fought the boys, or used their own perceived sexuality to provoke them.

In the next stage of transition, some of the boys slowly began to acknowledge that there were limits to the dominating effects of their gender stereotypical behaviour. Others, however maintained their masculinist self-image, and did not see the signals that the girls were putting out, much less interpret them or respond to them – in the way that the girls had been prompted to do in response to the boys' (much more blatant) signals. Nevertheless, all pupils were slowly moving through the transitional stages of their status passages, and were gaining different understandings of their sense of 'self', both in and out of school, from the ones they had previously known. What the school would ultimately become, when its 'phase of incorporation' (Van Gennep 1960) was completed, was not yet known, although it was already clear that its 'objective universe' (Berger and Luckmann 1967) would differ from any of the three contributory institutions.

ACKNOWLEDGEMENT

I should like to thank Peter Woods and Martyn Hammersley for their helpful comments on earlier drafts of this chapter.

REFERENCES

Abercrombie, N., Hill, S. and Turner, B. (1984) *The Penguin Dictionary of Sociology*, Harmondsworth: Penguin.

Anyon, J. (1983) 'Intersections of gender and class: accommodation and resistance by working-class and affluent females to contradictory sex-role ideologies, in S. Walker and L. Barton (eds) *Gender Class and Education*, New York: Falmer Press.

Askew, S. and Ross, C. (1988) *Boys Don't Cry*, Milton Keynes, Open University Press.

Ball, S. J. (1984) 'Initial encounters in the classroom and the process of establishment', in M. Hammersley and P. Woods (eds) *Life in School*, Milton Keynes: Open University Press.

Berger P. and Luckmann, T. (1967) *The Social Construction of Reality*, Harmondsworth: Penguin.

Burgess, R. G. (1981) 'Keeping a research diary', *Cambridge Journal of Education* 11(1): 75–83.

—— (1983) *Experiencing Comprehensive Education: A Study of Bishop McGregor School*, London: Methuen.

Davies, L. (1978) 'The view from the girls', *Educational Review* 30(2).

—— (1984) *Pupil Power, Deviance and Gender in School*, Lewes: Falmer Press.

Deem, R. and Weiner, G. (1984) *Co-education Reconsidered*, Milton Keynes: Open University Press.

Delamont, S. (1980) *Sex Roles and the School*, London: Methuen.

Denscombe, M. (1980) 'Pupil strategies and the open classroom', in P. Woods (ed.) *Pupil Strategies*, London: Routledge & Kegan Paul.

Draper, J. (1985) 'Attitudes and behaviour of fifth year girls in a single sex secondary school', unpublished MEd thesis, University of Warwick.

Forward, D. (1989) 'A guide to action research', in P. Lomax (ed.) *The Management of Change. BERA Dialogues No. 1*, Clevedon: Multilingual Matters.

Glaser, B. and Strauss, A. (1971) *Status Passage*, London: Routledge & Kegan Paul.

Goffman, E. (1971) *Relations in Public*, Harmondsworth: Penguin.

Griffin, C. (1985) *Typical Girls? Young Women from School to the Job Market*, London: Routledge & Kegan Paul.

Halson, J. (1989) 'The sexual harassment of women', in L. Holly (ed.) *Girls and Sexuality*, Milton Keynes: Open University Press.

Hammersley, M. and Atkinson, P. (1983) *Ethnography Principles in Practice*, London: Tavistock.

Hebdige, D. (1976) 'The meaning of mod', in S. Hall and T. Jefferson (eds) *Resistance through Rituals*, London: Hutchinson.

Hudson, B. (1984) 'Femininity and adolescence', in A. McRobbie and M. Nava (eds) *Gender and Generation*, London: Macmillan.

Humphries, S. (1981) *Hooligans or Rebels*, Oxford: Basil Blackwell.

Jackson, S. (1980) 'Girls and sexual knowledge', in D. Spender and E. Sarah (eds) *Learning to Lose; Sexism and Education*, London: Women's Press.

James, A. (1979) 'The game of the name: nicknames in the child's world', *New Society* 14, June, pp. 632–4.

Jones, C. (1985) 'Sexual tyranny: male violence in a mixed secondary school', in G. Weiner (ed.) *Just a Bunch of Girls*, Milton Keynes: Open University Press.

Jules-Rosette, B. (1978) 'Towards a theory of ethnography', *Sociological Symposium* 24, 81–98.

Kelly, A. (1985) 'The construction of masculine Science', *British Journal of Sociology of Education*, 6(2): 131–54.

Kelly L. (1988) *Surviving Sexual Violence*, Cambridge: Polity Press.

Lees, S. (1986) *Losing Out*, London: Hutchinson.

McRobbie, A. (1978) 'Working class girls and the culture of femininity, in Women's Studies Group, CCCS *Women Take Issue*, London: Hutchinson.

McRobbie, A. and McCabe, T. (eds) (1981) *Feminism for Girls*, London: Routledge & Kegan Paul.

Mahoney, P. (1985) *Schools for the Boys?*, London: Hutchinson.

Mead, G. H. (1934) *Mind, Self, and Society*, Chicago: Chicago University Press.

Measor, L. (1983) 'Pupil perceptions of subject choice', in I. Goodson and S. Ball (eds) *Defining the Curriculum*, Lewes: Falmer Press.

—— ' "Are you coming to see some dirty films today?": sex education and adolescent sexuality', in L. Holly (ed.) *Girls and Sexuality*, Milton Keynes: Open University Press.

Measor, L. and Woods P. (1984) *Changing Schools*, Milton Keynes: Open University Press.

Menell, J. (1990) Quoted in 'Privates on parade', *The Guardian*, 28 August 1990.

Morgan, J., O'Neil, C. and Harre, R. (1979) *Nicknames: Their Origin and Social Consequences*, London: Routledge & Kegan Paul.

Patrick, J. (1973) *A Glasgow Gang Observed*, London: Eyre Methuen.

Pollard, A. (1985) 'Opportunities and difficulties of a teacher-ethnographer: a personal account', in R. G. Burgess (ed.) *Field Methods in the Study of Education*, Lewes: Falmer Press.

Riddell, S. (1989) 'Pupils, Resistance and gender codes', *Gender and Education* 1(2): 183–97.

Rocheron, Y. (1983) 'Sex and gender: a case study of sex education in one comprehensive school', unpublished PhD thesis, Warwick University.

Spender, D. and Sarah, E. (eds) (1980) *Learning to Lose: Sexism and Education*, London: Women's Press.

Stanley, J. R. (1989) *Marks on the Memory: The Pupils Experience of School*, Milton Keynes: Open University Press.

Stanworth, M. (1983) *Gender and Schooling*, London: Hutchinson.

Stone, G. P. (1962) 'Appearance and the self', in A. M. Rose (ed.) *Human Behaviour and Social Processes*, London: Routledge & Kegan Paul.

Turner, V. W. (1969) *The Ritual Process*, London: Routledge & Kegan Paul.

Van Gennep, A. (1960) *The Rites of Passage*, London: Routledge & Kegan Paul.

Walkerdine, V. (1984) 'Some day my prince will come', in A. McRobbie and M. Nava (eds) *Gender and Generations*, London: Macmillan.

Weiner, G. (ed.) (1985) *Just a Bunch of Girls*, Milton Keynes: Open University Press.

Whyte, J., Deem, R., Kant H. L. and Cruikshank, M. (1985) *Girl Friendly Schooling*, London: Methuen.

Wood, J. (1984) 'Groping toward sexism: boys' sex talk', in A. McRobbie and M. Nava (eds) *Gender and Generation*, London: Macmillan.

Woods, P. (1977) *E202 Unit 11. The Pupil's Experience*, Milton Keynes: Open University Press.

—— (1979) *The Divided School*, London: Routledge & Kegan Paul.

—— (1983) *Sociology and the School*, London: Routledge & Kegan Paul.

—— (1985) 'Ethnography and theory construction in educational research', in

R. G. Burgess (ed.) *Field Methods in the Study of Education*, Lewes: The Falmer Press.
—— (1990) *The Happiest Days? How Pupils Cope with School*, Basingstoke: Falmer Press.

Chapter 4

Humour as resistance

W. S. Dubberley

Source: Dubberley, W. S. (1988) 'Humor as resistance', *International Journal of Qualitative Studies in Education* 1(2): 109–23.

BACKGROUND

What struck me most forcibly about Coalton School, a comprehensive school in the UK's Yorkshire coalfield, when I began my research there in January 1985 was the sense of conflict. Coalton is one of a number of satellite villages around the town of Shedley, and most of the teachers who worked there would drive in from the surrounding area. A conflict existed between the imported culture and values of the majority of the school staff and the local culture of most of the pupils, particularly the working-class pupils from the mining community. Humour played a central role in this situation.

By way of a working definition, what I mean by humour is an imaginative and creative process whereby people present a simultaneous view of two parallel realities, one the 'real' situation and the other a creatively distorted one. One view has such an incongruous relationship to the other that we are shocked into laughter in order to resolve the tension. The perception of the joke and the response to it will depend upon a range of variables which include culture, biography, ideology, ethics and status.

Here, I will concentrate on how working-class pupils used humour to test teachers and to categorize them on the basis of their reactions. This process describes and defines the relationship between the pupils and the teachers. The teachers, however, are tested not simply in terms of the culture of the school, but also in terms of the culture of the working-class community. In this respect, the counter-school culture is linked with the shop floor (see Willis 1976) or, in this case, the coal face. I will not argue simply that forms of resistance in the school can be paralleled directly by the culture of the workplace, though in many cases they can, but that resistance reflects the way the total community, men and women, old and young, have generated an entire culture around the digging of coal. Thus, working-class 'lasses' do not always express their resistance in quite the same way as the 'lads', so it does not always relate directly to the coal face, whereas the resistance of the 'lads' tends to do so. Further, the lasses' response to male dominance essentially is in terms of working-class culture and very much as working-class women, and is dissimilar to that of middle-class teachers. In pupil resistance, therefore, teachers are judged first by the values of the school, but, subsumed under that, they are judged also by the values of the working-class community.

USE AND MEANING OF HUMOUR

I have said that conflict in the Coalton School was evident between the working-class pupils and the majority of the teachers. I interviewed two groups of fifth-year working-class pupils, the lads and the lasses on a weekly basis. They explained to me that they always 'tested out' teachers by what can be described only as trial by ordeal:

Carley: With all new teachers we start off mekin' a noise [humming].
WSD: And then what?
Carley: If they tell us to do summat, we'll say no and start an argument. We'd start cheekin' 'em. Like if they'd say 'Get on wi' yer work,' we'd say 'No'.
Janet: If we do this and we find art that they're soft, they're like that for t' rest o' t' time we've got 'em. But say somebody new comes along and they're OK wi' us, we're OK wi' them.

From this trial emerged four main categories of teachers:

1 Hard.
2 Think they're hard.
3 All reight.
4 Soft.

There was also a subgroup, completely off the 'richter' scale, who were wimps and worse, 'dinner women', not fit even to be junior school teachers.

There are parallels between these categories and those that Woods (1979) describes. The Lowfield pupils described by Woods identified teachers as:

1 Those that keep you working.
2 Those you can laugh and joke with.
3 Those you can work and have a laugh with.
4 Those that just don't bother.

The lads and lasses identified teachers as 'all reight' if they 'did not talk down to yer', 'were respectful', and 'could have a laugh wi' yer' as well as teach you something. This seems to correspond exactly to Woods's third category, 'those you can work and have a laugh with'. The 'hard' teachers correspond to 'those that keep you working', although they were not simply looked upon, negatively, as authoritarian. In fact, they were given grudging respect because they could make you work. 'We might get more education if we had stricter teachers.' However, as far as 'having a laugh' was concerned, they were a 'reight maunge'. For the remaining categories, there are no direct parallels between the two typologies. For the lads and lasses of Coalton, teachers 'who think they're hard', 'soft', and 'wimps' collapse into one category typified by their inability to do their jobs, as the pupils perceived it.

Having a laugh was as important for the lasses and lads of Coalton as for those in Lowfield School, and for the same reasons. They explained that they've 'got to riot to have a laugh' and they had to 'muck abaht – 'cos it's boring'. Teachers who would allow this and still get some work done with their pupils were much admired and liked because it relieved the boredom of school. Other considerations did not simply have to do with the institution and the interaction of pupils and teachers. The trial by ordeal took the form of assessing the teachers by the cultural values of the working-class pit community, and the terms that were used – 'hard', 'soft', 'think they're hard', and 'wimps' – reflect this.

'Soft' teachers and 'wimps' were criticized for talking differently, 'all drawling and that', and were parodied by posh accents which often were high-pitched and effeminate. This was not a one-way process, however, and was almost certainly a reaction to the behaviour of the staff in question. Pupils complained about the attitude of many of the staff, in that they 'talked down to yer', a fact confirmed by some of the more sympathetic teachers.

What these pupils are assessing is the understanding and respect of a stranger towards their culture. One of the most potent tests was to see whether a teacher could take a joke. This characteristic is crucially important in working-class communities and is significantly different from 'having a laugh'. You have to take a joke to show that you're not above yourself, that you're one of the crowd, one of us. On the other hand, you have to be able to give as good as you get, for otherwise you're soft and not able to 'stand up for yoursen'. The joking, abrasive badinage of working-class humour is designed to establish these criteria.

The testing was an ongoing process: it was important to test continually for weaknesses, in the same way that working-class communities continually test each other (Willis 1976). Failure means persons are beyond the pale and there is no respite; 'they're like that for t' rest o' t' time', while those who are 'all reight' continue to show that acceptance by their ability to enter into the badinage.

We can illustrate the process by referring to the broader community. One member of the Women Against Pit Closures (WAPC), Madeline, described the constant testing of workmates that occurs in the pit. Her husband, Neil, is an experienced pit electrician, and yet even now he comes home with wounds inflicted by his workmates in fun. Recently he came home with his ear so unmercifully pulled and twisted by a mate that the skin had parted and the flesh bled.

Madeline's two sons also work down the pit as apprentices. The men have twisted the flesh on their necks between thumb and forefinger deliberately to produce a bruise resembling a love bite. This is a standard test for apprentices; sometimes the senior men actually bite young lads for real. Practical tricks are played, including nailing lads by their clothes to any available timber underground. Apprentices are obliged to wear yellow helmets, instead of the usual white, to denote their inexperience. With superb wit, the men call them 'chicks', betokening in one felicitous word youth and inexperience, acceptance and solidarity, and protection and responsibility.

Another example comes from my own experience some years ago as a teacher at the local technical college, where I taught physical education to mining apprentices. They always wanted to play five-a-side football and picked the teams themselves, including me as one of the players. I quickly realized that the teams denoted status, similar to the situation described in *Street Corner Society* (Whyte 1955). The lads with high status made up the best team. In the first few weeks, I was always placed on the weakest team. My first touch of the ball invited a series of ferocious tackles that I suffered in silence. Over the weeks I was steadily promoted until in the last week of the term I made the 'first team'. I was given the place of honour within this elite band; the lads would go out of their way to ensure that I was forced to have 'a blinder'. I was even presented with a new pair of socks, as the lads noticed that mine always seemed to have a hole in them.

I made mistakes. During one of the earlier sessions, while playing for 'the scrubbers', I was tackled so hard that I feared I had damaged my leg. I lay on the floor ruefully holding my shin and complaining to the young miner who had inflicted the pain and who now stood over me. There was a pause. He looked at me soberly; then saying, 'Don't be so soft', he turned away and rejoined the game.

Life down the pit is dangerous and requires an extreme degree of loyalty, cooperation, and physical and mental toughness. In the event of danger, life might well depend upon these qualities; and there is not time for the weak or faint-hearted. Survival as a community depends upon similar qualities. This was demonstrated by the miners' strike of 1984–5 and applies to everyone in the community, men and women, young and old alike. Such qualities inform the culture of all working-class communities, given their powerlessness over their employment and their future. Often their only defence is stubborn and bitter resistance, which demands courage and collective solidarity.

Lack of respect or understanding of the local culture by teachers invited attack, and a failure to handle that attack meant they were soft. A teacher so exposed could be punished unmercifully. Pit life, and working-class life generally, encourages an instrumental perspective on work. Miners are paid to hew coal, steel workers to produce steel, and teachers to teach. Knowledge is a commodity to be implanted by the teacher-worker, a view compounded, incidentally, by the 'professionals' attempt to 'ring-fence' their jobs by mystifying their practice. If a worker doesn't do his job he will be sacked, eventually. If a teacher is too soft, he cannot control the class. If he cannot control the class, he cannot teach them anything; and if he cannot teach, it is legitimate to 'rubbish' him, for he is not doing his job. There is no room for sympathy; the teacher should have thought about that before. Life is hard.

Jack: [about soft teachers] They let yer swear in class and push them around.
WSD: But what can they do?
George: But if they're reight soft, they can't do nowt, so there's no point in them teaching.
Jack: They can't really teach yer if they're soft, can they? Yer don't get on wi' any work.
WSD: But what if they're scared?
Jack: Well, they shouldn't be teaching then. Because it's just like life, isn't it? They should have thought about that before they started teaching.

Staff are tested by these criteria: by being 'all reight' and by being a 'reight' or 'proper' teacher.

The lasses were particularly adept at exploiting the weaknesses of soft teachers. Maybe the creativity and variety of their resistance results from their continued exploitation as women and the fact that resistance cannot be too overt. Davies (1983: 44) argues that women are more creative users of 'scripts' than men and that their scripts 'may be temporarily more powerful because they derive from the culture of the powerless'. When it came to disruption, the staff as a whole preferred to teach lads rather than lasses. Lads knew when to stop and 'when it was a fair cop', but the lasses were unremitting.

I observed the lasses at work in a history lesson. They had described the teacher, Mrs Galton, previously.

> Carley: I know somebody that said to Mrs Galton, 'I'm goin' ter hammer you if yer do this or do that,' and she just says [posh voice], 'OK, then, OK.' [Laughter.] She were frightened.
>
> Mary: And she'd do everything that we said, didn't she?
>
> Lynn: I used to sit there and spit on t' floor and rub it in wi' m' foot and she used ter say, 'I'll write a report on yer,' and I'd say 'You dare,' and she wouldn't write a report.

What was interesting about the resistance was that it did not mean necessarily that they disliked the person.

> Pauline: She's a nice teacher ter get on wi', reight – she doesn't pick on yer, *but if you pick on 'er she doesn't do nowt* [author's emphasis].
>
> Carol: That time we were riotin' – we turned all t' tables upside darn and chucked all t' chairs abaht.
>
> Debbie: Yer, and all she does is say [posh, weedy voice], 'Shush, be quiet, girls.' [Laughter.]

When I asked them whether they felt sorry for such teachers, they replied that is exactly what they want; they think, 'Oh, if I roar they'll give up'.

> Carley: But we don't – we do it all t' more.

Certainly the lasses were more unrelenting than the lads as Davies (1983) also suggests, although contempt for the 'posh weed' who cannot stand up for herself is a view held by lads and lasses alike. What is striking about the tone and style of the lasses' threats is that it suggests warring peers, not a teacher and pupil confrontation. Mrs Galton, a young and diminutive woman, was referred to as 'like a lass', and this attitude seemed to motivate their behaviour towards her.

The history lesson is a bottom-set class dominated by the lasses. There are only two boys in the class, and they are not 'lads'. They keep quiet throughout the lesson and sit at the front by the teacher, who sits on the top of a desk in the front row. The lasses scatter themselves around the room well away from her. One of them, Linda, keeps strolling casually about the room. Eventually she is cajoled into sitting down, which she does very casually, turning her back to the teacher.

Mrs Galton has decided on trade unionism as the subject of the lesson. As she tries to start, the door opens and Carley walks in, several minutes late, her face like thunder and pointedly dragging her feet on the floor. Mrs Galton asks, 'Where have you been?' to which Carley tersely replies, without looking at her, 'I've just come', and with her back to the teacher and her face to us she mouths a very clear 'fuck off' over her shoulder. She sits down, chewing gum in a highly exaggerated manner. She is asked to empty her mouth. She shuffles to the bin at the front of the class, stands bolt upright over it, and loudly flubs the gum out of her mouth. There is a moment's silence, and then the bin rattles. Carley turns away, shuffles loudly back to her seat and, nodding curtly in my direction, storms, 'It's only 'cos he's here'.

There is much tapping of feet, elaborate yawning and scraping of chairs as Mrs Galton asks, 'Anyone heard of the Tolpuddle Martyrs?' A slim girl, who has remained silent up till now, responds lazily, 'No – nice name, though'. There is a pause, punctuated by Carley tapping her pen rhythmically on her desk. Mrs Galton, with a cheerful smile, presses on. 'Does anybody know what transportation means?' 'Vehicles', grunts Linda, still with her back to the teacher. Carley mutters to her, 'Yer thick', and then starts making loud raspberry noises to herself. There is another pause; then Mrs Galton mentions the need for agitation to achieve political change. 'What's flagellation?' asks the slim girl. 'Agitation', corrects Mrs Galton. 'Oh', says the slim girl, grinning wickedly. The lesson continues in like manner until break time. Just before the end, Carley gets up from her desk abruptly and sits next to me, 'I've come to talk to yer. I hate this lesson wi' 'er.'

It is difficult to do full justice to the consummate skill with which the lasses contained Mrs Galton. She herself afterwards remarked, 'The girls regard me as an equal, so they are more difficult to control. With the lads I can use other things.'

WSD: Such as?
Mrs Galton: Well – erm – [smiles] charm.

What the lasses demonstrated is that given equality and the absence of ascribed status, Mrs Galton is certainly no match for them. She was completely outmanoeuvred and outwitted, especially in the use of language. Of course, the precedence for such political and combative skills is demonstrated in the female community by the existence of such organizations as WAPC.

Mrs Galton suggested a further explanation of the problems teachers encounter in the school: it illustrates the instrumental view of teaching that the local community have. In a staffroom conversation with Mr Daniels, she remarked, 'The attitude towards us is *wonderful*, you know [heavily ironic]. We don't work with our hands.'

Mr Daniels: If they're failing, it's our fault. Kids come to lessons with no pens; they say. 'Lend us a pen.' It's my responsibility to provide them with a pen and above all a brain with which to do it. *They* don't have to do anything.

Mrs Galton: We're paid to do the whole thing, including the learning. I think our kids think they're finished when they've actually attended.

With male staff members the lasses often used their femininity as resistance. In the following instance two soft teachers are reduced to being like silly lads on the receiving end of the lasses' sexual power.

Carol: They shout to 'im, 'Sexy', he ses 'Oh, I know' [laughter].

Louise: If you go 'Sexy' to 'im, he starts waddling his arse.

George: He sits there in 'is chair, [imitates] legs sprayed out – in front of all t' lasses.

Various
voices: Yer, he does!

Carol: He thinks he's great.

Louise: He's thick.

Later, in a group of lasses only, they expand.

Mary: You can feel his bum an' everything – and we get 'im and we feel 'im and he just laughs at us. And we feel his cheeks – not his face [shrieks of laughter] and we walk into 'im and we feel him and he doesn't know what – he goes [foppish voice], 'Oh, get off'.

Kate: We go, 'Why are you so sexy?'

Linda: He doesn't take it as a joke, does he? He takes it all in.

Kate: He keeps askin' me to get in t' back room wi' 'im.

Margaret: And he fancies Blacker, an' all.

Various: [with keen interest] Does he?

Kate: He's a reight gay.

Margaret: Do you remember that time in cosmetics?

(They had made talcum powder in a 'Science for Today' lesson and, covering their hands with it, had used it as follows.)

May:	We printed hand prints on there [front of trousers] and on his cheeks [laughter]. We walked into 'im and put hand prints on his cheeks and at t' front. [Shrieks of laughter, half horrified.]
Linda:	[mocking] You disgusting. . . .
Kate:	No . . . [then, worldly-wise], he enjoyed it.
Margaret:	He brought Mr Ruben in, didn't he? We got 'im as well.
Kate:	That's the only excitement he gets.
Linda:	He [Ruben] meks out he's got a girl friend. [In fact, he is married.]
Kate:	He used to tell us he were married – at t' beginning.
Linda:	[aside] Nobody 'ull 'ave 'im.
WSD:	Why?
Linda:	Cos he's ugly.
WSD:	I thought you said he fancies himself.
Kate:	He does.
Linda:	He does 'cos everybody keeps ramming against him. [Laughter at the joke within the joke.]

Both men were regarded as soft, being variously criticized as 'dopey', 'thick' and taking everything in. Because they were dopey, they couldn't understand the nature of the joke the lasses were playing on them. Had they been able to respond from a position of equality and understanding and stood their ground, this would not have happened. They failed to respond appropriately to the sexual badinage, so the lasses were only too willing to embarrass them in terms of both their status and their gender. Much of the humour came from the dispassionate evaluation of their competence as lovers by women who know about these things, not directly, but as junior member of the matriarchy.

The lads were more direct and uniform in this resistance to staff, who were being tested by rules of acceptable behaviour from the point of view of a working-class male of the community. In the lads' opinion, virtually all the women were incapable of teaching effectively because they were not hard enough. Three exceptions were Mary Cowley; perhaps Joy Austen, though there was some disagreement over her; and Mrs Dixon, but only because of her status as deputy headmistress. About half the men were equally suspect because they were too soft, as the following example shows.

Some teachers were foolhardy enough to adopt a bogus image and affect a familiarity that they did not have with the cultural code. One male teacher, for instance, thinking that he was engaging in the friendly exercise of badinage through mickey take and insult, called a lass a 'slag'. The furore this caused taught him a painful lesson.

Another teacher affected a tough role with the lads that was clearly false. His true biography, that of a sheltered, rural, middle-class upbringing, clearly shone through the Cagney persona he wished to project. Once, demonstrating to two of the lads how to make a simple battery, he told them to take care not to put their fingers inside. One of the lads leered at the other, 'Tha not ter put thee finger in, Gotty.' The teacher missed the joke completely.

Sadly, this teacher had great problems with the lads and lasses, who treated him generally, with contempt, the lads particularly.

Jack: He's a wimp.
Pete: Way he talks.
Jack: He talks like a wimp an' all.
Pete: Drawling noises.
Jack: He talks reight punch drunk. That's why we call him Rocky, 'cos he reckons he used ter be a boxer.
Pete: Ay, that's why I hate him an' all – he tells Jacks, doesn't he? He said he were a boxer – he's a reight wimp.
WSD: You don't believe he was?
Jack: [laughing] Do we, hell! No! He got me 'cos I'd bin taking the mick. He got me and he got his pen knife out and he threatened me with his pen knife. He said – like a wimp – 'If you want a fight outside school, I'll be prepared to meet you' [posh accent]. 'I used to carry a knife around with me,' he ses, 'and I still do sometimes, and I'll use it.' I goes, 'Ah, go away and that' [laughter, derisive tone]. It were one of those small Swiss army knives. Only wimps carry knives and threaten yer with it.

Jack was bitterly sardonic and dismissive about such behaviour, a fact demonstrated graphically in the sharp change of accent from the local and macho to the fluting and posh. There is also something sadly humorous in the bathos about 'the blade', 'the shift' Rocky carries, a Swiss army pen knife. A Tom Brown's School Days hero threatens the local ruffian, but the script goes all wrong.

Jack went on to add. 'You were watching soccer, weren't you?' (Rocky had stood in for an absent colleague.) 'Did yer see t' way he runs?' (He made exaggerated motions with his fingers to signify someone running with an excessive swaying of the hips.) 'Men don't run like that. He runs like a lass, doesn't he? He's a wimp. It's the way he walks and talks.'

Rocky is being judged by the standards of masculinity in the pit community. He is a wimp because he doesn't talk 'properly', because he has a 'posh' accent. His ignorance of the culture and his sad attempts to compensate for his lack of success in it by affecting a role and image he cannot sustain is unacceptable to the lads. Men don't behave like that. They don't need knives (particularly Swiss pen knives), and they don't claim to be hard and to be something they are not. Indeed, Rocky's behaviour deviates so markedly from what a man should be that there is a suspicion about whether he really belongs to that gender, with some confirmation from the way he runs when playing football.

Of course, a lot is expected of teachers, although it is important to be aware of the social structures within which these interactions take place. Teachers are cultural imperialists; they attempt to impose the culture and values of the dominant social group upon all cultural groups. Such a clash provokes resistance, and this is what really is occurring here. I will discuss the serious ramifications of this later. On the surface, friction obviously is going to occur as the two cultures impact.

The more removed staff were from an understanding of or a sympathy for the culture, the greater the difficulty they had. Burgess (1983) points out that Newsom teachers tended to be from working-class backgrounds and that their experiences were used to help them to understand their pupils. This accords with what I found at Coalton. The most successful teachers were able to present themselves as far from 'soft'. They were capable, not only of having a laugh, but crucially of taking a joke while at the same time 'looking after yoursen'.

Tony Jones was a case in point. A bluff and tough, if somewhat macho, son of a local miner, he was irritated by the attitude of many of the staff towards the local lads and lasses. He could not understand the staff's defensiveness and hostility and felt that 'they must lead very unfulfilled lives'. But I also sensed a certain defensiveness on his own part towards the staff and thought this was because of his own background. He was conscious of his poly degree but argued that, anyway, he would 'wipe the floor with them' as a teacher.

Tony taught with a peculiar mixture of love and discipline, described by one of the deputy heads as 'tough love', although he erred somewhat on the tough side. Nonetheless, he taught with enthusiasm and related his concepts to local features within the culture. A point about world geography would be illustrated by a reference to the canal bank, or the pit, or a local character. He also could enliven the situation by ad libbing jokes in a cut and thrust manner.

Pupil: I thought t' Empire State Building were t' highest [in the USA].
Tony: Not any more. Any road. King Kong knocked it down.

Tony's jokes served not only to demonstrate his own humanity, but to debunk the mysticism that goes with 'academic' learning – its extended code and its phony seriousness. Sometimes, though, this could descend into oversimplification.

Pupil: What's communication studies?
Tony: Watching tele.

Mary Cowley, also from the local community and a celebrity because she was one of only three women the lads thought capable of being an effective teacher, presented an equally powerful personality. She was able to banter and badinage quite brilliantly with her pupils. She would call the class to order with a 'Nah, then, get thee tackle art' (get your books and things out). In one lesson, a lad entered and asked the whereabouts of her name-sake, Judith Cowley, a slim attractive woman in her mid-twenties. Mary, a little dumpy and forty, explained to the lads, 'I'm the young attractive-lookin' one'. In mock amazement the lad looked keenly about the room and asked, 'Wheeyer?'.

This kind of badinage was used by the pupils, the lasses particularly, to show affection and regard, while at the same time not going over the top and being too soft and gushing. As I got to know the lads and lasses, I too became involved in this tough love and wry humour. The lasses showed interest in my private life and commented on the amount of time I seemed to spend at the pub. When they also learned that I was separated and living alone, there were genuine clucks of sympathy.

Linda: [with affectionate concern] Yer haven't got a right good life, 'ave yer?
Kate: He wants to find 'imself a bird, doesn't he?
Margaret: A vulture. [Laughter.]

Those teachers able to take part as equals in the working-class badinage were also the teachers who most successfully 'contained' the bottom sets and most difficult groups in the school. This containment (I use the word advisedly) was demonstrated aptly in the teacher's relations with the rural studies group. They were first described as follows:

Mr Swallow: The Duggie Diggers – have you heard of them? They're of very low ability. They're t' hardest group I have. There's about ten of them – two can't read: one can't talk – or at least won't.

WSD: Why 'Duggie Diggers'?
Mr Swallow: Well. I take 'em for rural studies and 'duggie' is a
                     local term – it means 'thickee'. They call themselves
                     'Duggie Diggers'.

The humour arises from the pupils' own conscious self-effacement, which attempts to anticipate and defuse further condescension from the school, the staff and their peers. The alliterative and irreverent debunking of pompous liberal rhetoric is a fine piece of satire. 'Rural studies for the less able' becomes what it really is, 'digging for thickees'. The humour is precise and subversive and cocks a snook at the hypocrisy of a situation in which rhetoric hides the real vision of class-biased education. To illustrate this further, a staff member was indignantly describing a 'riot' that had occurred in someone else's classroom. One of the lasses had acquired a garden spray from the rural studies group. She describes the situation: 'Tracey left Mrs Ireland's room. Outside, she met Linda Thomas, who had got hold of a spray that the Diggers . . . [she hesitated, looked at me, then corrected herself] that the rural studies group . . .'

When doing rural studies, the 'Diggers' conducted themselves with an elaborate casualness that seemed to parody both the lesson and the process of manual work. One of the blocks in the school was built around a quadrangle of earth which was being cultivated by the group under the direction of Jim Swallow. I went to observe one day and arrived early. The lads had a collection of gardening implements and had organized a parody of a game of cricket with spades as bats. The 'ball' was a stone from the garden. When I arrived, they carried on with their slow-motion parody, affecting to be deeply engrossed. When the teacher arrived, they made no attempt to disguise what they had been doing, but allowed themselves to be organized into work groups to dig and rake a patch of earth. Mr Swallow handled them with the rough good humour of a building-site ganger.

Everything was done with casual labouredness, while the lads competed with each other in a laid-back, laconic manner. While their arms mechanically operated their implements, up and down, to and fro, they indulged in occasional sarcastic remarks. 'Look at Scoggy.' Mock contempt: rakes pause, except for Scoggy's; the rest of the group eye him solemnly. 'Tha supposed ter rake it.' Scoggy, lightly dragging the rake over the lumpy soil to no effect, shouts back over his shoulder, 'I *am*, Tinsley'. The teacher mentions that peat should be added after the digging. One lad leans on his spade, looks inquisitively around the rest of the group and asks, 'Pete? Who's Pete?'

The same air of indifference and casualness informed the pupils' behaviour in academic lessons. I observed a geography class with Jim

Fletcher, affectionately referred to as 'Paddington' because of his stature and his liking for duffle coats. The lesson, incidentally, was light years away from an O level class I had seen the same teacher give a few days previously. On that occasion, Jim had injected a sense of urgency into the proceedings, a pre-exam revision exercise, standing throughout the whole period, sleeves rolled up, urging and cajoling his class to work.

In this particular case Jim remains seated, is relaxed, indulgent, and slightly condescending. The 'Diggers' are given a test. They settle down noisily, co-operating with the same studied casualness as in rural studies and responding to each question by counter-questions affecting complete ignorance. In the midst of this co-operative chaos, someone farts. The lads pointedly hold their noses and cry, 'Yer dirty get', and as the smell spreads, it is accompanied by a cry of mock horror and revulsion, 'Oh, it's driftin' well!' Some lasses in the group smile ruefully, and one holds her cardigan over her nose. The teacher, Jim, handles the situation well: 'Do I have to send someone to the science labs for a cork?'

The test continues while the lads hold their own conversations, making no attempt to hide their remarks. Snatches of conversation can be heard clearly: 'I wouldn't shit on him', 'Shagger'. 'He wants one under t' chin'. One says to another, 'Stop minging', and this is taken up rapidly with 'What's a minge?', 'Ginger minge' (a nickname given to a red-haired female member of the staff), 'Ginger minger', and so on.

Eventually the test is completed and Jim, with a pointed smile at me and a nod to them, says, 'Right, pass your books two places clockwise, then three places anti-clockwise.' There is pandemonium while the teacher grins broadly at me. One lad, however, cuts through all this and snorts impatiently, 'Chuck 'em in t' middle and pull another one art.' With this simple expedient, the chaos is resolved.

Though in the above examples the teachers were successful in avoiding the resistance of the pupils by their insight into the culture, this did not mean that the resistance disappeared. The teachers' good sense allowed the contradictions of school and the counter-culture of the working-class community to resolve itself in good humour. The teachers who were well-liked showed the ability 'to have a laugh' and indeed 'to take a joke' and thus negotiate a relatively painless passage for these working-class pupils through the meaninglessness of the school process. However, the humour of the 'Diggers' and their general behaviour in school shows not simply that pupils will use the local culture to resist teachers, but that the local culture actively resists the dominant school culture by parody and subversion. Nonetheless, the process of reproduction (Bourdieu and Passeron 1977) is unaffected. Indeed, one could argue that 'all reight' teachers unconsciously facilitate this process.

The majority of the staff, however, reacted to 'disruption' in terms of their own middle-class culture. One teacher observed, 'The majority of the staff talk down to kids': and this was echoed and re-echoed by the lads and lasses, particularly about those teachers they did not like. Staff counter-resistance was typified by disdain. Their own sophisticated and civilized behaviour was scandalized by the behaviour of the working-class kids and their manifestations of pit culture. Staff attempted to reassert themselves by ridicule, asserting the superiority of their culture over that of the pupils.

One female head of department, commenting on disruptive behaviour, observed, 'Anyway, the kids here are not really intelligent enough to be really disruptive. It's very easy to make a fool of the kids. They haven't the wit and intelligence, and they hate it'. One lass reported, 'Simon Carr calls Miss Crabbe "Fatso" and she ses. "You can call me what you want about my stature – how I'm built; it doesn't bother me – just because you've got no brain".'

Miss Crabbe recalled an incident to other teachers in the staff room.

[In a superior tone] One lad was making funny noises, and he said to me [crude accent], 'I'm not making funny noises – tha daft'. I said [arch tone], 'All right, let's have a competition to see who is daft, me or you.' He said [crude accent], 'I'm not daft.' I said [urbane], 'Well, then, I suggest you go to see a psychiatrist, then. Anyone who makes funny noises and can't even hear them must need one.' Of course, all the class laughed at this.

There were numerous complaints by the pupils, supported by a few of the staff, that teachers often used aspects of the dominant culture, particularly language, code and intonation, social style, and urbanity, to put them in their place. One teacher said, 'We should not go down to their level'. Aspects of working-class culture and middle-class stereotyping of that culture were freely used to parody and ridicule.

Mrs Boyle: [arch tone] Do you know that awfully tall boy?
Miss Roach: George Ash?
Mrs Galton: The giant.
Mrs Boyle: Well, he came into my class the other day, I pushed his chest to get him out and then I thought, 'Good God, he might strike me'.
Mrs Rice: [heavily ironic] Oh no – he won't hit a woman. I had him by the neck and he wouldn't hit me.
Mrs Boyle: No – just rape you.

The insult is multi-layered. This giant is potentially dangerous because of the physical strength he has allied to his dumbness. A Frankenstein monster of the lower orders, through his lack of intelligence he becomes a potential threat, if not by physical violence, then by sexual violence, to his betters, the women. Mrs Boyle later said about a family in the local community (shades of Orwell), 'They all need a good scrub'.

One technique of staff counter-resistance that the pupils were bitter about was that often the lasses would be described as tarts, slags and sluts by the staff. Such insults were generally restricted to the lasses, but occasionally the lads were described as puffs or gays. Of course, the pupils themselves were not innocent of this. They referred to female teachers liberally as bitches, as did the lads about the lasses. However, the pupils felt there was a profound difference between the way they used abuse and the way staff did. The pupils argued they didn't really mean it: they didn't use the terms literally to impugn sexual reputations; whereas the staff did. The pupils claimed they used the words as 'swear' words, whereas the staff actually meant that the lasses were not respectable women.

The staff knew these descriptions really hurt, for irrespective of how raucous or 'crude' their sexual rhetoric might be, the lasses defended their sexual reputations zealously. The lads respected this and also were angry with the staff because it simply wasn't true that any of the lasses were 'sluts' or literally promiscuous.

The staff, I believe, used the term in a number of ways. First, they knew that to call the lasses 'bitches' and the lads 'puffs' or 'gays' was a particularly sensitive cultural offence. Second, 'bitch' is often synonymous with being mouthy or bolshy. Third, and perhaps the way in which it was used most, it denoted social status – the lasses were the lowest of the low, like common prostitutes.

Women in the school generally had to put up with the sexist attentions of both the male pupils and the male staff. Interestingly, however, the lasses complained exclusively about the behaviour of the male staff, while the female staff were most critical of the lads' behaviour and of the community attitude towards women as a group. There were few complaints about the male staff from the female staff, though there were blatant examples of sexism that the women accepted without comment. Further, institutional sexism was reflected in the distribution of key posts in the school, though this was a residual factor that the head was trying to reverse. The women staff never commented to me about this form of structural sexism. It would seem, then, that the perception of sexism is profoundly influenced by social class perspective, or at least by that of peer group relationship and power status.

There were complaints by the lasses about male teachers 'hittin' yer on t' bum' and looking 'darn yer top'. It was claimed that one member of the staff 'was always on abaht people's busts', making such remarks as 'she's got a nice pair o' melons'. The lasses were slightly scandalized in a good-humoured way by this, but were more disapproving, not so much at the observations as at the fact that 'he were married' and as a teacher was 'supposed to respect yer'. However, they were more than capable of resisting the suggestions. One teacher who made a humorous and suggestive public proposition to a lass was deflated immediately by 'Ah . . . when yer capable . . . He didn't like it, did he?' The lasses were able to resist the cruder aspects of male sexism in this way and even succeeded in going on the offensive. The talcum powder incident mentioned earlier is an example. Another was 'raping' the duggie lads, a practice whereby a number of lasses would subject an isolated lad to an investigative feeling-up process. One female teacher, though complaining bitterly about sexism herself, was shocked by an incident she observed involving a fifth-year lass.

Mind you, it's not just the lads. Jean Norman, she got a piece of mistletoe that had fallen on the floor at Christmas. The berries had got squashed. She went up to Dicky Thomas, plonked it in his hand and said, 'Here you are, a load of spunk for you.'

This seems to be a brilliantly conceived elemental joke worthy of further comment. The nature of the symbolism, the squashed white berries off the floor, suggests not only sperm, but sperm as something dirty, as pollutant. This is plonked unceremoniously into a man's hand with the comment, 'Here you are, a load of spunk for you', as if to say, 'Have the whole mucky mess back'.

ANALYSIS

Humour reflects the nature of the culture which employs it and, in the case of conflictual humour, the differences between cultures. Humour highlights power in particular by its ability temporarily to distort social relations and structures and point to their absurdity. Like a Magritte painting, by altering features of 'normality', such as scale and proportion, humour shocks us out of perceptive lethargy, forcing us to re-evaluate what is around us.

I hope that by giving fairly full examples in this paper of the lads' and lasses' humour and the counter-resistance of the teachers, I have illustrated the gulf that exists between the two cultures. It is important in academic research to give as full an ethnographic account as possible. Runciman (1984) argues that one of the three key functions of theory is to communicate what it is like to experience a particular system. On the whole, research is failing in this respect. Consequently, teachers and academics (or any workers) operate peacefully within the gap that exists between theory and lived-out reality without having to face the unpleasant contradictions of their society. Indeed, radical theory exposes educational institutions and their practitioners, and the implementing of a carefully doctored form of the rhetoric in social policies that do little for those to whom they are supposedly aimed but a great deal for the interests of those who have appropriated them. We know what goes on, or ought to know. It is time to face up to the realities of the contradictions, to inform our practice, to vocalize our objections, and to influence policy [. . .].

Willis (1976) argues that the key function of counter-school culture is to provide an alternative to the school for working-class lads. But by opting for the shop floor as a more attractive alternative, the lads ensure the process of reproduction and therefore of their continued exploitation. While I agree with this analysis, I also want to emphasize the imperialistic nature of the culture of schools. School culture is so antagonistic to working-class culture, the orientation of the community to the experience of hired physical labour, that it cannot be accepted.

Emphasizing this aspect of the school process allows the educational aspirations of working-class communities to be taken into account. For instance, while the lads and lasses reviled much of what was happening in schools, they were also critical about the fact that they were not receiving a 'reight' education. They were aware that they were disadvantaged by the processes they experienced. Unfortunately, this awareness has led the working-class community to press for a return to the more traditional and conservative education based on the grammar school model. I have dealt with this point before (Dubberley 1988); briefly, the point is that the grammar school system, typified by uniform, discipline and product learning, was seen to produce a few successes. This idea has led to a similar unconscious collusion with the process of reproduction that Willis (1976) mentions, that the community insists on the very processes that disadvantage them.

Also obvious, I hope, from the lads' and lasses' resistance is the wit, vitality and creativity with which they opposed the school culture. At the very least, the lads and lasses could hold their own against the teachers, and in many cases they left them a very poor second. Lévi-Strauss (1958), in comparing pre-industrial and post-industrial societies, argues that man 'has always been thinking equally well' (p. 230). The human mind does not so much 'progress' as it applies its 'unchanged and unchanging powers to novel areas'. The inference seems clear; the potential of the human mind to operate remains the same irrespective of time and place.

Like Lévi-Strauss, I would argue that in the particular situation of the Coalton School it is the same human mind at work in a different cultural milieu. Discrimination arises not because of an intrinsic weakness or inferiority on the part of working-class people and their culture, but because of power, the power to define what is good and what is not good.

I agree with Willis (1976) that it serves no purpose to romanticize working-class culture, although my own prejudices are obvious. However, if a viable alternative is to be formed to that to which working-class culture is opposed, many problematic issues will have to be dealt with, not the least of which is the exploitation of women. Coalton, like other pit communities, is a male-orientated community. In this respect it is sexist, but it is a sexism that has arisen as a particular manifestation of capitalism. The family unit is arranged and exploited so that coal can be produced. It is therefore offensive that some middle-class feminists should attack sexism in such communities while ignoring the very social and economic structures that force miners to dig coal and allow others the privilege of higher education and access to that cultural capital which enables them to make such criticisms. Gender roles and relationships cannot be equated between the mining family, on the one hand, and the graduate, polytechnic teaching suburbanites, on the other hand.

Let me give a final illustration. During the miners' strike, I attended a public seminar at the university given by the deputy head of Coalton School, Ronnie Clayton, about the effect of the strike on the school. Afterwards, a number of us went to the local pub. A young married couple, both successful graduate teachers, were in the group. The woman, waxing lyrical in her feminist radicalism, urged that if we cared about feminism we should start picketing working men's clubs. At the time, the mining communities were being fed by soup kitchens and people were selling their family belongings bit by bit in order to survive. I do not minimize the problem of sexism, but in order to combat it, the exploitative economic and political structures that create it have to be dealt with. The working men's clubs are secondary.

A few other general observations and suggestions can be made. The 'middle-class ethnocentricity' of teachers is still prevalent and remains a problem for research and training. The hierarchical structure of the teaching force encourages a compliance (Lacey 1977) and a conservatism which has been exacerbated by the current contraction of the labour market. Restricted career opportunities in teaching have reinforced the power of middle management and have ensured the increasing marginalization and disaffection of 'radicals'.

However, the problem is not simply a matter of changing the minds and hearts of teachers. As has been shown, even 'good' teaching practice of 'all reight' teachers facilitates reproduction unless accompanied by policy change. We must re-commit ourselves to a comprehensive system (Willis 1986) that is genuinely egalitarian (Ball 1981) by 'communitizing' education. This necessitates the devolution of power, the demystification of professionalism, and the establishment of a curriculum that emanates directly from the culture of the local community. This would provide the opportunity for issues such as gender to be addressed and dealt with on a face-to-face basis, allowing the re-negotiation of relationships from an understanding of the economic and cultural structures that people live in. A genuine community-based education would mean community control over the educational processes, community members and teacher-workers becoming co-authors of educational projects.

Of course, within the current education climate, with centralization of control and the escalation of divisive policies amounting to virtual educational apartheid, such suggestions might provoke a loud and bitter laugh.

REFERENCES

Ball, S. J. (1981) *Beachside Comprehensive: A Case Study of Secondary Schooling*, Cambridge: The University Press.

Bourdieu, P and Passeron, J.-C. (1977) *Reproduction in Education, Society and Culture*, Richard Nice (trans.) London: Sage Publications.

Burgess, R. G. (1983) *Experiencing Comprehensive Education. A Study of Bishop McGregor School*, London: Methuen.

Davies, L. (1983) 'Gender, resistance, and power', in S. Walker and L. Barton (eds) *Gender, Class, and Education*, New York: Falmer Press.

Dubberley, W. S. (1988) 'Social class and the process of schooling', in A. Green and S. Ball (eds.) *Progress and Inequality in Comprehensive Education*, London: Routledge & Kegan Paul.

Lacey, C. (1977) *The Socialisation of Teachers*, London: Methuen.

Levi-Strauss, C. (1958) *Structural Anthropology*, London: Penguin Books.

Runciman, W. G. (1984) *A Treatise on Social Theory, vol. 1*, Cambridge: The University Press.

Whyte, W. F. (1955) *Street Corner Society*, Chicago: University of Chicago Press.

Willis, P. (1976) 'The class significance of school counter-culture', in M. Hammersley and P. Woods (eds) *The Process of Schooling: A Sociological Reader*, London: Routledge & Kegan Paul.

—— (1986) 'Unemployment: the final inequality', *British Journal of Sociology of Education* 7(2).

Woods, P. (1979) *The Divided School*, London: Routledge & Kegan Paul.

Chapter 5

Gender imbalances in the primary classroom
An interactional account

Jane French and Peter French

Source: French, J. and French, P. (1984) 'Gender imbalances in the primary classroom: an interactional account', *Educational Research* 26(2): 127–36.

INTRODUCTION

It is now well-established that in mixed-sex classrooms male pupils receive more teacher attention than do females. Brophy and Good, for example, have observed that 'boys have more interactions with the teacher than girls and appear to be generally more salient in the teacher's perceptual field' (1970: 373). Stanworth (1981) and Spender (1982) have also noted an imbalance in this respect and, although their formulation is more tentative, Galton and colleagues' conclusion is in essence the same: 'There does appear to be a slight tendency for . . . boys to receive more contact than girls' (1980: 66).[1]

The present study reveals imbalances in teacher–pupil contact which, in broad terms, are compatible with these observations. However, rather than simply reporting the occurrence of the imbalances and thereby giving yet more voice to an already well-documented trend, it takes the gender-differentiated distribution of teacher attention as a starting point for further analysis and investigates its grounds. As Spender points out: 'While it has been known for a long time that boys get so much more attention from teachers than do girls . . . few attempts have been made to explain this phenomenon' (1982: 54). The principal aim of this study is to provide the basis for such an explanation through an examination of classroom interaction.

THE DATABASE

The data to be considered comprise a verbatim transcription of a fourth-year junior school lesson (pupils aged 10–11 years). The lesson is one from an extended series that one of us (JF) observed and recorded as part of an ethnographic study of gender differentiation in primary classrooms. The grounds for selecting this particular lesson for analysis will be discussed later in the article. The lesson is organized as a teacher–class discussion of the topic 'What I do on Mondays and what I would like to do on Mondays'. In an earlier lesson pupils had addressed this topic in writing, but their essay answers proved unsatisfactory to the teacher. The present lesson therefore covers a number of points which, the teacher explains, he would like to have seen included. After the lesson, pupils make a second attempt at the essay. The class contained 29 pupils, 16 girls and 13 boys. The teacher was male.

ANALYSIS

(i) Distribution of interaction turns between boys and girls

We begin the analysis with a numerical breakdown of the interaction turns that occurred during the lesson.[2] Table 5.1 indicates that, when taken as categories, boys took more turns than did girls: 50 instances of turn-taking are clearly attributable to boys as against only 16 girls. When one considers that girls are in a (16:13) majority in the class, the proportions of the imbalance become all the more apparent.

Table 5.1 Interaction turns during the lesson

Turns taken by teacher	81
Turns taken by pupils as 'chorus'	33
Turns taken by unidentified pupils	8
Turns taken by boys (13 out of 29 pupils)	50
Turns taken by girls (16 out of 29 pupils)	16
Total	188

Although, as Spender suggests, few studies have tried directly to account for distributions of this type, statements are now emerging from feminist research which could at least throw some light on the present patterning. These statements tend to be of two types. The first concerns teachers' attitudes. We have in mind here proposals expressed in, for example, Clarricoates (1978, 1980) and Stanworth (1981) that teachers have a general and overall preference for male pupils. Given that in teacher–class discussions it is the responsibility of the teacher to allocate turns to pupils (cf. McHoul 1978; Edwards 1981), then a preference for interacting with boys might give rise to the sort of pattern represented in Table 5.1. On the basis of such an analysis, the responsibility for gender imbalances rests largely with the teacher. They may be seen to result from his/her being socially and psychologically predisposed to solicit contributions to the lesson from boys (by, for example, directing questions to them) at the expense of involving girls.

Whilst the data under consideration do not directly contradict this explanation, there are further aspects of the lesson to be discussed in section iii below which suggest that it may lead us to underestimate the part played by pupils themselves in achieving the gender-based imbalance.

The second type of statement that feminist researchers have advanced which may be relevant to the interpretation of the present turn distribution deals in more directly interactional categories. Here we have in mind the proposals that boys are more likely than girls to, for example, ask questions, to 'volunteer' information and to make heavier demands on the teacher's time (Stanworth 1981). Contained in these proposals there is, we think, a very promising basis for explaining gender-differentiated rates of pupil interaction. However, it is clear to us that if one is to gain any adequate understanding of gender-differentiated patterns, then these notions must be qualified, clarified and refined in various respects. It is this task that we see ourselves as addressing in the sections of analysis below.

(ii) Detailed breakdown of interaction turns

Table 5.2 Detailed breakdown of interaction turns

Male speakers	Turns	Female Speakers	Turns
Tom	17	Marie	5
Matthew	10	Rachel	3
Andrew	10	Angela	2
Simon	5	Sharon	2
Peter	3	Anne	1
Wayne	3	Claire	1
Jason	1	Laura	1
Warren	1	Rowena	1
Thomas	0	Anna	0
Andrew C.	0	Debbie	0
Allan	0	Gina	0
Martin	0	Helen	0
Paul	0	Jenny	0
		Joanne	0
		Linda	0
		Lorraine	0

It is clear from Table 5.2 that it is not the boys generally who monopolize the interactional space of the lesson. Indeed, some boys take fewer or no more turns than most girls. The distributional imbalance between boys and girls is manifestly due to a particular, small subset of boys taking a disproportionately high number of turns (Tom 17, Matthew 10, Andrew 10 and Simon 5). Some interactional processes through which these boys come to take such a large number of turns will become clear from a consideration of the extracts of talk represented below.[3]

(iii) Interaction examined

Extract 2 follows immediately upon Extract 1. Prior to their beginning, the teacher had posed the generally addressed question: '*Anybody get up earlier than eight o'clock?* At the start of Extract 1, Tom is sitting with his hand raised.

Extract 1 (conventions of transcription appear in Appendix)

1	T:	What time do you get up Tom?
2		(0.7)
3	Tom:	Half past four.
4	T:	What?
5	Tom:	Half past four.
6	T:	(What do you get up at that time for)?
7	Ps:	((exclamations etc.))
8	Tom:	(no:) I've got to feed the a-animals and (clean
9		the aviary).
10	T:	What?
11	Tom:	I've got to clean the (aviary) and feed all the
12		animals and (.) all that.
13	T:	What animals?
14	Ps:	⌈All the animals ((various pupils call out – diffi-
		│he's got a cult to distinguish individuals))
15		⌊(hamster)
16	T:	(I think) half past four perhaps is a little bit
17		early I mean that's half way through the night
18		Tom.
		(1.9)
19	T:	What animals have you got?
20	Tom:	erm=
21	T:	=you've got your parakeet.
22	Tom:	Two cats (.) two dogs (.) hams – no hamster
23		(.) two rabbits.
24	Wayne:	Birds
25	Tom:	Erm (1.0) parrot (1.0) that's all (.)
26		I've got about (0.5) two rabbits (.)
27		(I've) got about (.) fif:ty-three birds something
		like that.
28	T:	What (.) have you got them in an aviary have
		you (.)

29		(Have you got them in the garden)?
30	Tom:	Yeah.
31	T:	Well it must take a long time to feed so you'll
32		have to get up a bit before eight o'clock that's
		true (.)
33		What happens on a Saturday then?
34	Tom:	I cleans 'em all out.
35	T:	Yeah but what time do you get up on a Saturday
		then.
36		You've still got to feed them.
37		(0.5)
38	Tom:	I gets up about (.) half past eight.
39		(1.0)
40	T:	Half past eight. (.) What time do you get up
		early?
		((to Rachel))

Extract 2

1	T:	What time do you get up early?
		((to Rachel))
2	Rachel:	Quarter to eight.
3	T:	Quarter to eight (.) What about you Laura?
4	Laura:	Half past seven.
5	T:	Half past seven. ((nods to Jason))
6	Jason:	Quarter to eight.
7	T:	Quarter to eight. ((points to Rowena))
8	Rowena:	Seven o'clock.
9	T:	Seven o'clock.

In the first extract, Tom takes ten turns at talking, nine in response to the teacher and one prompted by Wayne. In contrast to this, in Extract 2 four pupils take one turn each. Each pupil is selected to speak by the teacher and produces an answer to the question *'What time do you get up early?'* The teacher then acknowledges the answer and passes on to the next pupil. This pattern of interaction, i.e. of pupils being given a single rather than several successive turns at answering, has been reported widely in studies of classroom discourse (cf. Mehan 1979; MacLure and French (1981). In respect of Extract 1, it seems clear that the teacher allocates Tom an extended series of turns on the basis of what he (Tom) has to say. The teacher's further questions are occasioned by the type of answer Tom has given to the first question. Tom's claim that he gets up at half past four is out of the ordinary and newsworthy when compared with what everyone knows about weekday getting up times. It is the sort of claim one might wish to investigate further (*'What do you get up at that time for?'*), the other answers produced by Tom are no less extraordinary, and thus in turn warrant investigation. For example, the claim at line 26–7 that he keeps *'about fifty-three birds'* occasions yet another question from the teacher: *'What (.) have you got them in an aviary have you?'*[4] Returning briefly to Extract 2, it can be seen that the getting-up times claimed by pupils there (e.g. *'quarter to eight,' 'seven o'clock'*) do accord with everyday expectations and are treated as warranting nothing more than an acknowledging repetition.

To move to a more general level of analysis, it is clear that the turns in Tom's series do not have a purely 'voluntary' basis, but are answer turns which have been solicited by the teacher's questions. However, it is also clear that at least some of the teacher's questions do not have a purely voluntary basis either: they are responses to the newsworthy, or extraordinary, answers Tom has produced in the previous turn. Thus teacher and pupil are seen as acting collaboratively, each simultaneously producing and inviting further talk in response to constraints provided by the other. In view of this, we would suggest that the sort of model which best explains turn distribution in this instance is not one which implies responsibility to lie unilaterally with the teacher, but an *interactional* one which emphasizes the collaborative aspects of classroom behaviour.

The analysis we have advanced in respect of Tom's achieving an extended series of turns rests heavily upon the proposal that pupils' answers making newsworthy claims occasion requests for further information. This proposal finds some additional justification in Extracts 3 and 4:

Extract 3

1	T:	What about you Peter?
2	Peter:	Half past six.
3	T:	Why do you get up at that time?
4	Peter:	My mum gets up early.
5	T:	Does she? (0.5) What time does she go to work?
6	Peter:	Eight o'clock.
7	T:	That's early. (0.5) What about you Matthew?

Extract 4

1	T:	What about you Matthew?
2	Matthew	Half past five to six o'clock got to feed my
3		horses and dogs and all that.

4	T:	Do you do that before you come to school everyday=
5	Matthew	Yeah.
6	T:	= do you? (.) Oh well people obviously (go) – some
7		people then have got to get up er at er (10.) well
8		before it's light

Whilst the claims to getting up times made by pupils here ('*quarter to seven*', '*half past six*') are not as far removed from everyday expectations as was Tom's, the teacher nevertheless explores them further. What is more, there is evidence that pupils themselves may look upon these types of claims as requiring explanation. In Extract 4, for example, Matthew, who it will be recalled is a member of the subset of boys taking a larger number of turns, appends to his answer ('*half past five to six o'clock*') the justification '*got to feed my horses and dogs*'. The knowledge that self-reports of unusual practices are to be accounted for may provide a powerful resource for pupils who wish to talk more about themselves.

Claims like those produced by Tom and Matthew in Extracts 1 and 4 give pupils prominence within the classroom setting; they mark them out as different from their peers. Tom's activity in Extract 5 also has this effect:

Extract 5

1	T:	Put your hand up all those people who like
2		coming to school on Tuesday.
		(2.0) ((most pupils' hands are raised)).
4	T:	Put your hands down. (0.5) Put your hands up
5		all those people who don't like coming to
6		school on Tuesdays.
→7		(2.5) ((Tom's hand goes up, alone))
8	Ps:	((laughter))
9	P1:	⌈It's swimming Tom.
10	P2:	⌊It's swimming.
11	Tom:	We don't do owt on Tuesdays.
12	Ps:	We do we do ((several pupils calling out at once))
13	Tom:	(I) do now.
14	Ps:	((laughter))
15	T:	So Mondays then. (.) Monday's a pretty hard day then

16		really isn't it?

The teacher's request for a show of hands at lines 4–6 (*'put your hands up all those people who don't like coming to school on Tuesdays'*) must be interpreted against the background information that Tuesday is the day that the class goes to the swimming baths. Given what we know about the likes and dislikes of children of this age, there is an expected outcome to this request, i.e. that pupils will not raise their hands. Only Tom raises his hand. Interestingly, in this case it is the other pupils rather than the teacher who take Tom up on his response. In answering them, Tom achieves two further turns at speaking. In some respects the pattern here is very similar to that in Extract 1. Tom's extra turns are produced in response to the talk of others, but again this talk was in turn generated by the unusual or 'out of line' character of his previous activity.

Further instances of this kind can be seen in Extracts 6 and 7, where Simon and Matthew indicate that they consider the subjects English and maths to be unimportant:

Extract 6

1	T:	How many people think that it's really necessary
2		to do any maths?
3		(1.0) ((most pupils' hands are raised))
4	T:	That it really is necessary that it's er (0.4) how
5		many people think that em it doesn't really make
6		any difference whether you do any maths or not?
7		(0.5) And that you can get on quite well without
8		it?
→9		(1.0) ((Simon's hand goes up, alone)
10	Ps:	((laughter))
11	T:	(You do) like it Simon don't you? (.) (Well think
12		about) tell me why you think that.
13	Simon:	'Cos I (just don't like it).
14	T:	No no no no that's not really what I said. (.) I
15		said how many people think that it's *necessary* (.)
16		to do Maths (1.0) to learn about it. (2.0) So you
17		think it's necessary do you?
18	Simon:	Yes.
19	T:	Well what about em (being able to count)? (0.5)

20		Is it important that you should be able to count?
21	Simon:	((nods))
22	T:	So it's important that you should be able to do
23		Maths is it?
24	Simon:	((nods))
25	T:	I think it's important too.

Extract 7

1	T:	Put your hands up all those who think that doing
2		English is important.
3		(2.0) ((most pupils' hands are raised))
4	T:	Right put your hands down. (.) How many people think
5		that English isn't important?
→6		(1.0) ((Matthew's hand goes up, alone))
7	T:	Doesn't really matter?
8	Ps:	((laughter))
9	T:	Why?
10	Matthew:	((shrugs his shoulders))
11	T:	Well I think you've got to have a reason (0.4) other
12		wise (in fact I think)
13	Ps:	((general chatter))
14	T:	sh sh (0.5) otherwise (you've got to be very) careful
15		when we're talking about things like this that you
16		don't argue against something just for the sake of it.
17		(.) What I'm interested in is that you think (0.4) not
18		what
19	Matthew:	I just I just I just like maths anyway=
20	T:	Yes well whether you like it or not is not what I said=
21	Matthew:	=( )=
22	T:	=I said I said that do you think that being able to do
23		English for example to be able to read (0.4) to be able
24		to write so that people can understand what you've

25		written and to be able to read is that important is
26		that going to be important in your life? (0.5) Is it
27		an important thing to have to do?
28	Ps:	Yes.

The positions advanced by Simon and Matthew here are investigated further by the teacher and, as a result, each boy is accorded several more turns.

Not all the additional turns taken by the highly participating boys identified in Table 5.2 can be accounted for by reference to the sorts of practices so far described. A further tendency appearing in the data was for these boys to make unsolicited comments on the lesson's topic. The type of turn we have in mind here is illustrated in Extract 8, where Simon addresses Claire's answer to the teacher's question:

Extract 8 ((question: *'Which bits of maths do you like doing?'*))

1	T:	What about you Claire?
2	Claire:	Er I like in the Fletcher books where you've got
3		to do measuring.
4	Simon:	Ugh that's horrible.
5	T:	What about you? ((to next pupil))

As previous studies of classrooms have pointed out, teacher–class lessons are guided by certain normative 'rules' of participation whereby pupils' rights to speak are governed by the teacher (cf. McHoul 1978; Edwards 1980, 1981). Unsolicited contributions from pupils are sanctionable events. It is the prerogative of the teacher to decide whether they be let pass (as in Extracts 8 and 9), suppressed (as in Extract 10) or accepted, endorsed and developed (as in Extract 11):

Extract 9

1	T:	Perhaps some people might think that er em (1.0)
2		they should never be – there should not be any
3		Mondays.
4	Ps:	((talking among themselves, laughing))
5	Andrew:	Sir if there weren't any Mondays Tuesday would be
6		like a Monday it would be exactly the same
→7	T:	Perhaps then we

8		Should go straight from Sunday to Tuesday.
9	Ps:	Yes.
10	Andrew	'Cos Tuesday'd be a Monday it'd be exactly the same.
11	Ps:	((talking among themselves))
12	T:	Right now then before you start . . .

Extract 10

1	T:	Right put your hands down
		⎡(0.4) if I (***)=
2	Tom:	⎣I'd rather (***)
3	T:	=Marie and Nina?
4	Marie:	Only sometimes.
5	T:	Not on Mondays thought. (.) We're talking about Mondays
6		in particular aren't we?
7		(1.0)
8	Andrew:	Sir I like coming to school on Tuesdays Wednesdays
9		and Fridays.
10	Wayne:	Tuesday's swimming.
11	Pl:	Sir I like – ((at this point several pupils begin to call out and it is impossible to distinguish individuals))
→12	T:	Alright now look if you want anything (.) sh sh if you
13		want to say anything now you've got to put your hand up
14		otherwise we'll have twenty nine people trying to talk
15		all at once and (that'll never do).

Extract 11 ((T. speaking of importance of English, i.e. end of Extract 7))

1	T:	Is it an important thing to have to do?
2	Ps:	Yes.
3	Andrew:	You wouldn't have any General Knowledge without English.
4	T:	Pardon?
5	Andrew:	You wouldn't have any General Knowledge without English.
→ 6	T:	(Well you wouldn't have much chance (.) I know. (.))

7	In the evenings – there's three evenings a week for example
8	when I – when I take classes for adults (1.0) in
9	the evenings I take classes for adults who can't read
10	and write . . .

However, even though the decision to pass over or endorse unsolicited contributions lies ultimately with the teacher, it is nonetheless a decision that pupils can influence to some extent. If we consider the character of, for example, Andrew's comment in Extract 11, we can see that his utterance, *'You wouldn't have any General Knowledge without English'* expresses the sort of view a teacher might be expected to endorse and develop. It may well be that when pupils produce comments of this type, the teacher can allow concerns of pedagogy to override those of interactional protocol. The capacity to gauge the concerns of teachers may again constitute an important interactional resource for pupils who wish their voices to be heard and their comments to be addressed by the teacher.

DISCUSSION AND CONCLUSION

In this final section, we shall be concerned to do three things. The first is to provide an account of the grounds upon which our data were selected and the generality of the patterns they express. The second is to give some more explicit consideration to whether or not one may look upon the pupil activities discussed here as tactical, goal-oriented behaviour. And the third is to develop some policy implications from the findings we have presented.

Selection of data and generality of findings

As mentioned at the outset, the lesson examined here is only one from a large number of lessons that were observed and recorded as part of an ethnographic project. Our reasons for having selected this particular lesson are essentially practical. A great many of the recordings are characterized by small subsets of boys 'dominating' the proceedings, and the activities by which they achieve their prominence are aligned with those examined here. In most cases, though, the uneven distribution of turns is not quite so marked, and the activities are rather less frequent in occurrence. Because they are so richly represented in the present lesson, it provides us with a focal point for the presentation and discussion of patterns which, we would claim, are widely distributed across primary classrooms.

Intentional status of pupil activities

A large part of our analysis concerns the ways in which pupils, through making newsworthy claims or taking up unusual positions, secure the extended attention of the teacher (and/or other pupils). The question we have so far side-stepped is whether one can say that they produce these claims with specific aim of gaining attention.[5] The issue of intentionality is one of dogged debate within the social sciences (cf Coulter 1974, 1979), and the present context is not the place to resurrect the well-known arguments in any detail. Suffice it to say that the making of statements about the motivational states of actors is never unproblematic. However, the impression that we gain in many instances in our data is that pupils are actively seeking attention. The basis of this impression lies in the fact that certain pupils take up unusual positions on issues of classroom discussion so frequently and consistently that their behaviour argues for more than coincidence.[6]

The most explicit warrant we can offer in support of our position here is that there is occasionally come evidence that it is commensurate with a participant's analysis, i.e. with that of the teacher.

Extract 7a

14	T:	Sh sh (0.5) otherwise (you've got to be very) careful
15		when we're talking about things like this that you
16		don't argue against something just for the sake of it.

In Extract 7, for instance, the teacher's comment upon the position taken up by Matthew (*'don't argue against something just for the sake of it'*) would seem compatible with the interpretation we have been advancing more generally.

Policy implications

Our suggestion here has been that gender imbalances in teacher attention and turn distribution among pupils may be in part attributable to subsets of boys engaging in strategies to secure that attention.[7] Rather than attempting an exhaustive account of these strategies, we have provided only a broad outline of some of the more obvious exemplars. The analysis should be received, then, as a beginning, not as an end, to investigation of this area. Even at this early stage, however, we would see the sort of approach adopted here as bearing relevance to those who are concerned about the remediation of gender imbalances at the level of classroom practice.

Feminist work in pursuit of this goal has already pointed, though in general rather than detailed terms, to the tendency for boys to demand more of the teacher and hence receive more than their share of attention (cf. Clarricoates 1978, 1980; Spender 1982). Whilst existing analyses have therefore acknowledged that pupils may play a part in the shaping of classroom events, rather more emphasis has, in our view, been placed upon teachers being socially and psychologically predisposed to favour boys. As we have already noted, we do not oppose this claim. However, we would suggest that the redress of imbalances in teacher attention does not necessarily follow from the remediation of male-biased attitudes in teachers, unless they also become sensitive to the interactional methods used by pupils in securing attention and conversational engagement. Although there is occasionally evidence that teachers are aware of pupils' behaviour in this respect (see Extract 7), it may well be that in a great many instances pupil strategies remain invisible to them. Teachers' immersion in the immediate concerns of 'getting through' lessons may leave them unaware of the activities performed by boys in monopolizing the interaction.[8]

This view finds support in a recent report by Spender. Even though she consciously tried to distribute her attention evenly between boys and girls when teaching a class, she nevertheless found that

> out of 10 taped lessons [in secondary school and college] the maximum time I spent interacting with girls was 42% and on average 38%, and the minimum time with boys was 58%. It is nothing short of a substantial shock to appreciate the discrepancy between what I *thought* I was doing and what I actually *was* doing.
>
> (Spender 1982: 56; original emphasis)

We think that one would be safe in assuming that Spender's lack of success could not be attributed to her having a male-biased outlook.[9] It seems clear to us that much would be gained from developing, in the context of teacher education programmes, an interaction-based approach to this issue which sought to increase teachers' knowledge and awareness of what may be involved through the use of classroom recordings.

REFERENCES

Brophy, J. E. and Good, T. L. (1970) 'Teachers' communications of differential expectations for children's classroom performance: some behavioural data', *J. Educ. Psychol.* 61(5) 365–74.

Clarricoates, K. (1978) 'Dinosaurs in the classroom: a re-examination of some aspects of the "hidden" curriculum in primary schools', *Women's Studies International Quarterly* 1: 353–64.

—— (1980) 'The importance of being Ernest . . . Emma . . . Tom . . . Jane. The perception and categorization of gender conformity and gender deviation in primary schools', in R. Deem (ed.) *Schooling for Women's Work*, London: Routledge & Kegan Paul.

Coulter, J. (1974) *Approaches to Insanity*, London: Robertson.

—— (1979) *The Social Construction of Mind: Studies in Ethnomethodology and Linguistics Philosophy*, London: Macmillan.

Deem, R. (ed.) (1980) *Schooling for Women's Work*, London: Routledge & Kegan Paul.

Drew, P. (1978) ' "Accusations" the occasional use of members' knowledge of "religious geography" in describing events', *Sociology* 12(1): 1–22.

Edwards, A. D. (1980) 'Patterns of power and authority in classroom talk', in P. Woods (ed.) *Teacher Strategies: Explorations in the Sociology of the School*, London: Croom Helm.

—— (1981) 'Analysing classroom talk', in P. French and M. MacLure (eds) *Adult–Child Conversation*, London: Croom Helm.

French, P. and MacLure, M. (eds) (1981) *Adult–Child Conversation*, London: Croom Helm.

French, P. and Woll, B. (1981) 'Context, meaning and strategy in parent-child conversation', in G. Wells (ed.) *Learning through Interaction: The Study of Language Development*, Cambridge: Cambridge University Press.

Galton, M., Simon, B. and Croll, S. (1980) *Inside the Primary Classroom*, London: Routledge & Kegan Paul.

Garfinkel, H. (1967) *Studies in Ethnomethodology*, Englewood Cliffs, NJ: Prentice-Hall.

Hustler, D. (1981) 'Some comments on clarification requests: a response to Langford', in P. French and M. MacLure (eds) *Adult–Child Conversation*, London: Croom Helm.

McHoul, A. (1978) 'The organisation of turns at formal talk in the classroom', *Language in Society* 7: 183–213.

MacLure, M. and French, P. (1981) 'A comparison of talk at home and at school', in G. Wells (ed.) *Learning through Interaction: The Study of Language Development*, Cambridge: Cambridge University Press.

Martin, R. (1972) 'Student sex behaviour as determinants of the type and frequency of teacher-student contacts', *School Psychology* 10(4): 339–47.

Mehan, H. (1979) *Learning Lessons: Social Organisation in the Classroom*, Cambridge, Mass.: Harvard University Press.

Meyer, W. J. and Thompson, G. C. (1956) 'Sex differences in the distribution of teacher approval and disapproval among sixth-grade children', *J. Educ. Psychol.* 47: 385–96.

Sears, P. and Feldman, D. H. (1974) 'Teacher interactions with boys and girls', in J. Stacey *et al.* (eds) *And Jill Came Tumbling After: Sexism in American Education*, New York: Dell.

Spender, D. (1982) *Invisible Women: The Schooling Scandal*, London: Writers and Readers Publishing Co-operative Society with Chameleon Editorial Group.

Stacey, J., Benaud, S. and Daniels, J. (eds) (1974) *And Jill Came Tumbling After: Sexism in American Education*, New York: Dell.

Stanworth, M. (1981) *Gender and Schooling: A Study of Sexual Divisions in the Classroom*, London: Women's Research and Resources Centre.

Wells, G. (ed.) (1981) *Learning through Interaction: The Study of Language Development*, Cambridge: Cambridge University Press.

Woods, P. (1980) *Teacher Strategies: Explorations in the Sociology of the School*, London: Croom Helm.

APPENDIX: CONVENTIONS OF TRANSCRIPTION

The system used here is a simplified version of that developed by Gail Jefferson for use in Conversation Analysis.

1 Participants' identities appear on the left, as in a play script. The teacher is identified as T. Pupils' names appear where they are known. Where a pupil's identity is not known he/she appears as P1, P2, etc. Where pupils speak collectively they are identified as Ps.

2 Participants' speech appears to the right of their identities, again as in a play script.

3 Speech enclosed in single parentheses indicates that the transcriber thinks that this is what was said but is not 100 per cent sure, e.g. (what do you get up at that time for)?

4 Asterisks enclosed in parentheses indicate that a speaker said something but that the transcriber was unable to decipher it properly. The asterisks represent the number of syllables heard, e.g. (***).

5 Empty parentheses indicate that a speaker said something but that the transcriber was unable to hear even how many syllables were uttered.

6 Speech enclosed in double parentheses represents a description of some relevant activity, e.g. ((shrugs)), ((various pupils call out)).

7 A colon following a syllable indicates that the syllable was pronounced in a long, drawn-out style, e.g. no:

8 Pauses between utterances are timed in seconds and tenths of seconds, e.g. (1.5) represents a pause of one and a half seconds. A full stop between parentheses indicates an immeasurably brief pause.

9 An equals sign may be used to indicate 'latched' speech, i.e. where a second speaker comes in immediately the first speaker has stopped speaking e.g.

   T: What animals have you got?

   Tom: erm=

   T: =You've got your parakeet

   Equals signs may also be used to indicate that a speaker is continuing with his/her turn when it has perhaps been interrupted by a second speaker, e.g.

   T: Do you do that before you come to school⌈everyday=

   Matthew: ⌊yeah

   T: =do you? (.) Oh well then . . .

10 Dashes may be used to indicate that a speaker hesitates or stammers over a word, e.g.

   T: In the evenings – there's three evenings a week for example when I – when I . . .

11 Where participants' speech overlaps, a square bracket indicates the onset of overlap, e.g.

   Andrew: it would be exactly⌈the same

   T: ⌊perhaps then

ACKNOWLEDGEMENTS

Thanks are owing to the staff and pupils of the primary school near Bristol who participated in the study. Their names and initials have been changed for the usual reasons.

A preliminary version of this paper, entitled 'An initial investigation into the strategies used by boys and girls when initiating exchanges with the teacher', was first presented at the BERA Annual Conference, Cardiff, 1980. Thanks are due to Sandra Acker, Tony Edwards, Martyn Hammersley, Alison Kelly and Rod Watson, who all commented on the earlier draft.

NOTES

1 And see also in this context papers by Meyer and Thompson (1956), Martin (1972) and Sears and Feldman (1974).
2 Counting of pupil turns is, of course, only one of several measures that we could have employed (e.g. pupil contributions could have been subjected to word counts). The only advantage that turn-counting has is that it allows us – with the aid of notes made *in situ* – to include pupils' non-verbal turns, which word count measures would miss.

  We acknowledge that turn-counting is not unproblematic, but have tried to adhere to the following general guidelines: only talk and activities directed into the official proceedings of the lesson have been counted- asides from one pupil to another and 'background talk' have been excluded from the figures. Non-verbal activities have been counted where they are integral to the enactment of the interactions (e.g. a nod from a pupil in response to a teacher's question). Where they are concurrent with verbal turns (e.g. a pupil nodding at the same time as answering 'yes'), they do not appear in the figures.
3 In examining excerpts of interaction our aim is to provide insights which may be of interest to researchers, students and teachers who are concerned with issues of gender, education and classroom practice. In the interests of clarity of exposition, we do not attempt the highly rigorous modes of analysis current in, for example, the disciplines of conversation analysis and ethnomethodology. At certain points, though, it will be apparent that these perspectives have influenced the approach we adopt.
4 At an earlier, oral presentation of these data, a psychologist asked us if Tom was 'telling lies' – i.e. if his claim to keeping 53 birds was 'really true'. We do not know the answers. However, it seems to us that the question misses the point. There is always a range of alternative ways available to people for describing the same state of affairs (cf. Drew 1978). In this instance, we could point to formulations such as 'a lot of birds', 'some birds', 'stacks of birds' or just 'birds' as being available to Tom for depicting his pets collectively. When compared with these, the formulation he actually selects, *'about fifty-three birds'* may be seen as one which exploits quite heavily their news potential.
5 Accounts of younger children's strategies for securing the conversational engagement of adults can be found in French and Woll (1981) and Hustler (1981).

6 In suggesting that their behaviour is designed to gain attention, essentially
   what we are doing is attributing a pattern of underlying significance to
   diverse segments of observed behaviour. This mode of interpretation is
   described in some detail by Garfinkel (1967) under the name of 'documen-
   tary reasoning'. Garfinkel claims it to be an inevitable element in reasoning
   about social settings by social scientists and participants alike.
7 We would not want to make the claim that these activities are exclusive
   to boys. There are, in our recordings, clear instances of girl pupils marking
   themselves out from their peers by making newsworthy claims although,
   interestingly, in the lesson discussed here no girls are found either to make
   unsolicited comments or to employ the strategies discussed in relation to
   Extracts 5–7. As a general rule, however, we find that it tends to be
   particular boys who make these types of claim or who offer unsolicited
   contributions most consistently. The question of why such pupils tend to
   be boys stands outside the scope of the present study. Only more broad-
   ranging, longitudinal work could determine whether, for example, girls at
   an earlier age receive more negative responses to these activities from
   teachers and hence cease to engage in them.
8 The extent to which teachers are aware of these types of pupil activity is,
   of course, dependent upon several factors including the consistency with
   which particular pupils perform them. Overperformance would undoubtedly raise their visibility and may result in pupils being labelled 'characters',
   'attention seekers' and so on. It may well be that successful deployment
   (from the pupils' viewpoint) of the strategies outlined here involves their
   gauging quite carefully just how far they can go before their behaviour
   becomes too 'obvious'.
9 Our argument here, of course, assumes that the sorts of activities we have
   documented (or versions of them) are to found in other tiers of education.
   We have not systematically examined data from colleges or secondary
   schools from this angle, but on the basis of some familiarity with talk in
   these settings, we think the assumption is correct.

Chapter 6

An evaluation of a study of gender imbalance in primary classrooms

Martyn Hammersley

Source: Edited extract from Hammersley, M. (1990) 'An evaluation of two studies of gender imbalance in primary classrooms', *British Educational Research Journal* 11(2): 125–43.

In recent years there has been increasing concern about the under-achievement of girls in the British education system, and this has stimulated investigations of whether girls and boys are treated in significantly different ways in classrooms.[1] A particular interest has been whether boys receive more teacher attention than girls. Much of the research in this area has employed systematic observation. In this paper I want to examine a recent British study that has used a more ethnographic approach, carried out by French and French (Chapter 5). I shall try to assess what we can learn from this work, approaching it using the following framework:

1 Is the focus of the research justifiable?
2 Are the empirical claims made on the basis of this study convincing?
3 Are the implications drawn from these claims soundly based?

The starting point for French and French's argument is what they believe to be a well-established finding that 'in mixed sex classrooms male pupils receive more teacher attention than do females' (p. 115). They offer further evidence for this from a study of classroom inter-action in a Bristol primary school in the 1970s, though the data used in the article come from one fourth-year junior school lesson (pupils aged 10–11 years). The authors also put forward an explanation for how this gender imbalance was produced. The approach adopted is broadly sociolinguistic (influenced by ethnomethodological conver-sation analysis), but it also includes some quantitative analysis.

RATIONALE FOR THE RESEARCH FOCUS

French and French do not state what they take to be the significance of their research focus, but it seems likely that it derives from the belief that pupils of different sexes should be accorded equal treatment and/or the view that differential treatment in the classroom may play an important causal role in producing differential educational achievement and occupational mobility on the part of males and females.

In my view no explicit justification is required for the value that underlies these beliefs – a concern to achieve equality of opportunity between girls and boys, women and men. Its justification is obvious and widely accepted, at least in principle. However, there are problems with the beliefs themselves. As regards the first, it should be noted that an injunction that girls and boys should be treated in the same way in every respect is not acceptable. We rightly take account, to one degree or another, of the characteristics of people in dealing with them: of variations in their background knowledge and their interests, their abilities and disabilities, the opportunities they have and have not had, etc. The issue is not whether we should treat people as the same or as different, but rather what aspects of difference we should take into account for what purposes. In this context it is not obvious that equal aggregate teacher attention between the sexes is a good thing. This is especially so given an undifferentiated notion of teacher attention that draws no distinction, for example, between questioning and telling, praising and blaming, etc. But even putting this on one side, clearly we would not wish to insist that teachers reprimanded girls for equal amounts of time as boys irrespective of whether they committed the same number of serious offences as the boys. Nor, presumably, would we require that teachers follow up girls' answers to questions as much as they do those of boys irrespective of the relevance of those answers to the lesson topic. The arguments about equality of opportunity, in relation to class and race as well as to gender, are precisely about what are and are not relevant elements of similarity. From this point of view, it is not clear that equal teacher attention between the sexes is an ideal in terms of which we should evaluate classroom practice.[2]

The other possible justification, that the differential distribution of teacher attention might help to produce particular forms of under-achievement among girls, is more plausible. However, it is not entirely convincing as it stands. We need evidence that such a causal link operates. Furthermore, the concern with *amount* of teacher attention must be questioned: it seems unlikely that it will be closely related to levels of educational achievement. There are those who have suggested, not unreasonably, that under some circumstances less teacher attention may enhance learning and creativity (Bowles and Gintis 1976; Anyon 1981a, b; Tickle 1983). Much more plausible than the focus on amount of teacher attention is the claim that particular *types* of teacher attention, such as praise and blame, might affect achievement levels. However, French and French concern themselves solely with *amount* of teacher attention, on the grounds that measurement of types of teacher attention is not feasible in a rigorous manner (French 1988).[3]

In summary, I accept, and most readers would probably also accept, the importance of the value issue to which this study is addressed. However, there are doubts about the effective relevance of the study to that issue.

EMPIRICAL CLAIMS

The study makes at least two empirical contributions. First, the authors offer evidence about the distribution of teacher attention to boys and girls. Second, they develop an interesting explanation for the gender imbalance that they document.

Information about differential male-female participation rates

The evidence that the authors present comes from a single lesson in a primary school, devoted to teacher-class discussion. However, they claim that this lesson is 'richly representative' of a larger number of lessons in the same school. They do not give any further information about the larger data set however.

French and French operationalize the concept of teacher attention in terms of number of turns at talk in public interaction with the teacher. They provide information about the number of turns taken by girls and boys as aggregates and as individuals in the lesson concerned. Ignoring turns taken by pupils as a chorus and a small number of instances where the pupils were not identifiable, boys produced 50 turns (76 per cent) while girls produced 16 turns (24 per cent). Even this fails to represent the full degree of differential participation since there were more girls than boys. On the basis of equal participation we would have expected 45 per cent of the turns to be taken by boys and 55 per cent by girls. In these terms there was an over-representation by boys (or an under-representation by girls) of 31 per cent. Put in another way, the mean number of turns per boy was 3.8 and for girls 1.0, so that on average, boys had nearly four times as many turns as girls. (The median number of turns for boys was 2, while for girls it was 0. The mode number for both was 0). The percentage distributions are shown in Fig 6.1.

The authors also provide a breakdown of numbers of turns for each pupil. If we rank the pupils in terms of the percentage of turns they took, we get the distribution presented in Table 6.1. On the basis of these data, French and French claim that there is a gender imbalance in turns at talk, and thus in the distribution of teacher attention. But

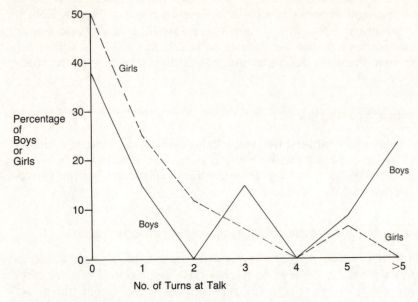

Figure 6.1 Distribution of turns at talk for boys and girls.

they also argue that this is produced by a small proportion of the boys, notably Tom, Matthew, Andrew and Simon who contribute exaggerated attention-seeking responses.

Table 6.1 The ranking of pupils in terms of percentage of turns at talk

Tom	26%
Matthew, Andrew	15%
Simon, MARIE	8%
RACHEL, Peter, Wayne	4%
ANGELA, SHARON	3%
Warren, Thomas, ANNE, CLAIRE, LAURA, ROWENA	2%
4 boys and 8 GIRLS	0%

(Derived from Table 5.2)

In assessing these empirical claims I shall begin by taking the focus of description to be the particular lesson from which these data derive. It is worth noting that while it is clear that there is an imbalance in the participation of individual pupils, and that it is also true that a larger proportion of the boys participate (and participate more) than the girls, it could be misleading to describe this as a gender imbalance. Such a description automatically implies that the differential participation is a product of gender, whereas it *could* be accidental that boys participated more than girls in this lesson. If we knew the eye colours of the pupils we might find that children with blue eyes participated more than those with brown. If so, I suspect that we would be less inclined to assume a causal relationship than we are in the case of gender differences. This is because there are plausible theoretical reasons for thinking that gender might produce differential participation and because others have found that boys participate more than girls, and men more than women, in other situations (Coates 1986). These are good reasons. But we should not forget that we are making an assumption here. Furthermore, it seems likely that gender is not the only (or perhaps even the primary) factor operating. After all, 38 per cent of the boys do not participate at all, and 54 per cent of them participate at or below the mean level of female participation.

Let me accept, however, that gender is the main immediate factor producing imbalance in participation rates among the pupils in the lesson. At least two questions then arise. First, whether this is a product solely of the actions of a small proportion of boys. And, second, whether number of turns at talk is an adequate measure of teacher attention.

As regards the first point, it is quite clear that a small proportion of the boys far exceed the girls, and most of their male colleagues, in the proportion of turns at talk they gain. However, what is also true is that there is a discrepancy in the proportion of girls and boys who take no, or very few, turns. Fifty per cent of the girls take no turns at talk, compared with 38 per cent of the boys; 25 per cent of the girls take only one turn, compared with 15 per cent of the boys. Even without the three boys who contribute more turns than any of the girls, the ratio of turns per pupil remains slightly higher for boys (1.3) than for girls (1).

This may suggest a general tendency for the girls to participate less than the boys, which would have implications for the explanation of the gender imbalance that French and French offer, and I shall return to it.

The other issue I want to discuss here is whether number of turns at talk is an adequate measure of amount of teacher attention. Within a sequence of teacher–pupil interaction that involves whole class discussion like this, it is not unreasonable to treat turns at talk as a measure of attention. But there are grounds for doubting whether *number* of turns is an adequate measure. First, a smaller number of longer turns could represent more teacher attention than a large number of shorter ones. If quantity of teacher attention is what is of concern, then number *and duration* of turns need to be taken into account. Second, turns include a variety of rather different phenomena, including, for example, invited repetitions where the teacher did not hear the response the first time. But if he did not hear the first response, should it be counted as an instance of teacher attention?

Perhaps, but this is clearly a matter of judgement. There are a number of other similar, probably minor, problems: such as how to deal with shouted-out answers that the teacher does not take any notice of; or, even more difficult, answers that the teacher explicitly declares inappropriate because shouted out. Similarly, in classroom interaction there are sometimes situations where a teacher indicates non-verbally that a particular pupil is to respond but another pupil shouts out an answer that the teacher accepts. Should the first pupil be deemed to have been given no teacher attention, even if, for example, there was a pause before the other pupil shouted out the answer. It seems unlikely to me that resolving these problems in a different way to that of the researchers would make much difference to the results, but some assessment probably needs to be made of them.

I want now to address the issue of the generalizations that the authors make on the basis of the data about this lesson. They claim that this lesson is 'richly representative' of the whole corpus of lessons that they recorded in this school. Furthermore, they imply that their results add further support to the empirical claim that in mixed-sex classrooms boys get more teacher attention than girls.

It seems clear from what the authors say that by 'richly representative' they mean that this is the most extreme example of gender imbalance in their data. If so, and even if it is not so, it would clearly be of interest to know in aggregate terms what the participation rates of boys and girls were over the whole corpus of lessons. After all, the evidence presented in the article concerns a relatively small number of interactional turns (effectively 66 in all). One might reasonably expect that there would be some fluctuation over time in the gender balance of contributions, and in the patterns of participation within the sexes; and the extent of this variation is clearly relevant to the authors' arguments.[4]

Another problem is that whole-class discussions are not the only, or even the dominant, form of teacher-pupil interaction in primary classrooms. And, while turns at talk is a reasonable measure of teacher attention in such discussions, a different measure may be required for other types of interaction. There are serious questions, then, even about the representativeness of the results as regards the behaviour of this teacher and class over a longer period of time than the single lesson about which evidence is provided. It is worth remembering that other kinds of teacher attention might well outweigh imbalances in whole-class discussion.

It is not clear from what French and French write whether the larger corpus of lessons from which these data were selected includes other teachers and other children. If so, more potential sources of variability are introduced, and the representativeness of the lesson is even more questionable; though such a corpus might give us a sounder basis for generalization to some larger population than would a single teacher, single class sample. However, insufficient information is provided about the other data for us to make any judgement.

French and French seem to go beyond generalization to the whole corpus of lessons they studied. They imply that their research supports the claim that in general in mixed-sex classrooms boys get more attention than girls. And they cite evidence from both sides of the Atlantic in further support of this claim. But, while it is true that in a number of situations studied an imbalance has been found, we cannot base an unrestricted empirical generalization on this. Empirical claims must be about objects and events in specific time-place locations. Universal claims are always conditional: they are theoretical statements about what will happen if certain conditions are met, anywhere and at any time.[5] It may be that in both Britain and the United States at the present time an imbalance in teacher attention between boys and girls is widespread, but the evidence from which we are generalizing here is rather limited. Of course, we may also believe that it is likely that girls will get less attention than boys on theoretical grounds: in very crude terms, because in patriarchal societies this is what occurs. This too is a reasonable form of inference, but its cogency depends on how effectively the theory on which it rests has been tested. In this case, as in that of many other theories in the social sciences, the answer is that the theory has not been subjected to rigorous test. French and French's findings cannot offer strong support to the statement that there is gender imbalance in the distribution of teacher attention, either as a theoretical claim or as an empirical generalization about schooling in Britain. This is because they neither show that the lesson they studied was a crucial case of the theory, nor give us strong evidence to believe that it is representative of the relevant population.[6]

The explanation

I want to look now at the explanation that the authors offer for the gender imbalance they found. The failure to distinguish between theoretical and empirical claims arises here too. The authors imply that what they are offering are ideas about what causes gender imbalance on all (or many) occasions. But to establish this theory they would need to study multiple cases, and cases selected so as to control both their theoretical and relevant extraneous variables. Since they do not do this I shall treat them as offering an explanation for the gender imbalance that they discovered in the particular lesson about which they provide evidence.

The authors suggest two interesting explanatory ideas. First, that the gender imbalance in teacher attention might have been the product of attention-seeking strategies on the part of a small group of boys, rather than (or as well as) a preference on the part of the teacher for interaction with boys. Second, that the gender imbalance was a collaborative product of teacher–pupil interaction.

There are three steps that the authors need to take in establishing their explanation, it seems to me. First, they must show that the evidence from the case they have studied fits their explanation. Secondly, they must assess whether the theory that their explanation presupposes (that attention-seeking strategies on the part of boys might produce gender imbalance) is true. Thirdly, they must show that their explanation is the most plausible of those that fit the facts of the case.

In my view French and French do show fairly convincingly that in the lesson for which they provide evidence a small group of boys did employ attention-seeking strategies and that the success of these strategies did depend upon the response of the teacher. As regards the second step, I think that the truth of the theory is obvious, though it is less clear under what conditions it would operate.[7] The third step is more difficult. The authors themselves mention a different plausible explanation that has been discussed in the literature: that the teacher might have had a preference for participating with boys. And earlier in this article I mentioned another: that in general terms the girls might be more reluctant to participate than the boys.[8] We need to decide which of these explanations apply, and if more than one does we must consider what the relationships are among them. Comparative assessment of these different explanations is necessary. For example, if the teacher used questions directed at particular pupils before offers of answers were made, we might investigate whether there was a gender imbalance in the pupils nominated. Where the teacher invited offers of answers we could examine whether the teacher gave non-verbal cues that encouraged boys rather than girls to respond. We might look at how many girls and how many boys offered answers, and whether they had equal chances of being nominated to answer.[9] Finally, the girls and boys could have been interviewed about their participation in lessons, to see if there was any evidence of gender differences in willingness to participate, etc.

IMPLICATIONS

The authors claim to have produced further evidence for the empirical finding that boys tend to get more teacher attention than girls, and to have shown that one reason for this may be the use of attention-seeking strategies on the part of some boys. On this basis they recommend that teachers be trained to be aware of such strategies so that they can counter their use and thereby achieve gender balance in the allocation of their attention. In my view these conclusions are not well-established. Summarizing the main points I have made:

1 Empirical claims must be about particular time–place locations: unrestricted empirical generalizations such as that 'boys get more teacher attention than girls' are illegitimate. We need to know the population to which generalization is being made, and to assess the strength of the inference. Of course, one could treat this unrestricted claim as a theoretical statement, but to count as such conditions would have to be specified under which gender imbalance occurs, and comparative analysis of multiple cases designed to control the theoretical and relevant extraneous variables would have to be carried out.

2 If we treat the authors' claims as referring to the lesson about which they provide information, it seems reasonably clear that a gender imbalance in the distribution of turns occurred. Whether this represents accurately a differential distribution of teacher attention is a little more questionable because duration of turns is neglected. However, it seems likely that taking account of duration would not substantially modify the authors' findings.

   Assessing the generalization of this finding of a gender imbalance in teacher attention to the whole corpus of data that the authors collected is problematic, since we are given little information about the rest of the data. Furthermore, whole-class discussion by no means exhausts teacher–pupil interaction in primary schools, and it is possible that any imbalance in such discussions could have been counter-balanced by different patterns in individual and small group contacts between teacher and pupils.

3 The authors' proposed explanation for the gender imbalance in teacher attention is interesting, relevant and plausible in itself. However, they do not establish its validity and it does not explain all of the gender imbalance they document. Over and above the activities of a small group of boys using attention-seeking devices, there seems to have been a more general disparity in the propensity of boys and girls to participate. This could be described as a reluctance on the part of girls as plausibly as that boys seek teacher attention. We cannot be sure that had the small group of boys not been attention-seeking the girls would have answered more questions, or even a larger proportion of the questions. This is one of the issues that French and French fail to resolve because they do not systematically compare the explanation they offer with plausible alternatives.

4 Finally, there is the problem of the justification for the focus of the research. French and French simply assume that a focus on the amount of teacher attention given to boys and girls is justified. However, while a concern with equality of educational opportunity between boys and girls needs no explicit justification, it is less clear what the relationship is between this value and the research focus adopted. It is not obvious why equal distribution of teacher attention should be implied directly by a commitment to equality of opportunity. Such a direct relationship might be more plausible if what were at issue were particular types of attention. Even then, I think we would probably want to argue for equality of treatment only where circumstances were the same in relevant aspects, rather than in aggregate terms. Of course, the research focus might also be justified on the basis of the assumption that the differential distribution of teacher attention between boys and girls contributes to girls' educational underachievement. However, the authors provide no explicit argument for this, nor is it convincing. An argument about the effects of learning and achievement of particular *types* of teacher attention would be more plausible.

In conclusion, this study is a useful contribution to an important field, in particular for its attention to patterns of differential participation among boys, and for the novel ideas in explaining gender imbalance that it presents. However, it has some serious defects, and these indicate areas where further reflection and research are required.

ACKNOWLEDGEMENTS

I would like to thank Peter French, Joan Swann, Dave Graddol, John Scarth and the students of Open University course E812 for discussions and comments that have contributed to this paper. Also, my thanks to two anonymous referees for helpful suggestions.

NOTES

1 Spender (1982: 54–9) raised the issue most forcefully. Of course, the underachievement of girls is not a straightforward matter. Over and above problems about the meaning of 'underachievement', it should be noted that patterns of achievement between boys and girls vary across stages of schooling and across subjects. Concern about girls' underachievement has not been limited to Britain. In the United States a large literature has developed dealing with this topic, a considerable amount of which addresses the possible effects of patterns of gender-differentiated interaction in the classroom. For useful reviews, see Bossert (1982), Lindow *et al.* (1985), Brophy (1985).

2 Of course, it might be argued that differences between boys and girls in

these respects should approximate a random pattern, and therefore cancel one another out over a very large number of lessons. However, this may not be the case, for example, with the tendency to disruptive behaviour (or perhaps in other instances either). Also, the data analysed in the two studies discussed here involve rather small samples where such cancelling out cannot reasonably be expected.

3 This focus is rather surprising given that systematic observation research in the area has been concerned with 'quality' as well as quantity of inter-action (see Note 1). However, it is to be explained I think by qualitative researchers' greater awareness of the problems of measuring 'quality'.

4 Some of the American research confirms that fluctuations across contexts and over time are common. See Bossert (1982) and Morse and Handley (1985).

5 For an account of the distinction between theoretical and empirical claims that is assumed here, see Hammersley (1984, 1992). For specifications of what I believe is required for the development and testing of theory, see Hammersley et al. (1985), Hammersley (1985, 1987).

6 The findings of the ORACLE study (Galton et al. 1980), being based on a much larger British sample, might have offered more convincing evidence for the empirical generalization. However, their results are difficult to interpret. The authors themselves conclude that there is little difference in the distribution of teacher attention between boys and girls, but that there is 'a tendency for boys to receive more contact than girls' (Galton et al. 1980: 66).

7 It seems to me that in this case there is no point in requiring that the theory be subjected to rigorous test: it is beyond reasonable doubt.

8 On some, but perhaps not all, interpretations this may be equivalent to the idea that boys are attention-seeking. There are also evaluative assumptions involved here about what an appropriate level of classroom participation is.

9 These issues are taken up by Swann and Graddol (1988).

REFERENCES

Anyon, J. (1981a) 'Elementary schooling and distinctions of social class', Inter-change 12(2–3): 118–32.

—— (1981b) 'Social class and school knowledge', Curriculum Inquiry 11(1): 3–41.

Bossert, S. (1982) 'Understanding sex differences in children's classroom experiences', in W. Doyle and T. L. Good (eds) Focus on Teaching, Chicago: University of Chicago Press.

Bowles, S. and Gintis, H. (1976) Schooling in Capitalist America, London: Rout-ledge, Kegan & Paul.

Brophy, J. (1985) 'Interactions of male and female students with male and female teachers', in L. C. Wilkinson and C. Marrett (eds) Gender Influences in Classroom Interaction, Orlando: Academic Press.

Coates, J. (1986) Women, Men and Language, London: Longham.

French, P. (1988) Personal communication.

French, J. and French, P. (1984) 'Gender imbalances in the primary classroom', Educational Research 26(2): 127–36.

Galton, M., Simon, B. and Croll, P. (1980) Inside the Primary Classroom, London: Routledge, Kegan & Paul.

Hammersley, M. (1984) 'Making a vice of our virtues: some notes on theory in ethnography and history', in I. F. Goodson and S. J. Ball (eds) *Defining the Curriculum*, Lewes: Falmer Press.

—— (1985) 'From ethnography to theory', *Sociology* 19: 244–59.

—— (1987) 'Ethnography and the cumulative development of theory: a discussion of Woods' proposal for "phase two" research', *British Educational Research Journal* 13 (3): 283–96.

—— (1989a) 'What's wrong with ethnography? The concept of theoretical description', *Sociology* 24(4).

—— (1989b) 'The relevance of ethnography', *unpublished paper*.

—— (1992) *What's Wrong with Ethnography?* London: Routledge.

Hammersley, M., Scarth, J. and Webb, S. (1985) 'Developing and testing theory: the case of research on pupil learning and examinations', in R. G. Burgess (ed.) *Issues in Educational Research*, Lewes: Falmer Press.

Lindow, J., Marrett, C. and Wilkinson, L. (1985) 'Overview', in L. C. Wilkinson and C. B. Marrett (eds) *Gender Influences in Classroom Interaction*, Orlando: Academic Press.

Morse, L. and Handley, H. (1985) 'Listening to adolescents: gender differences in science classroom interactions', in L. C. Wilkinson and C. B. Marrett (eds) *Gender Influences in Classroom Interaction*, Orlando: Academic Press.

Scarth, J. and Hammersley, M. (1986a) 'Some problems in the assessment of closed tasks', in M. Hammersley (ed.) *Case Studies in Classroom Research*, Milton Keynes: The Open University Press.

Scarth, J. and Hammersley, M. (1986b) 'Questioning ORACLE: an assessment of ORACLE's analysis of teachers' questions', *Educational Research* 28(3): 174–84.

Spender, D. (1982) *Invisible Women: the Schooling Scandal*, London: Writers & Readers Publishing Cooperative.

Swann, J. and Graddol, D. (1988) 'Gender inequalities in classroom talk', *English in Education* 22(1): 48–65.

Tickle, L. (1983) 'One spell of ten minutes or five spells of two . . . ? Teacher–pupil encounters in art and design education', in M. Hammersley and A. Hargreaves (eds) *Curriculum Practice*, Lewes: Falmer Press.

Part II

Ethnicity

Chapter 7

Ethnicity and friendship

The contrast between sociometric research and fieldwork observation in primary school classrooms

Martyn Denscombe, Halina Szulc, Caroline Patrick and Ann Wood

Source: Denscombe, M., Szulc, H., Patrick, C. and Wood, A. (1986) 'Ethnicity and friendship: the contrast between sociometric research and fieldwork observation in primary school classrooms', *British Educational Research Journal* 12(3): 221–35.

INTRODUCTION

The origins of the research reported in this paper can be traced back to a project at Leicester Polytechnic titled 'Development education in the primary school'. As part of this project a number of primary school teachers were brought together to work on new curriculum materials dealing with world development (Denscombe and Conway 1982). It was during discussions about these materials that the teachers' reluctance to accept research findings on the link between ethnic group and friendship choice became explicit. The teachers were not impressed by the evidence that pupils from the age of 4 years tend to establish racial awareness and that this awareness develops in subsequent years into a preference for a pupil's own group. Nor did they agree that friendship choices in the primary school classroom could be linked to ethnic group and that such ethnically biased patterns of friendship choice were symptomatic of a developing racial prejudice. On the contrary, they were steadfast in arguing that in their experience primary school pupils were generally racially unbiased in their choice of friends and, though sometimes mouthing the prejudiced statements heard at home, pupils in their classes were naive and colour-blind when it came to choosing friends.

This unwillingness to accept research evidence does not appear to have been unique (Townsend and Brittan 1973; Jeffcoate 1977; Davey and Mullin, 1982) yet, to date, it does not appear to have invoked any serious inquiry. As the 'non-expert' practitioners, teachers' opinions tend to have been dismissed as either lacking rigour and insight (reserved for the 'scientific' investigator) or as blinkered by the teachers' own cultural straitjacket (which blinds them to the reality of prejudice in the classroom). But it seems, today as much as it did at that time, unsatisfactory to leave the matter as a 'teacher problem' related to ethnocentricity and lack of familiarity with research evidence rather than treat it as a topic for further investigation. If teachers perceive classroom reality in a way substantially at odds with research findings it suggests the need to interrogate the research findings and to investigate the rationale for the teachers' perceptions rather than simply *assume* that research evidence produces superior knowledge.

An initial probe into the dissonance between the research findings and teachers' perceptions of friendship was undertaken as part of the 'Development education in the primary school' project. It replicated the sociometric analysis of friendship choice to be found in the key research findings and the results have been reported previously (Denscombe 1983).

The research report here is an extension of the initial investigation. Focusing on just two classrooms it set out to test the received wisdoms about ethnic preference in friendship choice in the primary school by replicating the sociometric analyses. But more than this, it also attempted to contrast the quantitative analyses using chi-squared tests of significance and the Criswell Index with alternative styles of analysis. Principally this involved (i) a description of classroom friendship groups in terms of sociomatrices based on sociometric tests, and (ii) extended fieldwork observation aimed at revealing the qualities of friendship choice in context and over time.

METHODS

Research focused on a multiracial junior school in Leicester during the school year 1983–4. The pupils, just over 200 in all, were approximately 60 per cent South Asian and 40 per cent white.

Classes in the school were vertically integrated covering 7- to 9-year-olds and 9- to 11-year-olds. Two classes were studied; class A with the older pupils, class B with the younger ones. Background information about the pupils was collected at the start of the school year. This information included religion, language spoken in the home and parental country of origin – factors which allowed all the pupils to be classified under one of five ethnic group headings: (i) white/Christian, (ii) Hindu, (iii) Sikh, (iv) Muslim and (v) Buddhist (see Table 7.1).

Sociometric tests were administered in October 1983 and April 1984. Pupils were asked to name their three best friends in class. As part of the same exercise the pupils were asked to write something about why they liked their friends and to draw a picture of their friends at play. In the second of the tests, pupils were invited to do the same for their 'friends in the playground' and 'friends at home'.

Table 7.1 Description of the two classes (October 1983)

Age
  Class A=9–11-year-olds×27 pupils
  Class B=7–9-year-olds×27 pupils
Sex
  28 boys, 26 girls

Religion		M	F
1 Buddhist		—	1
27 Christian	(1/2)	15	12
3 Muslim	(1/20)	—	3
11 Hindu	(1/5)	5	6
12 Sikh	(1/5)	8	4
Language in the home			
27 English	(1/2)	15	12
13 Gujerati	(1/4)	5	8
11 Punjabi	(1/5)	8	3
2 other Indian		—	2
1 Chinese		—	1
Parental country of origin			
26 Britain	(1/2)	14	12
26 India/E. Africa	(1/2)	13	13
1 Singapore		—	1
1 West Indies		1	—

Of the twenty-seven pupils in each of the two classes at the start of the year, it was possible to get sociometric choices from twenty-five in each class which covered the six-month time span. Four pupils left the school; three others arrived. These were not incorporated into the sociometric test data.

The sociometric tests were used specifically to replicate the methods used in the studies most often cited as evidence of ethnic bias in the choice of friends amongst primary school pupils (cf. Rowley 1968; Kawwa 1968; Durojaiye 1969, 1970; Jelinek and Brittan 1975; Davey 1983). But the research was also designed to allow a direct comparison between findings based on sociometric tests and more qualitative findings based on protracted fieldwork in classrooms. It was central to the conception of the research that *both* methods be employed and that the evidence on ethnic group and friendship choice be evaluated on the strength of a direct comparison between findings from sociometric tests and from fieldwork observation covering the same pupils in the same settings.

To this end, class B was observed for sixty sessions of one or 1¼ hours in the mornings and afternoons over a nine-month period between October 1983 and June 1984. Class A was observed for fifty-six sessions over the same period, again covering one or 1¼ hours in the mornings and afternoons. Observation involved the field researcher, Halina Szulc, operating very much in the mode of participant observer. She was introduced to the pupils as a person 'helping the teacher' and acted in this capacity throughout the period of observation. Her observation of events focused on contact between the pupils during periods of 'free association' in class time and, to a lesser extent, observation of pupils on visits outside the school, in the canteen and in the playground. The main purpose of these observations, of course, was to record patterns of association between pupils on occasions in school when pupils were allowed to mix with whom they wanted rather than having the choice made for them by teacher-directed seating plans.

On the basis of friendship choices in the sociometric tests, twelve pupils were also selected for special attention as case studies. They were selected to represent a cross-section of the kinds of choices to emerge from the tests and thus included 'all in-group' choices, 'all out-group' choices and, after the second of the two tests, 'all-consistent choices'. During May and June these pupils were specifically asked about their friends and what friendship meant to them. Records were kept of who they played with at break time and with whom they ate lunch. To complete the dossier, a profile of each pupil's personality, appearance and behaviour was included.

FINDINGS

Quantitative analyses of friendship patterns

The sociometric test has figured prominently in attempts to analyse patterns of friendship choice. Its early advocates stressed the claim that sociometric techniques applied to the small group situation could reveal an underlying social structure (Moreno 1934; Gronlund 1959) and it was regarded as particularly appropriate for use in school classrooms. Sociometric tests, it was argued, could reveal social structures of interaction which were not apparent to the 'casual' observer or even to those actually involved in the small group and, in effect, this meant that sociometry in the classroom could reveal to teachers facts about the relationships between pupils in their classes which the teachers themselves could not perceive.

This 'insight' of sociometry has been applied quite extensively to the matter of race relations and the existence of racial or ethnic[1] bias in choice of friends in class. In the words of Joan Criswell,

> Such measurement is valuable in the study of relations between races or between any majority group and the minorities with which

it is in contact. The analysis may reveal cleavages in population which superficially appear homogeneous.

(Criswell 1934: 398)

Criswell herself developed a statistical method for estimating the extent to which a subgroup expressed in-group (or out-group) preferences and this 'Criswell Index' has been used frequently in research on ethnic group and friendship choice. A value of 1 represents the expected balance of in-group/out-group choices presuming no presence of ethnic preference: as values increase above 1 they represent increased in-group preference; below 1 they represent out-group preference.

In order to replicate the methods used in previous studies sociometric tests were used with pupils in the two classes of the junior school in Leicester and the results were subject to quantitative analysis to gauge both the *extent* of in-group preference (using the Criswell Index) and the confidence that the results were not due to chance (using chi-squared). Just as Braha and Rutter (1980) found in their study of friendship choice in a West Midlands primary school, this revealed no obvious contrast between the age groups in their degree of in-group preference. This was a little surprising in view of the more widely accepted belief that in-group preference increases with age up to adolescence. Also surprising, perhaps, was the finding that, at the time of the October sociometric test, the Criswell Index for the two classes pointed to only a slight in-group preference on the part of white pupils and a considerable degree of out-group preference on the part of the South Asian pupils. By April 1984, the in-group preference by white pupils had increased quite markedly gauged by the Index while the South Asian out-group preference had remained much the same.[2] The simple and obvious conclusion to be drawn from this would be that white pupils had developed their in-group preference during the course of the year from a lower level to one where an ethnic bias was statistically significant. Certainly the chi-squared test of significance of choices would support such a conclusion, moving over the six-month period from a position of clearly insignificant statistical results to a quite acceptable level of probability (see Tables 7.2 and 7.3).

It is worth noting, however, that the extent of in-group preference was still not great considering the 50:50 balance of South Asian and white pupils in these particular classes and the fact that Davey and Mullin (1982) had concluded that this kind of situation was one where ethnocentricity in friendship choice was likely to be most prevalent. Nor was the in-group preference as extensive as it was in research conducted in the school three years previously (Denscombe 1983). So, even on these classic quantitative analyses of friendship choice there are grounds for some feeling of anxiety about the received wisdoms.

Table 7.2 Criswell Index: Classes A and B

		October 1983	*April 1984*
Class A			
	White	1.308	2.17
	South Asian	0.27	0.3
Class B			
	White	1.143	1.6
	South Asian	0.44	0.36

Table 7.3 Friendship choice by ethnic group

	October 1983		*April 1984*	
	White	*Asian*	*White*	*Asian*
Class A				
White	17	13	26	12
	(17.6)	(12.4)	(20.8)	(17.2)
South Asian	20	13	14	21
	(19.4)	(13.6)	(19.2)	(15.8)
significance	>0.90		significance	<0.02
Class B				
White	16	14	24	15
	(14.8)	(15.2)	(18.2)	(20.8)
South Asian	15	18	11	25
	(16.2)	(16.8)	(16.8)	(19.2)
significance	>0.50		significance	<0.01

Expected values in brackets.

Sociomatrices of friendship choice

A more descriptive approach to sociometric data is provided by the sociomatrix which allows some visual representation of the friendship choices and which does not mask the nature of specific subgroups through a process of statistical aggregation. Using the Forsyth and Katz (1946) cluster technique, data from the sociometric tests could be portrayed in the following sociomatrices (see Figs 7.1–7.4).

Looking at class A first, the sociomatrices would appear to reveal four main groups. Group 'A' was a tight-knit group of boys, two Hindu and one white. This integrated group persists and appears in the April 1984 tests as well as the test in October 1983. Group B was a larger group of five boys, two white, two Sikh and one Hindu. This group, however, seems to have literally disintegrated over the six months between the tests so that in the April 1984 sociomatrix we see

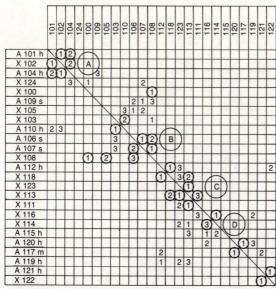

X = white/Christian; A = Asian; h = Hindu; m = Muslim; s = Sikh.
Circled number indicates reciprocated choice.

Figure 7.1 Sociomatrix I: Class A October 1983.

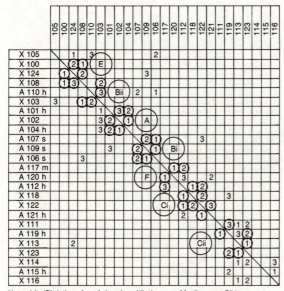

X = white/Christian; A = Asian; h = Hindu; m = Muslim; s = Sikh.
Circled number indicates reciprocated choice.

Figure 7.2 Sociomatrix II: Class A April 1984.

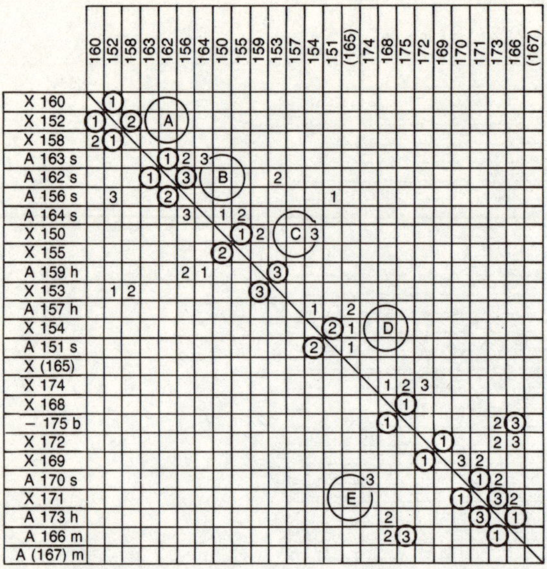

X = white/Christian; A = Asian; b = Buddhist; h = Hindu; m = Muslim; s = Sikh.
Circled number indicates reciprocated choice.

Figure 7.3 Sociomatrix III: Class B October 1983.

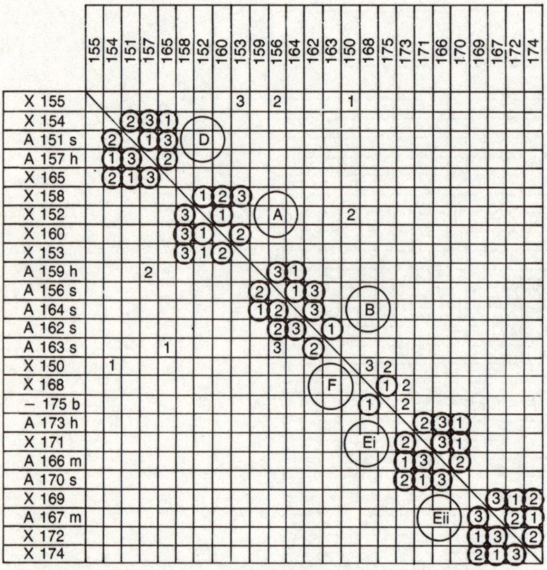

X = white; A = Asian; b = Buddhist; h = Hindu; m = Muslim; s = Sikh.
Circled number indicates reciprocated choice.

Figure 7.4 Sociomatrix IV: Class B April 1984.

group 'Bi' having incorporated pupil 109 to become an exclusive Sikh group. Group 'Bii' – the other splinter from the original group B – remained intact as an integrated group. Meanwhile, among the boys, we find the development of more obvious groupings of white pupils (group 'E') connected to group Bii through pupil 108.

Early in the school year, the girls in class A presented a number of unreciprocated choices but could still be seen in terms of one large group (group 'C'), a smaller group 'D', and two other reciprocal pairings. Group C, at this stage was predominantly white with just one of the five girls being a Hindu. The core of group D was also white but, again, with a Hindu girl also incorporated. The two reciprocal pairings involved Hindu/Muslim and Hindu/white pupils. Six months later, the clustering of pupils in the sociomatrix supplies a picture of more clear-cut friendship groups. Group D remains, though would not appear to be a very tight-knit group. One of the duos (117, 120) incorporated a second Hindu girl as well as the Muslim – providing an all-Asian friendship clique. However, the new member (112) linked this group with the new group Ci, one of the two subgroupings to emerge from the original group C over the six-month period. Group Ci linked two white girls and one Hindu girl with pupil 112 to comprise an integrated two Hindu/two white profile. Group Cii similarly had the Hindu/white combination, this time with three white girls and one Hindu.

Class B, like class A, showed a more cohesive clustering in friendship choice over the six months between the tests. Initially there appeared to be four groups of boys with an additional reciprocal pairing, and one rather large, diffuse group of girls also with an additional reciprocal pairing. At the time of the October 1983 test, class B exhibited some element of segregation according to the sociomatrix. Group A consisted of three white boys; group B comprised three Sikh boys. The rest of the groups, though, were integrated on both racial and ethnic criteria. The second sociometric test showed a clear picture of six friendship groupings in the class. Among the boys, the loose grouping C had disintegrated with one of the pupils (164) joining an expanded group B. This group then consisted of four Sikh and one Hindu pupil thus becoming a racially exclusive group predominantly Sikh in origin. Group A, likewise, had expanded to include four pupils and, again, this was a racially exclusive grouping of white boys. Group D remained racially mixed with two white pupils, one Sikh and one Hindu.

The girls in class B presented friendship groups that were more integrated than the boys. Group E fragmented into two smaller groups by April 1984. Group Ei included one Hindu, one white, one Muslim and one Sikh; group Eii included three whites and one Muslim. Group

F, augmented from a reciprocal pairing (168, 175) in the October, was something of an anomaly. It still centred around the tight-knit duo of one white girl and one Buddhist girl but had a white boy (150) linked with it on the grounds of his 'choosing in' to the group.

What does all this add up to? First, it would appear that any tendency towards in-group preference is more prevalent among the boys than girls – a point that surely warrants further investigation. In the context of this paper it is another finding from the data which is more pertinent, i.e. that friendship patterns described in the sociomatrices for classes A and B do not present the kind of support to the Criswell Index and chi-squared tests of significance that might be expected. While there would seem to be grouping along ethnic lines evident in the way pupils become ordered (reading down the column on the left) in the sociomatrix, there is a noticeable amount of integration in the groups. Groups Bi and E of Class A and groups A and B of class B, offer the only examples of exclusive ethnic in-group preference (11 of them boys).

The difference between the quantitative analysis of the sociometric data and the presentation of these data in the form of sociomatrices is that, whereas the quantitative analysis points to an *overall* tendency towards in-group choices, the sociomatrices show that the groups are rarely ethnically exclusive. Rather than swamping the individual cases with statistical aggregations, the sociomatrices (a) highlight the differences between groups, and (b) suggest a tendency for groups to be *predominantly of one ethnic group but incorporating pupils from different ethnic backgrounds as well*.

Fieldwork observation and the case studies

Field observation was dedicated to identifying friendship patterns as they actually existed (rather than as projected in the test choices) and to tracing their development over the school year. The data presented here are drawn exclusively from class B not only for reasons of brevity but also because there was greater use of 'free association' in this class. In all but six sessions observed, pupils were able to join whoever they wanted during at least one phase of the lesson to do 'carpet work' (e.g. listen to story), 'desk work', or music. Only during such periods were pupils in a clear position to associate with those they preferred.

It is useful, first, to consider the friendship links of two pupils in class B whose choice of friends in both sociometric tests, six months apart – were the same three and, significantly, were completely *in-group*. Sukhbir Singh (163) was an 8-year-old Sikh boy whose parents spoke Punjabi at home, Randip (164), Jaswinder (156) and Sukhbinder

(162), three Sikhs, were chosen by him on both occasions. There was considerable reciprocity of choice as depicted by group B in the two sociomatrices and, on the surface, this would seem to be an archetypal case of ethnic bias revealed by sociometric testing. However, during free-association periods in class, Sukhbir was not always to be found with the three others. Indeed, the field observations reveal that, in practice, he seemed quite willing to associate with Julian (152), Gary (158) and Alpesh (157) amongst others. On most occasions he was in the company of one or more of the clique (46 out of 64)[3] but there seemed little element of exclusivity. On 11 occasions he was observed exclusively with members of the group, on 35 occasions with others as well, including girls on 20 occasions – mainly Farzana (167) and Shuk Quan (175). On 18 occasions he was with none of his three sociometric choices. When asked about his friends (towards the end of the school year) he said that he sat with and played with Jason (165), Craig (154) and Ranjit (151) – and occasionally Julian (152).

What appeared from the sociometric tests to be a clear case of ethnic bias in friendship choice, then, becomes far less obvious in terms of actual contact observed. Indeed, in the playground when he was observed during May and June 1984 he was rarely with the three sociometric choices. Other than times he spent with his brother from another class (2 of 20), he played with boys and girls[4] in his class and these groups generally included white pupils (17 of 20 occasions).

Similar doubts about the sociometric data were raised by the case of Julian Harvey (152) who also expressed a complete in-group preference in both sociometric tests. Julian was a 7-year-old white/Christian boy in class B. At the time of the first sociometric test he chose Andrew (160) and Craig (158) as his friends (no third choice). Six months later it was Andrew (160), Colin (150) and Gary (158) – all 7-year-old white/ Christian boys. Here again, the pattern ostensibly suggests a clear-cut in-group preference expressed through a friendship group (group A) persisting throughout the school year.

It is interesting, however, that the sociometric choices did not include his brother Keith (153) who, though a year older, was also in the class. Keith, for his part, put Julian as his first choice in both sociometric tests and, as the sociomatrices indicate, Keith can be regarded as part of the clique through his reciprocated choices with Andrew (160) and Gary (158). Group A is consolidated all the more by Keith's inclusion as one of the all-white group in the second sociometric test.

As with Sukhbir (163), however, tracing Julian's interactions during free-association occasions over the year gives ground for doubting the prima facie case for his ethnic preference in the selection of friends.

Julian was observed on 69 separate free-association occasions in class and on outside-school trips. On 20 of these occasions he was exclusively with members of the sociometric clique, on 11 occasions he was with none of the clique and on 38 occasions he was part of a group which included clique members but also included other pupils in the class. Even this does little to portray the kind of racial integration revealed by field observation because:

- of the 20 occasions he was exclusively with clique members, most were times when he was just with his brother Keith or with Andrew in a small group;
- of the 38 occasions when he was with a mixture of clique members and other pupils in class, all but seven included Asian pupils; Sanjay (159) and Alpesh (157), both Hindus, were prominent despite the fact that half of the boys (i.e. 8) in class B were white;
- all 11 occasions he was observed with none of the clique, he was with Asian as well as white pupils.[5]

When Julian was observed in the playground throughout June it was clear that, though Andrew, Keith, Gary and Colin were frequently to be found with him, he also played quite frequently with Sukhbir (163), a Sikh, and Sanjay (159), a Hindu.

As a contrast to these case studies, Alison O'Keefe (171) chose out-group friends in both sociometric tests. Alison, a 7-year-old white/Christian girl, chose Chamandip (170), Sajeda (166) and Naina (173) in both tests six months apart. With Chamandip, a Sikh, Sajeda, a Muslim, and Naina, a Hindu, the pattern would appear to be one of full ethnic integration. As part of group E, the identity of the clique emerged clearer in the second of the two sociometric tests (as seen in the sociomatrix).

Of the 55 observations of Alison, there were 12 occasions when she was exclusively with clique members – though, as with Julian, most of these were when she was with one particular key clique member. In this case it was Chamandip who was the principal associate of Alison's throughout the year. In practice, Sajeda and Naina were more of a separate duo who had an affinity with the Alison/Chamandip duo. On 28 occasions Alison was associating with a mixture of clique members and others. On only 2 of these did the group not include South Asian pupils though Alison spent a lot of time with Paula (174), Ann (172), Christine (169) – all white/Christians – and with Farzana (167). This suggests that the May 1984 sociomatrix for class B might present a rather artificial division of groups Ei and Eii based on the Forsyth and Katz cluster technique. This seems even more likely in view of the fact that, on the 15 occasions that Alison was not to be found with any of the clique members she was almost invariably with members of group Eii. Observation in the playground reinforced the idea that group E was a broader amalgam of friendships covering eight girls in the class with all the group involved at times with playground games and activities.

This ought not take us away from the degree of inter-racial association. In Alison's case there were only 7 occasions of the 55 in which she was in the company of solely white pupils – despite the fact that 6 of the 12 girls in class B were white.[6]

Finally, as a commentary on the sociometric method, the case of Ben Jones is also worth considering. Ben (155) was a 7-year-old white/Christian boy whose sociometric choices varied between the first and second tests. In the first, he nominated Sanjay (159), a Hindu boy, and Colin (150), a white/Christian boy, with no third choice. In the second test he again nominated Colin (150) – this time as first choice – with Jaswinder (156), a Sikh boy, and Keith (153), a white/Christian boy, as second and third choices. Field observation revealed that Ben's friendship was actually very strong with Colin – despite the fact that Colin did not choose Ben in the second test. Colin, indeed, chose two girls and Craig (154) in this test leaving Ben to appear in the sociomatrix as something of an isolate. In practice, Ben and Colin were rarely separated during free-association times. Of the 61 occasions on which Ben and Colin were both in class when free-association observation occurred, on 46 occasions Ben and Colin were directly together seated on the floor or working at a desk. And in the playground, he was observed 18 times during May and June 1984, 10 of which he was just with Colin, the other 8 with Colin and others. The others were not Jaswinder and Keith, those he had nominated on the sociometric test around this time, but were Farzana (167), a Muslim girl, Sanjay (159), a Hindu boy, and Paula (174), a white/Christian girl.

DISCUSSION

On the face of it the findings of the field observation would seem to do two things. They would appear (i) to condemn sociometric analysis of friendships as simplistic and inaccurate and (ii) to reinforce teachers' visions of the primary school as a place of racial innocence if not racial harmony. The results would seem to explain the dissonance between 'research findings' and 'teacher perceptions' in terms of the limitations of previous research rather than the limitations of teachers' knowledge and, to push a point rather provocatively, might be heralded as a triumph of the 'practitioners' over the 'experts'.

A less sanguine reading of the results, however, might question whether this research was a fair test of the sociometric method. The results, after all, go against the grain so far as the orthodoxy of ethnic preference in the primary school classroom is concerned and seem to be at odds with previous (sociometric) research which has found time and again that primary school pupils exhibit in-group preference in their choice of friends.

One reason, quite plausible, is that the current research is based on one school and that it cannot aspire to offer a definitive statement based on a cross-section of situations. In contrast with the large-scale studies of Jelinek and Brittan (1975), Davey (1981, 1983) and Davey and Mullin (1982) who cover 15, 16 and 16 schools respectively, it is fair to say that the findings must remain suggestive rather than conclusive. Yet, before this point leads us to dismiss the findings as possibly unrepresentative it is worth noting that other studies in the UK tradition of sociometry have also restricted their analysis to individual schools (Rowley 1968; Durojaiye 1970; Braha and Rutter 1980; Thomas 1982) or just a few schools (Kawwa, 1968). This has not stopped the work of Rowley, Kawwa and Durojaiye, in particular, becoming established as key references in support of the idea that friendships in the primary school are influenced by ethnic factors.

If, then, the size of the study does not provide grounds for dismissing the results perhaps the nature of the specific context might negate its potency. After all, Leicester has a distinct ethnic mix; and this particular school had 60 per cent South Asian pupils. However, this profile can hardly be used to dismiss the findings when it is realized that in Kawwa's study Cypriots far outnumbered West Indians and South Asians in the three schools.

It seems reasonable to argue, then, that to reject the present findings on the basis of their size/representativeness it would also be necessary to reject some of the classic sources. That would leave the large-scale research of Jelinek and Brittan and Davey et al. unscathed – but the findings presented here must raise doubts about their analyses as well. Certainly in both cases the number of schools and pupils would appear to offer the possibility of representative findings. And the large number of pupils involved (4,300 and 4,000 respectively) might be expected to overcome statistical problems of dealing with small numbers. But the overall size of the sample, as argued elsewhere (Denscombe 1983), can do little to overcome the basic facts that when a class of say thirty pupils gets subdivided by sex and ethnic origins the expected frequency for the cells of contingency tables are likely to become too small for meaningful analysis.

From the findings from field observations, however, the critique of sociometry goes beyond matters of statistical analysis to questions about the very *validity* of sociometric tests as techniques for revealing patterns of friendship. There is some debate, dating back to Moreno's (1934) pioneering work, as to whether the choices ought to be made in connection with specified activities or whether the abstract nomination of 'best friends' provides sufficiently precise information upon which to base the analysis of the social groups. Some would argue that tests based on the choice of three best friends, like that adopted in the present research and by Kawwa (1968), Braha and Rutter (1980), and in a close form by Jelinek and Brittan (1975) and Durojaiye (1969, 1970), are too abstract and projective but it is difficult to escape the conclusion that the observed pattern of friendship in class was not accurately predicted by the sociometric test. The case studies, in their different ways, demonstrate that pupils' friendships are far more flexible and complex than a sociometric test can allow for. And it seems difficult to argue that this point does *not* apply if the test is based on 'concrete activity' questions like 'who are the two children you'd most like to sit next to?' (cf. Davey 1983).

CONCLUSION

At one level the findings described here provide a salutary reminder of the need to re-evaluate 'received wisdoms'. The danger is that wisdoms which contain politically attractive messages become taken as immutable truths on the basis of evidence that, upon reflection, seems flimsy or dated.

At another level the findings described in this paper provide ammunition for ethnographers who have argued for many years that quantitative data and analysis is ill-suited to certain kinds of social phenomena. The use of quantitative techniques to assess the extent of in-group preference (Criswell Index) or the likelihood of any pattern of in-group preference occurring by chance (chi-squared) will necessarily fail to capture the complexity of the situation. It then becomes reasonable to explain disparities between research evidence and teacher perceptions by the way quantitative analyses swamp the uniqueness of groups in their quest for 'statistically apparent' and 'statistically significant' *tendencies* whose very strength, that they represent general patterns, is also their very weakness. The 'balance' of group members might show a statistically significant bias but the fact that mixing occurs in the groups raises awkward questions about the extent to which the statistical evidence implies racial bias on the part of the pupils. For teachers in the classroom it is the existence of the ethnic mixing, rather than the balance of group members, which is likely to be the most striking feature of classroom friendships and, therefore, it is hardly surprising that their perceptions of integration in the classroom tend to be at loggerheads with accounts based on statistical aggregations.

It would be dangerous, however, to infer from this that quantitative analyses are 'all wrong' and that the observational method has got things 'all right'. Certainly the sociometric data did not accord with the data retrieved from the field observation and, as it has been argued, there are good grounds for doubting the validity of the sociometric data, but the field observations themselves do not really stand as 'objective evidence' which disprove sociometric findings. What were observed and recorded were the contacts and proximity of pupils during times of free association. Such contact and proximity have been used in this research as *indicators* and, in the playground especially, there are good reasons for regarding them as valid indicators of friendship. It needs to be recognized, though, that such indicators are themselves (i) quite crude guides to something as complex as friendship and (ii) based on researchers' knowledge of what friendship entails. Although the specific aim of the field observations was to identify pupils' preferences for working with, sitting with and playing with other pupils of different ethnic origins and to use these preferences to contrast with sociometric analyses of friendship patterns, the assumption that working with, sitting with and playing with others is indicative of friendship is something that warrants further investigation.[7]

Perhaps more than anything else the findings demonstrate the need for ethnographic research which investigates *the meaning of friendship* for those involved. The contrast in findings between sociometric tests and fieldwork observation, if they are to be resolved, requires first and foremost that the meaning of friendship be investigated as an integral part of the exercise and that researchers' contributions to the area start from the study of teacher perceptions and pupil meanings. Only in this way will it be possible to identify with any clarity the relationships between racialist behaviour, racial antagonism, ethnic tension, racist comments and friendship patterns in the ethnically mixed classroom. While there is no inherent contradiction between ethnographic research and the quantification of data (Silverman 1985), these are complexities vital to our understanding of inter-ethnic friendship patterns which exclusive reliance on quantitative research methods cannot hope to unravel.

ACKNOWLEDGEMENTS

We are grateful to the local education authority, the headmaster and the governors of the school who gave their approval to the research project. Fieldwork research referred to in this paper was conducted by Halina Szulc in classes taught by Caroline Patrick and Ann Wood. An earlier version of this paper was given to the ESRC sponsored conference 'Sociology and the Teacher', St Hilda's College, Oxford, September 1985.

NOTES

1 For the purposes of this paper 'racial' will refer to divisions based on colour (i.e. white/South Asian) and 'ethnic' will refer to *all* cultural divisions (i.e. Hindu, Sikh, Muslim, White, Buddhist).

2 Analysis of the in-group and out-group preference among the Buddhist, Hindu, Sikh and Muslim pupils, rather than amalgamating their choices under the heading 'South Asian', revealed that contrary to the general out-group preference identified for South Asian pupils as a whole, the Sikh pupils had a strong in-group preference.

In-group preference of Sikh pupils: Criswell Index

	October 1983	April 1984
Class A	8.89	22.22
Class B	3.04	4.81

Though results were analysed in terms of the South Asian subgroups the small numbers involved in each subgroup in each class rendered the statistical analysis of friendship patterns among them fraught with numerical traps.

3 The 64 observations comprise free-association time and incorporate both absences of the pupil and times when there were more than one free-association phase during the lesson.

4 He was playing with girls on 3 of the 20 occasions he was observed.

5 On 11 occasions his free-association group included girls.

6 On 11 occasions she was with groups including boys during free-association periods.

7 I am grateful to Martyn Hammersley for emphasizing this point and for his broader comments on an earlier version of this paper.

REFERENCES

Braha, V. and Rutter, D. R. (1980) 'Friendship choice in a mixed primary school', *Educational Studies* 6: 217–23.

Criswell, J. H. (1943) 'Sociometric methods of measuring group preferences', *Sociometry* 6: 398–408.

Davey, A. G. (1981) 'Pride and prejudice in the primary school', *Education 3–13*, Autumn, 4–8.

—— (1983) *Learning to be Prejudiced*, London: Edward Arnold.

Davey, A. G. and Mullin, P. N. (1982) 'Inter-ethnic friendship in British primary schools', *Educational Research* 24: 83–92.

Denscombe M. (1983) 'Ethnic group and friendship choice in the primary school', *Educational Research* 25: 184–90.

Denscombe, M. and Conway, L. (1982) 'Autonomy and control in curriculum innovation', *Teaching Politics* 11 (3).

Durojaiye, M. (1969) 'Race relations among junior school children', *Educational Research* 11: 226–8.

—— (1970) 'Patterns of friendship in an ethnically-mixed junior school', *Race* 12: 189–200.

Forsyth, E. and Katz, L. (1946) 'A matrix approach to the analysis of sociometric data: preliminary report', *Sociometry* 9: 340–7.

Gronlund, N. (1959) *Sociometry in the Classroom*, New York: Harper & Row.

Jeffcoate, R. (1977) 'Children's racial ideas and feelings', *English in Education* 2: 32–46.

—— (1984) *Ethnic Minorities in Education*, London: Harper & Row.

Jelinek, M. and Brittan, E. (1975) 'Multiracial education: (1) inter-ethnic friendship patterns', *Educational Research* 18: 44–53.

Kawwa, T. (1968) 'Three sociometric studies of ethnic relations in London schools', *Race* 10: 173–80.

Moreno, J. L. (1934) *Who Shall Survive?* New York: Beacon House.

Rowley, K. (1968) 'Social relations between British and immigrant children', *Educational Research* 10: 145–8.

Spradley, J. (1970) *You Owe Yourself a Drunk: an Ethnography of Urban Nomads*, Boston: Little, Brown.

Silverman, D. (1985) *Qualitative Methodology and Sociology*, Aldershot: Gower

Thomas, K. (1982) 'The influence of race on adolescent friendship patterns', *Educational Studies* 8: 175–83.

Tomlinson, S. (1983) *Ethnic Minorities in British Schools*, London: P. S. I./Heinemann.

Townsend, H. and Brittan, E. (1973) *Multiracial Education: Need and Innovation*, Schools Council Working Paper No. 50, London: Evans/Methuen.

Chapter 8

Beyond the white norm

The use of qualitative methods in the study of black youths' schooling in England

Máirtin Mac an Ghaill

Source: Mac an Ghaill, M. (1989) 'Beyond the white norm: the use of qualitative methods in the study of black youths' schooling in England', *Qualitative Studies in Education* 2(3): 175–89.

This paper illustrates the use and value of qualitative research for understanding the 'different reality' of black youth schooling in England. It reports two ethnographic studies – in an inner-city secondary school and a sixth form college. Student-teacher classroom survival strategies are seen to be linked to a wider framework of racism and sexism, thus revealing that 'race', class and gender are elements in maintaining hegemonic domination. Black female and male students 'resist through accommodation'. Qualitative research reveals these interpretations and can help to reorient the schooling of young black people.

M M: Do you think that the way I see things gives a true picture of your lives?

Judith: I mean its bound to be biased, your being for black people, but it was because of that, that we talked to you as we really felt. You knew what you thought about us, you were more aware, but for most white people they hide it and pretend that they see us as just the same as them, at the same time they treat us differently. As long as you make it clear in your study where you stand, then its OK. That's Weberian! (joking). You reported our view of things.[1]

When I began to examine the schooling of black young people, I did not initially report their view of things. I want to draw on a five-year study of black youths, of Asian and Afro-Caribbean parentage, in order to illustrate the central value of qualitative research for understanding the 'different reality' (Hall *et al.* 1986), from that of white people, of the black community[2] experience in England in the 1980s. In so doing, I shall indicate how my own theoretical position developed.

I carried out two ethnographic studies. The first study looked at the interaction of white teachers and two groups of anti-school male students – the Asian Warriors and the Afro-Caribbean Rasta Heads – at an inner-city secondary school in a black population area in an English city during 1980–2. The second study looked at a group of female students of Asian and Afro-Caribbean parentage, whom I called the Black Sisters, who responded positively to education. This study took place in the same city, at a sixth form college, during 1983–5.

THE WHITE NORM: INITIAL RESEARCH PROBLEM

Young (1971: 1–2) referring to Seely's (1966) valuable distinction between the 'making' and 'taking' of research problems, claims that sociologists during the 1950s and 1960s tended to 'take' educators' problems and, by failing to make explicit their assumptions, took them for granted. This concern with methodological procedure, which was an important element in the emergence of the 'new sociology' of education in the 1970s, still appears in the 1980s to be missing from much 'race-relations'[3] research. It was an inadequacy with which I began my study, by taking the dominant 'race-relations' ethnic explanation of black students' educational performance (see Ballard and Driver 1977, and Banks and Lynch 1986, for explanations of the 'ethnic approach').

This culturalist perspective focuses upon the black students' distinctive cultural attributes and suggests that social behaviour is to be understood primarily in terms of culture. Adopting a discourse of deficit, the main social images constructed by this approach portray the black community as a 'problem'. Ethnicity is assumed to be a handicap for their assimilation or integration into British society, resulting in their relative social subordination. So, for example, the difference in the educational attainment of Asian and Afro-Caribbean students frequently is explained in terms of the assumed pathological structure of the Afro-Caribbean family and kinship organization. This often is contrasted with the assumed cultural unity of the Asian extended family network, providing the necessary support for the 'second generation' (Khan 1979).[4] My research design implicitly shared the white norm of classifying black students as a 'problem'. The substantive issues focused upon the deviant students, and methodological and data techniques were employed to meet the culturalist assumptions of this theoretical approach.

During the second term at Kilby School, in early 1981, I began to reformulate my examination of black male students' transition from school to work. In order to build up selected case histories, qualitative material was collected on the then fourth-year students. In analysing the data, a pattern emerged of the relatively higher academic achievement among Asian students and the corresponding 'under-achievement' among the Afro-Caribbeans. At this stage I was attempting to identify the significant variables that 'caused' the Asians' apparent positive response to school and the Afro-Caribbeans' apparent negative response. As is the case with the dominant 'race-relations' perspective, as I observed the students I became concerned particularly with the question of how the Afro-Caribbeans' subcultural values and attitudes might be linked to their educational performance.

BEYOND THE WHITE NORM: PRESENT RESEARCH PROBLEM

Whyte (1943: 300) points to the importance of having the support of key individuals in groups that are studied ethnographically. My initial source was Gilroy, who explained to me the Afro-Caribbean youths' own informal social division, which was based on identification with different types of music, namely, the Funk Heads, the Soul Heads, and the Rasta Heads. The groups also were indicated through different styles of dress, hair styles, and the wearing of badges. The groups did not fall into a simple classification of pro-school and anti-school students, though the first two groups, a number of whose members attended church, tended to be more orientated to the formal demands of the school. Gilroy, a Soul Head, provided detailed information on the composition and practices of each group.

My first contact with the Rasta Heads resulted from an out-of-school incident. A number of them had been stopped by the police and were being questioned. The students recognized me from the school and asked me to assist them. During the following week, I explained to them that I was carrying out a study on the educational performance of black youth and required their help. Leonard, a Rasta Head, in a review of the study, explained why he co-operated:

> Reading it reminded me that I thought you were a nutta, talking about blacks all the time, but you were interested in us, helped us, so I thought, we can trust him, an' I still do.

Meyenn (1979: 125) argued that, within research, methodology has a relative autonomy, and that however important theoretical and substantive issues are, they do not completely determine methodology. The shift in my understanding of the research problem arose from the methodological concern with observing the anti-school Rasta Heads. Focusing on the students' perspective of the meaning and purpose of school, I came to see the logic of their response as a survival strategy (see Everhart 1983: 276–9). Rather than viewing it in terms of how subcultural values contributed to the Afro-Caribbeans' educational 'under-achievement', I came to see their subculture as a legitimate mechanism opposed to the school's institutional authoritarianism and racism (see Troyna 1984).

Leslie: Alright then, put yourself in my place. You get mad, the teacher slap you up in front of your friends, and you feel shame, you feel low down before them. What do you expect me to do? Walk off, walk off! Here. I tell the man to fuck off or just tump him down, that's what I say.

Kevin: It's lowness, you feel lower than the other man, don' it?

M M: So what?

Kevin: What do you mean, so what? Already yer looked down upon as more inferior, right? Not just us lot, all, all black men. The Indian kids are treated better than us. So, it don't make sense to make yourself look more inferior than you're already claimed to be.

This reassessment of the Rasta Heads' subculture led me to examine what I came to see as teacher typification of the students. There was a tendency for Asian students to be seen by teachers as technically of high ability and socially as conformist. In contrast, Afro-Caribbean students tended to be seen as of low ability and potential discipline problems (see Wright 1985).[5] These dominant teacher perceptions are made clear in the following comment from a teacher:

The Afro-Caribbeans are tough. I tried not to let anyone influence me in how I treated them but they look at you with wild eyes if you tell them to sit down. They are looking, expecting trouble. They are more prejudiced than white people. The Asians are better. You tell them to do something and they are meek and they go and do it.

From observation within the school and the local community, I had identified a number of anti-school Asian students. The Rasta Heads often spoke of the Warriors, the main anti-school subcultural group at Kilby School. I met Parminder, then a fifth-form student, at an anti-racist demonstration organized by the Communist Party, of which he was a member. I explained my study to him. He introduced me to Amerjit, the leader of the Warriors. At first the Warriors' co-operation was based on their respect for Parminder, who eventually became an unofficial research consultant. Though difficult to judge, as Whyte (1943) and Liebow (1967) report, my presence with the Warriors and the Rasta Heads seemed to produce few changes in their normal behaviour. After the first year of fieldwork, Sokhjinder asked me if I would get in trouble for being one of the gang.

By this time, I had started systematically to read texts such as Bourne and Sivanandan (1980) that explicitly acknowledged a black perspective on the social world. In their examination of 'race-relations' in Britain Bourne and Sivanandan attack the ethnic school, with its emphasis on cultural relations, for distracting attention from the black community's real struggle against racism. They distinguish between the experience of colour prejudice and the institutionalization of prejudice in the power structures of society, that is, a distinction between racialism and racism. They point out that the ethnic approach is concerned exclusively with racialism. Such theorists as Hall (1980) and Sivanandan (1985) have argued that the study of 'race-relations' cannot be reduced to models of pathology or subjective discrimination. They have contributed important insights to our understanding of the structural subordination of the black population in Britain.[6]

The above work helped me to locate the form of racism, both historically and socially, that operates upon and within English schools in the 1980s. As Paul Gilroy (1981: 208) argues, 'different racisms are found in different social formations and historical circumstances.' I examined the present-day racist ideologies and practices in terms of what Barker (1981) calls the 'new racism'. He maintains that racism in Britain now tends to be rationalized in terms of cultural superiority. This idea of the new racism, with its dominant conception of intrinsic cultural differences as the primary cause of social behaviour, is pervasive because of its strong ideological 'common-sense' appeal within Britain. So, for example, whereas liberal policy-makers, researchers and teachers would reject the overly racist inferiority/superiority couplet, they do operate with the culturalist model. At Kilby School, liberal teachers explained differences in the Asian and Afro-Caribbean examination results in terms of intrinsic cultural differences.

FOCUS ON THE TEACHERS

I had not intended at the planning stage of research to make the Kilby School teachers the subjects of this study. However, research activity should not be a static but rather a dialectical process, with methodology, data and theory informing each other. Before the end of the first year of fieldwork, having reassessed the significance of the anti-school male subcultural groups, I shifted the research away from the conventional 'race-relations' focus on the youths' culture as the main problem with their schooling and began to investigate the assumed unproblematic nature of the teachers' ideologies and practices. In this way, I 'made' the research problem.

This methodological shift of focus to include the teachers ensured that the study did not become merely an 'underdog' account. Lacey (1976: 56) suggests that ethnographers, rather than being over-concerned with the notion of objectivity, should attempt to describe the social system from several perspectives, including the parent, the teacher and the child. I adopted a similar methodological approach, with the student–teacher relations at Kilby School becoming the central substantive concern, and in so doing developed my analysis of how their different perspectives intersected to produce a social process. The following example illustrates how an examination of student–teacher interaction revealed the complex structure and processes of racism operating within the school, including the centrally significant system of racist stereotyping. Mr Young was regarded by other staff members as a successful classroom teacher who had few disciplinary problems and coped effectively with trouble-makers. The following discussion took place after I had attended some of his lessons. He assumed that I was helping a small group of students with language difficulties and so was not aware that I was observing his interaction with the students.

M M: Do you think that you treat all the kids the same?

Mr   I like to think . . . , no I mean I do try and consciously
Young: try to treat them all the same, but to you, I suppose,
          unconsciously I label kids and react in certain ways, differ-
          ent ways to different kids. Kids who cause a lot of hassle
          say, or personality clashes . . ., but generally I try to treat
          them all the same.

M M: What about your treatment of Asians and Caribbeans?

Mr   Well, no, as you know, I'm against the crude division
Young: that they make in this place. I try to treat the Indians and
          the Afro-Caribbean kids, and the white kids, the same. I
          try to see them individually. There's good and bad in all,
          and some days it's one kid and the next another. There
          are a few that are problems, but it can't . . . , it's not a
          question of them all being Afro-Caribbean or anything
          like that.

Mr Young was surprised when I showed him how he had responded to a number of incidents involving students who had 'interrupted' the lessons. Although out of a class of 34, there were only 5 Afro-Carib-beans, they had been identified nearly twice as many times as causing an interruption as the 27 Asian and 2 white students. Most important, as Mr Young could now see, was that his different perceptions of Asian and Afro-Caribbean youths, affected his definition of what constituted a 'classroom interruption'. The stereotypes that Mr Young worked with were part of what Lacey (1976: 60) calls teachers' 'crude conceptual picture of the class', in which the teacher classifies the students into groups such as 'the bright ones', 'the conformists', 'the trouble-makers', and so on. These crude typifications are developed as coping strategies for the management of classroom interaction (see Hargreaves 1978; and Pollard 1982). What Mr Young was unaware of was how this conceptual framework provided the basis for the racist stereotypes that the Kilby teachers employed within the school. At this level, the racist stereotypes functioned as a strategy for teacher survival. (My own experience in the classroom acted as a safeguard against romanticizing the students' position.)

BEYOND THE WHITE NORM: CONNOLLY COLLEGE STUDY[7]

Llewellyn (1980: 42) writes about how much of the existing sociological literature on youth and education systematically neglects the issue of gender, thus making it 'invisible'. The Kilby School study appears to follow a similar approach in excluding half the population from sociological research. However, this did not reflect the reality of the ethnographic work. To redress this imbalance, relating to the position of black females within the English school system, I carried out a second study, of a small group of young black women of Afro-Caribbean and Asian parentage, at a sixth form college. It examines their strategies of institutional survival developed in response to their schooling. Anyon (1983: 19–23) writing about the American situation, suggests that the inter-relationship of accommodation and resistance is an element in the response of all oppressed groups and that such a process is 'manifest in the reactions of women and girls to the contradictory situations that they face'.[8] The Black Sisters, responding to their schooling in terms of resistance within accommodation, provide evidence in the English context to support Anyon's insight. They rejected the racist curriculum, and they valued highly the acquisition of academic qualifications. In other words, they adopted an anti-school but pro-education position (see Chigwada 1987).

Discussing the Black Sisters' general attitude to college lessons and their strategy of resistance within accommodation, Judith and Chhaya explained their perception of and response to their history lessons:

Judith: With me, like I go to school and I listen to the teacher and I put down just what they want. Christopher Colombus discovered America. I'll put it down, right. Cecil Rhodes, you know that great imperialist, he was a great man, I'll put it down. We did about the Elizabethans, how great they were. More European stuff. France, equality, liberty and fraternity, we'll put it all down. At the same time they had colonies, enslaving people. I'll put down that it was the mark of a new age, the Age of Enlightenment. It wasn't, but I'll put it down for them, so that we can tell them that black people are not stupid. In their terms, we can tell them that we can get on. In their terms, I come from one of the worst backgrounds but I am just saying to them, I can do it right, and shove your stereo-types up your anus.

Chhaya: They don't think that we have any nice history like them, winning all those battles, and we write it down. They don't think all those battles, conquering all those people, they're our people.

I found that the Rasta Heads perceived the school's official language as a major instrument of their own deculturalization. In response, they refused to adopt a standard dialect and spoke Creole within the classroom, using language as a mechanism of white exclusion. The Afro-Caribbean Black Sisters similarly were aware of the cultural sig-nificance of the college's dominant form of language. However, in their response, as Leonie explains, they implemented their strategy of resistance within accommodation.

Leonie: Talking of language, people don't really seem to think that Afro-Caribbeans have a problem. They think they speak bad English basically. It's not true. I found language a problem and I don't mean like learning French. It's the fact that they made you reject your own way of talking. That really got me. It was rejecting another part of you, being black you know, being part of you. Like the teacher at junior school got mad and I said, wha' instead of pardon and all that, and I found out that if you did not want to be laughed at, the best way to keep in the background was to try and speak the best English I could. So, I learnt to stop saying things like filim and all that business, coz when I was in junior school and the teacher asked, what did you do at the weekend? I stood up and I said, well, I went to see a filim and the whole class started laughing. I felt so bad inside, you can't under-stand. I mean the teacher laughing as well. I mean they're laughing at me, they're laughing at my parents, they're laughing at everything associated with Patois, with every-thing black. Well, I took a different attitude to most of my friends. They just stood by it and talked Patois even more.

M M: You changed your style and they didn't?

Leonie: I changed my style in appearance but deep down I kept
             it, I've still kept that feeling. I told my friends and some
             like agreed, the best thing to do was to pretend to change
             and to get on. Then they couldn't look down on us, but
             still keep yer language.
Hameeda: That's what we all do really, most of the time, in different
             ways.

It should be noted that the use of the concept of resistance within
accommodation to describe the young women's response to schooling
does not suggest that theirs was a strategy of conformity in contrast
to the Warriors' and the Rasta Heads' strategies of resistance. Historically, in all dominant institutions and societies, the survival strategies
of the oppressed have been a mixture of rebellion and acceptance (see
Roberts 1984, and the Institute of Race Relations 1985).[9] Furthermore,
as the Black Sisters pointed out, their different strategies of resistance
to racism cut across gender divisions, with girls at the secondary
schools totally rejecting school, and boys sharing their pro-educational/
anti-school position.

The Black Sisters informed me that my anti-racist stance within the
college was of primary significance in their deciding to participate in
the study. My visiting their homes and accompanying them to such
places as the cinema, theatre, Asian restaurants, and anti-racist meetings enabled us to break down the normal hierarchically-structured
relationship between teachers and students. However, I was not seen
as just some kind of community worker, I also functioned pragmati-
cally as a teacher in preparing them for examinations. So, for example,
our discussions of black writers including Alice Walker, Linton Kwesi
Johnson, James Baldwin and Tariq Mehmood, enabled the young
women taking arts and social science subjects both to experience works
other than those of white male authors, which dominated the college
curriculum, and at the same time to use texts to improve their examination technique.

Nevertheless, the study of black females by a white male researcher
raises methodological and political issues. Meyenn (1979), in his study
of white girls, found that private areas of their lives were not discussed
with him. More importantly, as Lawrence (1981) argues, in the past
researchers have failed to take into account how their relationship with
black respondents may be informed by racism. It should be added
that my interaction with black females also may be informed by sexism.
I hope that by adopting a theoretical position that sees racism and
sexism as the major barriers to the schooling of black youth, I have
become more sensitive to the question of how social location, in a

stratified society including differential power relations, influences one's perspective and that this, in turn, influences the present study.

DEVELOPING A SOCIAL ORGANIC RELATIONSHIP: FIELDWORK

The qualitative nature of the research enabled me to go beyond the white norm by adopting a collaborative relationship with the students, their parents, and other members of the black community (see Pollard 1985, for an account of work with primary school children). Having shifted from seeing black people as a 'problem', the study provided the opportunity to define their social position in contemporary England, with particular reference to racism (see Lather 1986, and Troyna and Carrington 1989).[10]

Detailed field notes were taken and written up each evening. In order to build up case histories of the male and female students who were the main subjects of the study, I interviewed each of them individually and in groups. The core methodology of the study was participant observation (see McCall and Simmons 1969). Like Waller (1967), I found the approach of inferring meanings by understanding the context, through participation in the lives of the students and the teachers, to be very productive. Also, like Lacey (1976: 60), I found it important to combine methods and integrate them into the analysis of the data. So, for example, the identification by observation of an anti-school group, the Warriors, was followed by the collection of material from school reports and questionnaires on their attitudes to school, and this enabled me to build case histories. The combination and integration of methods also acted as a means of cross-checking data obtained from participant observation, thus limiting potential subjective bias.

The study of the Black Sisters is not simply another presentation of participants' accounts of schooling, although, given the limited number of studies of black young women, this would be sufficient reason to carry out such a study (see Sharpe 1976; Fuller 1980; Riley 1985). The young women's involvement in the study was not only at the level of content, but more importantly, we collaborated in the form of the study. Being equipped with some sociological theory and concepts, they were involved in the attempt to ground the theory in the data collected (Glaser and Strauss 1967). There was continual critical discussion, among the students and myself, of the descriptions and interpretations of the data. More specifically, we were concerned primarily with the interrelationship of the three dimensions of 'race', gender and class. For the Black Sisters, racism was the main determinant of their lifestyles outside of the domestic situation, though the interaction of class and gender with racism was acknowledged.

M M: You don't seem to take class and sexism as seriously as racism. Can you talk about it like that? Do class and sexism affect your life to the same extent as racism?

Hameeda: Well, yes, of course, you can't really escape from any of them. You can see it with the middle-class Asians here. But the first thing that people notice, immediately, I don't think that they are going to think, a woman. They're going to think, a black, and then they're going to think, a woman.

M M: But what about at the staff cricket match? There it was the young women not the blacks making the sandwiches.

Hameeda: Yeah, there the sexist stereotype was on top, but the racist stereotypes nearly always come on top.

Smita: The sexist part and class are hidden beneath the racism. They're always looked at secondly.

Judith: And also, you can change your class position and if you have got a sexist husband, you can change him or leave him. But if yer black, you can't change. But for us, I agree with you there, we get all the three sets of stereotypes, which puts us at the bottom of society.

Whyte (1943: 300) informed the group he was studying that he was writing a book about them. However, he found that 'acceptance in the district depended more on the personal relationships that I developed far more than explanations I might give.' Like other researchers, such as Parker (1974) and Moore (1977), I found that what I assumed were insignificant personal autobiographical details were of significance from a research point of view. These included looking slightly older than many of the Kilby School students, living in a black community, and being able to cope with and contribute to the students' sense of humour: also, being quick-witted was an essential social skill. After a year working on the research, I enrolled for Punjabi lessons, but the teacher concentrated on Hindi and I soon dropped out. My pronunciation was a great source of amusement for the anti-school Asian students, who attempted to teach me the basics of their languages in exchange for the basics in Gaelic. Most unexpectedly, the students identified with my Irish nationality, and this had major implications for my research. For example, on a number of occasions outside of school, when their friends questioned or objected to my presence among them, it was pointed out that I was 'Irish not white', and this seemed sufficient to satisfy their objections. I had long conversations with the students on the effects of English imperialism on our respective countries of origin, and they showed a broadly sympathetic understanding of the Irish political situation, which was demonstrated particularly on such occasions as the death of Bobby Sands, the Irish Republican hunger striker. This shared political consciousness was developed explicitly with the Black Sisters.

Perhaps, most important for my ethnographic fieldwork was the students' access to my house, situated in Kilby, which provided a mutually relaxed atmosphere and undoubtedly contributed to the quality of the data collected. During the research period it became a sort of local community centre where local youth gathered. They were around most evenings and over the weekends and vacation periods. This interaction was of central importance in developing an organic social relationship with the participants, thus enabling me to adopt the 'insider's view', as Khalid, a Warrior, indicates:

> We could tell you liked us. You are the only white person I've known who invited me home. You see, here we could really relax and see each other as we really are. I got more education here than at school. I think that all of us learned more about real life and you really learned about us. You know more things about me than even my family or my friends. And we still come back, don't we?

FOCUS ON THE PARENTS

About nine months into each study, I began to interview the students' parents in their homes, covering a wide range of areas. Again, this qualitative approach led me to shift my perspective. Initially, I looked at the parents' attitudes towards their children's schooling in order to examine the assumed weak link between the home and the school. Implicit in this approach is the dominant white conception of the black students as 'caught between two cultures', which leads to psychological problems and the need to choose between their parents' culture and that of their country of birth. In the following discussion, the Black Sisters challenged this view, pointing out that culture is not a static phenomenon made up of a deposit of ethnicity that is handed on from one generation to the next. They also challenge 'race-relations' theorists' juxtaposition of an historically unchanging traditional rural Afro-Caribbean and Asian culture with that of their own experience of a modern urban Western culture. The young women offer a more sophisticated analysis, identifying positively with black culture; they present an emphatic assessment of their parents' demands on them.

Hameeda: They want you to keep their values as well as yer own, though these are not always different. They know that you are not going to live their life and they know that they can't force you to. So, they let you live yer life but the thing is that when they see you going too much from their way, they put their foot down.

M M: What are they objecting to?

Chhaya: Well, they can't be afraid of Westernised life because they have become part of it as much as anyone else. Probably, self-respect, self-respect towards society. They care a lot about what other Indians will say. I don't agree, but I understand. It's difficult to keep your culture and live here, but I tell them, you can't hang on to the past. India's changing. We all say this, when we come back. It's not like our parents say. What you call the immigrants dreaming because they suffer here, I understand.

Judith: It's the same with me. My mom romanticizes about Jamaica. She knows nothing about what the Americans are doing there, it's hard for them. If you've got horrible work to do all your life and no respect from that society, you dream. Like Marx said about religion, it's an opium. You dream about the past and things. Not like my mom's friend, she talks about smashing up all the racism. I've learned a lot from her. She knows what it's like over there and here.

The students' perception of their inter-generational relations led me to reformulate my research questions to their parents, taking in wider issues, including immigration to England, their housing and work situations, and their experience of and response to racism and sexism. I came to see that the formation of student groups, such as the Black Sisters, the Rasta Heads, and the Warriors, and the development of their practices, as Cohen (1972) has illustrated about white working-class youth peer groups, is related intrinsically to the 'parent' culture. For example, from the data collected within the local community and other black communities, I came to see that the students' resistance to racism within the school/college, and the wider society, was linked to that of their parents' resistance. The following comment was made by Mr Swali, the father of one of the Warriors, at an anti-racist demonstration (see Reflections on the trial of the decade: the Bradford Twelve, 1982).

We have to stick together and support each other. It's this place now, we could be next. There are a lot more attacks now in Kilby, I've seen it get more and more. The police don't care. You phone them and they come two hours too late or not at all. We must defend, protect ourselves.

A black teacher, working in Kilby, confirmed this view of the unity of the black community.

But why wouldn't black parents understand the frustrations of their kids? My dad fought racism ever since he came here. Kids are now doing it in their way.

It should be added that the black women's activities, on picket lines, on demonstrations against government education cuts, and campaigns against repressive immigration and policing practices, challenged any sexist images of them as simply the 'mothers' or the 'girlfriends' of the male students who were the subjects of the Kilby study.[11]

Again, qualitative research served to challenge the dominant white explanations of black students' academic 'underachievement', particularly that of Afro-Caribbean males, in terms of a generation gap, with a passive first generation and a rebellious 'second generation'. In fact, the image of rebellious black workers and children is to be found in the early 'race-relations' literature (e.g. Patterson 1963; Davidson 1966). However, current literature about this history suggests the absence of such a response. More recently, a number of theorists have examined this area. Sivanandan's (1982) historical analysis is the most comprehensive account of the black community's political structure and resistance to racism. He traces the move from resistance to open rebellion in the early 1980s and locates within this process the growth of the unity between the Afro-Caribbeans' and Asians' struggles. The students' perception of the most recent inner-city rebellions ('riots'), with the police threat to use plastic bullets in future disturbances, confirms the validity of Sivanandan's analysis in the late 1980s.

Amerjit: That is true. After the riots, the coppers [police] have got much tougher. They lost out that night but like you say, they will get their plastic bullets and they will come after us. They have to show their power just like the teachers at school. If they lose one fight, then they have to win the next one. And they will force us into a fight that we will lose. That's how they work. If we stick together like they do, we will be stronger.

Leonie: If the National Front grows like in France, the white people will not protect us. If the oil runs out, they will say, we've had enough of you lot, go back to where you

came from.
Minakshi: I think that they will try to kick us out. We will be made
           scapegoats. That's why we have to stick together just to
           survive. Just like at school, in our different ways.
Joanne: *Tiocfaidh ar la!* [Gaelic = Our day will come. Written on
           the walls in Republican areas of Northern Ireland].

CONCLUSION

Qualitative research may be practised as an exercise in the use of the
sociological imagination (Mills 1970: 12), enabling us to bring into focus
the three-dimensional social world of biography, culture and history.
Like Weis (1985) and Anyon (1983) in the United States, and Connell *et
al*. (1982) in Australia, in looking at student responses to contemporary
schooling, I have tried to describe the students' lived culture in relation
to the wider society. Qualitative research enables us to go beyond the
distorted, de-racialized and de-gendered, white male world of much
academic work. Such a sociological re-focusing is of vital importance
to the future of social science.

Two general points can be made. First, a sociological re-focusing
provides a more fruitful approach to the dichotomous macro–micro
debate, which Dale (1982: 129) aptly criticizes: 'the one can explain
everything in general, but nothing in particular; the other can explain
everything particular, but nothing in general'. As Dale suggests, a
more adequate approach would include complementary explanations.
For example, in studying the schooling of black youth, student–teacher
classroom survival strategies can be seen to be linked to the wider
framework of racism and sexism, thus, acknowledging that 'race', class
and gender are constitutive elements in the maintenance of hegemonic
domination. Consequently, the transformation of these power relations
requires a theory of social change that includes these interrelated
elements (see Brah and Deem 1986).

Secondly, in a highly stratified society, the study of black female and
male students may provide a comparative perspective within which to
test the validity and reliability of traditional studies of the schooling
of white youth, thus offering a more rigorous and systematic analysis
and increasing the general level of explanation.

Sociological re-focusing is also important for understanding the
social world. For example, the issues that have been examined in this
study are of value, not only for the black community, but are part of
a wider concern with state schooling of the working class as a whole.
A study of the encounter between white middle-class professionals
and black working-class students serves to highlight the dynamics of
this process, which are often hidden.

More specifically, this research set out to make a contribution to the concern with the schooling of black young people. Qualitative research enabled me to see the education system as part of a wider system of constraints which, often unwittingly, helps to maintain black people in a position of structural subordination. The major problem in the schooling of black youth lies not with their culture but with racism. The ethnographic studies at Kilby School and Connolly College demonstrate that racism operates through the existing institutional framework that discriminates against all working-class youth (Williams 1986), through 'race'-specific and also gender-specific mechanisms such as the system of racist stereotyping. There may be no conscious attempt to treat black young people in a different way to white youth, but the unintended teacher-effects result in differential responses which work against black youth. Different strategies that are informed by class and gender are adopted by different sections of the youth in their resistance to a racially structured society. These collective responses, which are linked to the wider black community, are seen as legitimate survival strategies.

Finally, discovering the relative autonomy of methodology from more theoretical and substantive concerns provided an alternative reading to the dominant overly-pessimistic evaluation of schooling in the 1980s. We may conclude that at one level there is a ubiquitous political hegemony in operation in England that is hostile to progressive educational practice. However, at the same time, this is not all-embracing, for as the students demonstrate there is always resistance to oppression. The Black Sisters, the Warriors and the Rasta Heads represent a critical case, being part of an increasingly marginalized sector of the working class who have pushed themselves to the centre of the stage and are creating their own history within their community and the wider society. Returning to the question of how I carried out the study, Judith commented:

> In a way, you see our lives as worse than we do because you have an alternative to measure it against. But in another way, it's worse for us because you can go on with your life. Tomorrow you can leave Kilby and go to your white areas. But we are always black living in a racist society. You can't really know what it's like for a black woman. That's why I think that although what you have done is good, I think that black women should carry out their own studies.

ACKNOWLEDGEMENTS

I want to thank Stephen Ball, Chris Griffin and Barry Troyna for their useful comments on earlier drafts of this paper, which also benefited from the comments of a number of anonymous referees.

NOTES

1 All the passages quoted in this article are taken from Mac an Ghaill (1988), and all the names have been changed to maintain confidentiality.

2 Throughout the article, I refer to people of Asian and Afro-Caribbean origin as black. The term highlights their common experience of white racism in England. Racism may take different forms for the two social groups and is gender-specific, as is shown here.

3 'Race' and 'race-relations' are in quotation marks to highlight the fact that these concepts are socially and politically constructed rather than based on scientific findings. For a discussion of the problematic nature of these terms, see Husband (1982).

4 Theoretically, a division has been created between a 'strong' Asian culture and a 'weak' Afro-Caribbean culture. The development of the latter has been explained largely in terms of British imperialism: that is, it underwent a process of acculturation. In contrast, Asian culture is presented as not having suffered this fragmentation to any significant degree. However, as Lawrence (1982: 111–12) has argued, these social images are caricatures.

5 Barratt (1986: pp. 42–56) distinguishes between the psychological stereotype, with its focus on individuals' attitudes such as prejudice, and the sociological view that locates stereotypes within the wider context of society and the ideological function they serve in reproducing the dominant power relations. I use the concept in the latter sense. Idealist analysis, which reduces racial stereotypes to a matter of teacher prejudice creating deviant black students, is insufficient to explain the complex social interaction of white teachers and black students. Rather, the process of racism involves concrete practices linked to the objective material conditions and expectations within the institution and the wider society.

6 Hall (1980: 2–6) divides British work on the analysis of racially structured societies into two broad tendencies: the economic (Castles and Kosack 1973) and the sociological (Rex and Tomlinson 1979). Dummett (1984) and the Institute of Race Relations (1982a, b) provide a clear exposition of English racism. See Hiro (1971) and Fryer (1984) for a history of black people in Britain. See also C. L. R. James (1980). Marable (1985) and MacCarthy (1989) provide accounts of racism in the United States.

7 See Griffin's (1986: 95–111) article, 'It's different for girls: the use of qualitative methods in the study of young women's lives', for a discussion of the male norm in academic research. See also McRobbie (1980).

8 Anyon (1983: 19–23) describes gender development in the United States as an 'active response to the contradictory social messages regarding what they should do and be'. In order to develop the dynamics of this concept, she adapts Eugene Genovese's (1972) account of how black slaves appropriated the ideology of paternalism in order to resolve the contradictions in their existence as human beings and as slaves. Genovese argues that the majority of blacks neither totally accepted nor overtly fought the system

of slavery, but rather adopted strategies of 'accommodation *in* acts of resistance, and resistance *within* accommodation' (Genovese's emphasis).

9 See Giroux (1983) for a discussion of resistance in education. Aggleton (1987: 120–33) provides a most imaginative framework within which to examine theoretically different modes of resistance and contestation. The former being concerned with challenges against 'relations of power structuring relationships between groups'. The latter being challenges against 'principles of control operating within particular settings' (p. 24).

10 In commenting on this paper, Troyna claims that I have not operationalized an emancipatory research method as advocated by such critical theorists as Lather (1986). He also makes a useful distinction between empowerment and giving the researched 'a voice', claiming that my approach involves the latter. I would disagree with this assessment. My study operated within an anti-racist and anti-sexist framework and did empower the students who were involved in it.

11 See Carby (1980) and Gilroy (1981) for an account of the political structure of and activity among the black community. See, especially, Gilroy's (1981) argument that 'community' is a vital analytical concept for understanding such political activity.

REFERENCES

Aggleton, P. (1987) *Rebels Without a Cause: Middle-Class Youth and the Transition from School to Work*, London: Falmer Press.

Anyon, J. (1983) 'Intersections of gender and class: accommodation and resistance by working-class and affluent females to contradictory sex-role ideologies', in S. Walker and L. Barton (eds) *Gender, Class and Education*, Lewes: Falmer Press.

Ballard, R. and Driver, G. (1977) 'The ethnic approach', *New Society*, 16 June, 543–5.

Banks, J. and Lynch. J. (Eds) (1986) *Multicultural Education in Western Societies*, London: Holt.

Barker, M. (1981) *The New Racism*, London: Junction Books.

Barratt, D. (1986), *Media Sociology*, London: Tavistock.

Bourne, J. and Sivanandan, A. (1980) 'Cheerleaders and ombudsmen: the sociology of race relations in Britain', *Race and Class*, 21(4): 331–52.

Brah, A. and Deem R. (1986) 'Towards anti-racist and anti-sexist schooling', *Critical Social Policy*, 16: 66–79.

Bryan, B., Dadzie, S. and Scafe, S. (1985) *The Heart of the Race: Black Women's Lives in Britain*, London: Virago.

Carby, H. V. (1980) *Multicultural Fictions. Occasional Stencilled Paper*. Race series- SP No. 58. Centre for Contemporary Cultural Studies, University of Birmingham.

Castles, S. and Kosack, G. (1973) *Immigrant Workers and the Class Structure*, London: Hutchinson/CCCS, University of Birmingham.

Chigwada, R. (1987) 'Not victims – not superwomen', *Spare Rib*, no. 183, 14–18.

Cohen, P. (1972) *Sub-cultural Conflict and Working-Class Culture*, Working papers in cultural studies 2, University of Birmingham.

Connell, R. W., Ashenden, D. J., Kessler, S. and Dowsett, G. W. (1982) *Making the Difference*, Sydney: Allen & Unwin.

Dale, R. (1982) 'Education and the capitalist state: contributions and contradictions', in M. W. Apple (ed.) *Cultural and Economic Reproduction in Education: Essays on Class, Ideology and the State*, London: Routledge & Kegan Paul.

Davidson, R. B. (1966) *Black British*, London: Oxford University Press.

Dummett, A. (1984) *A Portrait of English Racism*, London: CARAF.

Everhart, R. B. (1983) *Reading, Writing and Resistance: Adolescence and Labor in a Junior High School*, London: Routledge & Kegan Paul.

Fryer, P. (1984) *Staying Power: the History of Black People in Britain*, London: Pluto Press.

Fuller, M. (1980) 'Black girls in a London comprehensive school', in R. Deem (ed.) *Schooling for Women's Work*, London: Routledge & Kegan Paul.

Genovese, E. D. (1972) *Roll, Jordon, Roll: the World the Slaves Made*, New York: Pantheon.

Gilroy, P. (1981) 'You can't fool the youths . . . race and class formation in the 1980s', *Race and Class*, 23(2/3): 207–22.

Giroux, H. (1983) *Theory and Practice in Education*, London: Heinemann.

Glaser, B. and Strauss, A. (1967) *The Discovery of Grounded Theory: Strategies for Qualitative Research*, London: Weidenfeld & Nicolson.

Griffin, C. (1986) 'It's different for girls: the use of qualitative methods in the study of young women's lives', in H. Beloff (ed). *Getting into Life*, London: Methuen, pp. 95–115.

Hall, S. (1980) 'Race, articulation and societies structured in dominance', in *Sociological Theories: Race and Colonialism*, Paris: UNESCO.

Hall, S., Ouseley, H., Vaz, K., and others (1986) *A Different Reality: an Account of Black People's Experiences and Grievances Before and After the Handsworth Rebellion of 1985: a Report of the Review Panel*, West Midlands County Council.

Hargreaves, A. (1978) 'The significance of coping strategies', in L. Barton and R. Meighan (eds) *Sociological Interpretations of Schooling and Classrooms*, Driffield, Nafferton.

Hiro, D. (1971) *Black British, White British*, London: Monthly Review Press.

Husband, C. (ed.) (1982), *'Race' in Britain: Continuity and Change*, London: Hutchinson.

Institute of Race Relations (1982a) *Roots of Racism*, London: IRR.

—— (1982b) *Patterns of Racism*, London: IRR.

—— (1985) *How Racism came to Britain*, London: IRR.

James, C. L. R. (1980) *The Black Jacobins: Toussant L'Overture and the San Domingo Revolution*, London: Allison & Busby.

Khan, V. S. (1979) *Minority Families in Britain: Support and Stress*, London: Tavistock.

Lacey, C. (1976) 'Problems of sociological fieldwork: a review of the methodology of Hightown Grammar', in M. Hammersley and P. Woods (eds) *The Process of Schooling: a Sociological Reader*, London: Routledge & Kegan Paul.

Lather, P. (1986) 'Research as praxis', *Harvard Educational Review*, 56(3): 257–77.

Lawrence, E. (1981) 'White sociology, black struggle', *Multi-racial Education*, 9(3): 43–8.

—— (1982) 'In the abundance of water the fool is thirsty; sociology and black "pathology" ', in Centre for Contemporary Cultural Studies, *The Empire Strikes Back: Race and Racism in '70s Britain*, London: Hutchinson/CCCS.

Liebow, E. (1967) *Tally's Corner*, London: Routledge & Kegan Paul.

Llewellyn, M. (1980) 'Studying girls at school: the implications of confusion', in R. Deem (ed.) *Schooling for Women's Work*, London: Routledge & Kegan Paul.

Mac an Ghaill, M. (1988) *Young, Gifted and Black: Student-Teacher Relations in the Schooling of Black Youth*, Milton Keynes: Open University Press.

MacCarthy, C. (1989) '*Rethinking liberal and radical perspectives on racial inequality in schooling: making the case for nonsynchrony*', paper presented at the International Sociology of Education Conference, Newman College, Bartley Green, Birmingham, England, 3–5 January.

Marable, M. (1985) *Black American Politics*, London: Verso.

McCall, G. S. and Simmons, J. L. (eds) (1969) *Issues in Participant Observation: a Text and Reader*, Reading, Mass.: Addison-Wesley.

McRobbie, A. (1980) 'Settling accounts with subcultures: a feminist critique', *Screen Education*, 34: 37–49.

Meyenn, R. J. (1979) '*Peer networks and school performance*', unpublished PhD dissertation, University of Aston, Birmingham.

Mills, C. Wright (1970) *The Sociological Imagination*, Harmondsworth: Penguin.

Moore, R. (1977) 'Becoming sociologist in Sparkbrook', in C. Bell and H. Newby (eds) *Doing Sociological Research*, London: Allen & Unwin.

Parker, H. J. (1974) *View from the Boys: a Sociology of Downtown Adolescents*, London: David & Charles.

Patterson, S. (1963) *Dark Strangers*, London: Tavistock.

Pollard, A. (1982) 'A model of coping strategies', *British Journal of Sociology of Education*, 3(1): 19–37.

—— (1985) *The Social World of the Primary School*, London: Holt.

Reflections on the trial of the decade: the Bradford Twelve (1982) *Race Today*, 14(4): 124–32.

Rex, J. and Tomlinson, S. (1979) *Colonial Immigrants in a British City: a Class Analysis*, London: Routledge & Kegan Paul.

Riley, K. (1985) 'Black girls speak for themselves', in G. Weiner (ed.) *Just a Bunch of Girls*, Milton Keynes: Open University Press, pp. 63–76.

Roberts, E. (1984) *A Woman's Place: an Oral History of Working-Class Women, 1890–1940*, Oxford: Blackwell.

Seely, J. (1966) 'The making and taking of problems', *Social Problems*, 14, cited in Young, M. F. D. (1971) Introduction, in M. F. D. Young (ed.) *Knowledge and Control: New Directions for the Sociology of Education*, London: Collier-Macmillan, pp. 1–17.

Sharpe, S. (1976) *Just Like a Girl*, Harmondsworth: Penguin.

Sivanandan, A. (1982) *A Different Hunger*, London: Pluto Press.

—— (1985) 'RAT and the degradation of the black struggle', *Race and Class*, 26(4): 1–33.

Troyna, B. (1984) 'Fact or artefact? The "educational underachievement" of black pupils', *British Journal of Sociology of Education*, 5(2): 153–66.

Troyna, B. and Carrington, B. (1989) 'Whose side are we on? Ethical dilemmas in research on "race" and education', in R. Burgess (ed.) *The Ethics of Educational Research*, Lewes: Falmer.

Waller, W. (1967) *The Sociology of Teaching*, New York: Wiley.

Weis, L. (1985) *Between Two Worlds; Black Students in an Urban Community College*, London: Routledge & Kegan Paul.

Whyte, W. F. (1943) *Street Corner Society: the Social Structure of an Italian Slum*, Chicago: University of Chicago Press.

Williams, J. (1986) 'Education and race: the racialization of class inequalities'. *British Journal of Sociology of Education*, 7(2): 135–54.

Wright, C. (1985) 'School processes: an ethnographic study', in S. J. Eggleston, D. K. Dunn and M. Anjali (with C. Wright) *The Educational and Vocational*

Experience of 15–18 year old People of Ethic Minority Groups, A Report to the Department of Education and Science, Warwick: Warwick University.
Young, M. F. D. (ed.) (1971) *Knowledge and Control: New Directions for the Sociology of Education*, London: Collier-Macmillan.

Chapter 9

Genre, ethnocentricity and bilingualism in the English classroom

A. Moore

INTRODUCTION: REALITIES AND CONVENTIONS

In his address to the annual conference of the National Anti-Racist Movement in Education, in April 1988, the St Lucian-born linguist Morgan Dalphinis described his own early classroom experiences on arriving in an English school. Very early on, one of Morgan's English teachers asked the class to write a composition based on some aspect of their personal experience. Morgan's response was to write a story which included everyday scenes of his life in St Lucia: for example, 'a man fell off the [banana] truck and his head was bleeding'. Morgan's teacher, resisting the temptation to alter the non-standard 'his head was bleeding', chose instead to pick Morgan up on the actual content of his writing: 'Did this,' she asked (in a tone that said 'This is very unconvincing, Morgan'), 'really happen?'

The answer to her question was yes, it did really happen. As far as Morgan was concerned, he had written about something from his own experience that was not fantasy but reality: part of everyday life on the St Lucian banana trucks. However, the teacher remained unconvinced. 'I got the feeling,' Dalphinis said, 'that she was questioning my normal reality. . . . The semantic *content* [of my work] was not within her particular frame of reference.'

Morgan Dalphinis's experience is not uncommon among English-speaking children from all sorts of backgrounds not immediately familiar to their teachers or their schools. However, it is equally common, though, as we shall see, sometimes less obviously so, among pupils from backgrounds which have provided them with little or no English. Furthermore, it is not just the content of such pupils' work that is frequently brought into question: it is also – for want of a better word – the style. Put another way, there is often a refusal by teachers to acknowledge not only the validity of their pupils' everyday life experiences, but the validity or even the existence of previous learning experiences (both school-based and home-based), and in particular the validity and existence of learning conventions – including spoken and written genres – that may differ in significant aspects from the conventions favoured in the cultural forms transmitted, lauded and practised in their schools.

In order to investigate what this can mean in actual classroom situations, I want to examine one set of 'mainstream' English lessons attended by a Bangladeshi child, whom I shall call Abdul, at an inner-city school with its own very deliberate – and very public – set of multicultural policy statements. These assert the importance of providing an education 'that gives positive recognition to differences of culture and heritage, and that respects and affirms the identity of each individual child'. I was able to observe these lessons as part of a broader investigation into different forms of secondary-school provision for bilingual pupils that looked, among other things, at the possible advantages and disadvantages of 'mainstream support' teaching against small-group withdrawal lessons. The enquiry lasted several years and involved a number of teachers and pupils and a range of subject areas.

I perceived Abdul's experiences as typical at this school but not inevitable. By way of balance, and in order to present a positive alternative to the kind of experience provided for him, I have chosen to include a second study, describing the experiences of another Bangladeshi boy, whom I shall call Mashud, of roughly the same age and cultural-linguistic background, at the same school. It is my contention that Abdul's experience, which I attribute in large part to inappropriate pedagogy, reveals clear but mistaken notions on his teacher's part as to what, linguistically, bilingual pupils need and of how those needs are best met. These notions are fundamentally different from parallel notions related to Mashud's experience, which in part I see as attributable to appropriate pedagogy.

ABDUL'S LOVE STORY

Abdul had arrived in England from the Sylhet region of Bangladesh eighteen months prior to this study. He had joined the school (Company Road) as a second-year (Y8) pupil, and was now in the fourth year (Y10) following, among other subjects, a public examination course in English in a mixed-ability class in which he was one of ten Sylheti-speakers and in which all but two pupils were bilingual. He was hardworking, polite, and convinced of the particular importance of doing well in English. His English teacher, Ms Montgomery, had set the class a project for their GCSE folders. First, she had read them a love story from an anthology: a story about a teenage boy's secret and unrequited love for a girl in his class. Then, after some discussion of this story, she had invited the pupils to write love stories of their own. After one hour-long lesson and a homework, Abdul had produced the first draft of the first part of his love story, which began as follows:

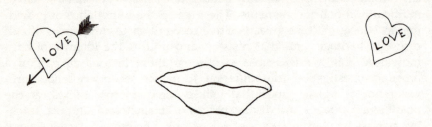

Love Story

19–3–87

by Abdul
once aponar time I fund a grill and I ask har exquiseme. wher you going she said?
I went to go some way wher you ask me for.' I said No I Just Ask you you going I am sorry about that have you dont mind she . said thats OK and anther I fund har on the bus and i was set on the Front and she was set on the back about Five Minuts ago two bay was come And ther set back of the set then this two bay said to hiair hellow wher you going And she was skate.

In addition to Ms Montgomery, there was a 'support teacher' in Abdul's class: Mr Geddes, a member of the school's ESL Department, who was timetabled to work with Ms Montgomery every time she took this particular class for English and whose commitment to the school's policies on 'multiculturalism' and equal opportunities appeared, in conversation, to be fierce and wholehearted. It was Mr Geddes who sat with Abdul to work with him on the preliminary draft of his love story.

Mr Geddes's initial 'corrections' of Abdul's work were of two kinds. First, he focused on the reproduction of acceptable Standard English sentences, spellings, punctuation and paragraphing; on presenting the story so that it made immediate sense to any reader; on helping Abdul with some of his more obvious linguistic confusions (between, for example, 'get' and 'see'); and in the presentation of direct speech. These corrections, written by Mr Geddes on to Abdul's draft, were made with little or no explanation as to what was wrong with the original. The second kind of corrections, made simultaneously with the first, related to Abdul's storytelling *style*. Again, there was little explanation as to why these were necessary ('Let's get rid of some of these "ands" '; 'That sounds a bit more grown up', etc.); and indeed there appeared to be little differentiation in Mr Geddes's own mind between these corrections and the others. In answer to my question 'Are you not changing the style here?', for example, Mr Geddes replied: 'No, I don't think so. It's the same basic story. I've just made it hang together a bit better.'

It seemed clear from Mr Geddes's remarks (typified by the use of the word 'better') that he himself had perceived a certain neutrality in his corrections of Abdul's work: a neutrality that enabled him to perceive corrections of style in the same way as corrections of grammar, spelling and punctuation. Just as there was 'correct' grammar, so there was a 'correct' way of putting together a story: something that was neither negotiable nor culture-specific. The fact that, almost by sleight of hand, he may have been transforming Abdul's story from an essentially additive style, that we might associate with cultures with a strong oral bias, to a more subordinative one, that we might expect to find in a more literacy-orientated culture, was an issue he had not found himself obliged to address. Had he done so, his favoured pedagogical approach, essentially of the replacement of one set of 'wrong' forms with a new set of 'right' ones, might well have been replaced by an alternative, such as extending Abdul's language repertoire to embrace new cultural forms while at the same time valuing and fostering existing ones – an approach deliberately fostered, as we shall see later, by the class's regular English teacher, Ms Montgomery.

After two further lessons, having made impressive sense of Mr Geddes's marks on his page, Abdul presented the second draft of his story, shown in its entirety below. His handwriting still bore the influence of the Bengali script, but his spelling, punctuation and grammar were, to use Mr Geddes's word, 'perfect'.

Love Story   25–3–87

Once upon a time I saw a girl and I asked her, 'Where are you going?'

She said 'I'm just going somewhere. What are you asking for? Do you want to know for any special reason?'

I said 'No. I was just asking where you were going. I'm sorry. I hope you don't mind.'

She said 'That's okay.'

Afterwards, I saw her on the bus. I was sitting at the front and she was at the back. After about five minutes, two boys got on. They

sat at the back near the girl and one of them said to her 'Hello. Where are you going?'
She was scared, and the boys tried to do something bad to her.
I went over and asked her, 'Are these boys troubling you?'
She said 'Yes. Can you help me, please?'
I took her and we got off the bus.
Then I said, 'Can you get home all right?'
She said, 'No, I can't go home. I'm too scared.'
I said 'O.K. I'll take you.'
After half an hour, she said, 'I want to say something.'
I said, 'What is it?'
'How do I tell you? I can't tell you.'
I said, 'Go on. Tell me what it is.'
Then she said, 'I love you.'
Then I said, 'I love you too.'
Another day she and I went to the park. I said to her, 'Do you have any brothers?'
She said, 'Yes. I have one brother.'
I said, 'How old is he?'
She said, 'He's fifteen or sixteen. I'm not sure.'
Then I said, 'Have you got a sister?'
She said, 'No, I haven't.'
Then she asked me, 'Do you have any brothers or sisters?'
I said, 'Yes, I have one. I have one brother and three sisters.'
She said, 'How old are they?'
I said, 'My brother is twenty-five years old and one of my sisters is twenty. Another sister is twenty-one years old, and the other one is eighteen.'
Then she said, 'Are they married?'
Then I said, 'Yes, two are married and one is not married.'
Then she said, 'What about your brother?'
I said, 'My brother is married. He had two daughters and one son. Now he's only got two daughters because his son died.'
She said, 'Oh.'
I said, 'Have you got a father?'
She said, 'Yes, I have.'
We went home. Now we go out every day.
End of part one.

This second draft was presented not to Abdul's class teacher but to Mr Geddes, who again sat beside Abdul to discuss further refinements with him before Abdul proceeded to Part 2 of his story:

Mr G: 'After half an hour she said, "I want to say something." I

said "What is it?" "How do I tell you? I can't tell you." I said, "Go on, tell me what it is." Then she said, "I love you." Then I said, "I love you too." '
Yes, I'm a little worried about this bit. Would she say 'I love you', just like that? It seems a bit sudden. Would they really say that? Maybe they should say it another time, when they've got to know each other better? What do you think about that?

A: [Shrugs]

Mr G: All this stuff about relations. . . . This isn't really necessary, is it. . . . For the reader. . . . What do you think?

A: [Silence]

Mr G: I mean, I think you could really cut a lot of this out, couldn't you. Cut most of this out. [Puts lines in the margin against this section.] Just put here [writing in the margin]: 'We talked about our families. She said she had a brother. I told her my brother was married . . .' You see, that's the other thing . . . I don't know . . . I mean, do people talk that way? In real life? Do they talk about how old their brothers and sisters are?

A: Yes, Sir.

Mr G: Do you think so? I'm not so. . . . And this here: you suddenly say, 'Now he's only got two daughters because his son died.' And she [Mr Geddes smiles] . . . She just says 'Oh'.

A: [Smiles]

Mr G: I mean, don't you think. . . . Do you think they'd just talk about it like that, as if it didn't matter?

A: [Silence]

Mr G: Would they say that?

A: Yes.

Mr G: Well . . . You see, I'm not so sure. Maybe. Let's just put: 'I told her that my brother was married and' [writing] 'he had two daughters but his baby son had died.' Then really you need something else here . . . because now there's not very much in this bit . . .

Mr Geddes's line of questioning during this second-phase assessment had once again raised issues, though not with Abdul, related to generic style, homing in as it did on three apparently similar stylistic points which Mr Geddes clearly perceived as areas of weakness. These were:

1 the girl's and boy's professions of love;
2 the boy's announcement of his nephew's death;

3 the long, detailed conversation about relatives.

Of each of these, Mr Geddes asked: 'Would they say this?' 'Is this how people talk?' – plainly concerned that Abdul's story was not 'true to life'.

Abdul's reactions to Mr Geddes's criticism – unnoticed or disregarded by Mr Geddes – were not, however, the same in each case: a shrug the first time he was asked about the realism of an episode; a clear yes (i.e. 'it is true to life') when asked about the realism of the other two. I believe that this difference in response, however small and insignificant it may appear in transcript, is in fact very important and tells us something about Abdul's *own* reality, the reality that is borne of experience, that he carried with him in his own head. When he said Yes, it is true to life for the girl and boy to enter into such lengthy conversation about their relatives, or for the boy to announce so bluntly (to Western ears) that his young nephew is dead, he may have meant one of two things:

> Yes, it is the kind of conversation that Bangladeshi youngsters (such as Abdul) might engage in in real life;

or

> Yes, it is the kind of conversation that might be found in that other reality, or rather, those other realities, of Bangladeshi *storytelling*.

When Mr Geddes questioned these two episodes, he was, likewise, not merely saying

> Western children do not actually talk to each other like this and therefore no children living *in* the West talk to each other like this;

but

> One of the essences of good storytelling is to make your story as close to reality, that is, to one particular reality, as possible. (Just as he had implied earlier that another is to make your story elliptical or subordinative rather than linear or additive.)

In other words, Mr Geddes's assumption had been that there was *a* way or set of ways of talking to one another, and *a* way or set of ways of telling a story: in both cases, the ways favoured and promulgated by certain powerful groups of people in British society. You do not formally discuss relatives with a potential lover on your first meeting, either in real-life situations or in fictional ones; and if someone in the family dies, you do not talk about it as if it is just another aspect of living. These were the ways, the conventions, the discourses that Mr Geddes had been brought up with and successfully initiated into, and there was no question in his mind but that these were the right ways, the right conventions, the right discourses – an assertion borne out, if he had needed it to be, by the very values and criteria enshrined in the English examination towards which Abdul was being taught. The possibility of linguistic diversity in the broadest sense, that embraced genre, perception and form – and that was plainly suggested by the whole-school policies Mr Geddes believed he practised – seemed not on this occasion to have entered his consciousness: nor, indeed, had the notion that Abdul might previously have learned ways of telling stories in 'alternative' fashions at all. For Mr Geddes, Abdul's previous learning experiences and existing expertise in the replication of cultural–linguistic forms might never have existed: the teacher's task was not a matter of extending an already rich and varied language repertoire to embrace new forms and styles, but to introduce universal 'correctness' into a consciousness that was previously empty in this compartment. In short, for all Mr Geddes's multicultural convictions, Abdul's *alternative* way of telling a story had been perceived as a *deficient* way of telling a story, and Mr Geddes's pedagogy had been affected accordingly.

As for Mr Geddes's third criticism, related to the youngsters' mutual profession of love, Abdul's shrug suggests an uncertainty that was either not spotted by Mr Geddes or was deliberately passed over. On the one hand, he had been asked to make his story true to life. On the other, when he had done just that – or thought he had done just that – he had had his work criticized for its *not* being true to life. It is a shrug that says 'I do not know'. It is also a shrug that invites us to look back to the experiences and observations of Morgan Dalphinis, described earlier. Morgan, it will be remembered, felt that his teacher was 'questioning the semantic content' of his work. She could not believe that a man would 'really' have fallen off a banana truck and cut his head open: Morgan had 'stretched' the truth; he had introduced an unacceptable (because it did not chime either with the teacher's lived realities or with her notions of literary appropriateness) element of fiction into a loosely autobiographical piece of writing.

What had happened in Abdul's case was similar but at the same time qualitatively different. The first difference was that Abdul had been asked to write a piece of fiction: not only that, but he had been asked to write a very particular *kind* of fiction, with its own very particular conventions and norms. Within that piece of writing, Abdul faced the additional task of having to introduce direct speech, a notoriously difficult, problematic and variable sub-genre (see, for example, Volosinov 1973: 109–59). He had been told that this direct speech was to be naturalistic or 'true to life', but he had also known that he was writing a story, and would certainly have had some understanding that stories are *not* life but have their own particular conventions and 'realities'. Abdul's task was made yet more difficult by the fact that he was not merely being asked to write a story in a particular style, but that he was also being asked to write a story *about* a style: that is to say, a style, also variable, of courtship.

The above should give some elementary notion of the extreme difficulty and complexity of Abdul's task: a difficulty and complexity his teacher had apparently not understood. In a task such as this, the differentiation of content from style is virtually impossible, since the content *is* the style: when Mr Geddes criticized what Abdul's characters were saying to one another, he was simultaneously criticizing the manner of their discourse. Whether Abdul had responded by writing according to the rules of a genre – perhaps an essentially oral genre – of storytelling learned in his native Bangladesh; whether he had made an attempt at representing a new kind of 'realism'; or whether he had sought some kind of middle course is not immediately inferrable from the story itself. What we might surmise, however, is that Abdul had never, in the country of his birth, been asked by a teacher to write out a love story as an important, examinable piece of work.

It would be rash, of course, to impute aspects of a pupil's linguistic/academic development solely to pedagogy. Such a claim would be in danger of overstating the impact that any one teacher could have on a child's working and thinking, and would deny other factors that may have been at work, to do with the pupil's perceptions and experiences of life inside and outside the institution. It still needs to be stated, however, that despite Mr Geddes's suggestion to 'take [the story] home with you [. . .] see if you can make Chapter 1 any better [. . .] start work on Chapter 2', and in spite of Abdul's remaining a friendly, courteous member of the class, this particular pupil undertook no further work on his love story, nor, for the rest of that school year, did he produce any piece of writing that was not copied from a magazine or a book.

'COMMON UNDERLYING PROFICIENCY' AND THE ISSUE OF GENRE

How, we may ask, did an experienced, well-meaning teacher such as Mr Geddes come to make such serious errors of judgement in his responses to Abdul's writing?

It would be easy to dismiss Mr Geddes as a poor or unthinking teacher. However, this is plainly not the case. Although his teaching of Abdul may, at first glance, appear to have been haphazard and ill-informed, it was underpinned by very consciously held theories and by a genuine desire to do the best for his client. In conversation about the merits of bilingual children being taught in mainstream classes, for example, Mr Geddes observed:

> Of course they need to be in mainstream classes: they need to read, listen to, and join in with the languages and behaviours of their peers – and they need that sort of audience and feedback for their work.

In subsequent interviews, it transpired that Mr Geddes had absorbed into his notions of good teaching a great deal of theory related to second-language learning. In particular, he had, along with most other members of the school's ESL Department, developed, through in-service training, a keen interest in the work of the Canada-based linguist James Cummins, and especially in Cummins's theory of 'common underlying proficiency' (CUP). Since an interest in this theory in part explains the school's overall policies towards the teaching of its bilingual pupils, while at the same time revealing some potentially dangerous misunderstandings, it is worth turning aside at this stage briefly to examine what that theory is.

Cummins's work on the 'interdependence' of first- and second-language skills and on the 'common underlying proficiency' model of second-language development (1979, 1984) stands in direct opposition to the 'separate underlying proficiency' (SUP) model once favoured by a number of linguists, such as MacNamara, who claimed (Appel and Muysken 1987: 104) that

> human beings have a certain potential, or perhaps neural and psychological capacity, for language learning. [Consequently] . . . knowing one language restricts the possibilities for learning other languages.

Cummins (1979) has argued that rather than restricting development in other languages, continued development in a child's first language actually enhances the possibilities of development in a second language, including development in the functions of that second language in the area of school-learning. This is partly because academic language skills such as reading and writing skills learned in one language can be 'transferred' to another, in the same way that concepts developed in and through one language can subsequently be expressed, experienced and developed in another. Adopting a variation of Shuy's iceberg metaphor, Cummins showed (1984) how languages such as English and Chinese that appear very different on the surface actually possess *beneath* that surface the same basic requirements as one another (for example, the ability to decode and interpret print, to argue a case, to tell a story, to interpret and respond to a speech). One of the conclusions drawn by Cummins (1984) was that:

we can predict that students instructed through a minority language for all or part of the school day will perform in majority language academic skills as well as or better than equivalent students instructed entirely through the majority language.

It is not my intention to examine Cummins's theories here in any depth, since the point at issue is not the theory itself but how that theory has been *understood* at Abdul's school. Cummins's theory is, in fact, a very complex one, arising out of research undertaken in situations where some genuine bilingual teaching was able to take place (that is to say, where bilingual pupils were instructed in school on a regular basis in their first language or in combinations of first and second languages). At Company Road, where there were not the resources for bilingual education proper, the theory had, as if by way of reflecting that situation, been interpreted and absorbed as if it were far more straightforward. Mr Geddes himself, for example, was to say:

> The importance of CUP is that it allows and encourages English teachers to let newly-arrived bilingual pupils with no English to write stories or letters in, say, Bengali, knowing that they'll be developing storywriting and letter-writing skills in that language which can be demonstrated in English later on in their school careers.

An adoption of simplified CUP theory had clearly proved useful to many teachers at Company Road. First, it gave them something to hang on to: the notion that, even with bilingual pupils who had no English at all, there was something they could usefully give them to do. Second, it could be easily incorporated into existing structures and practices – that is to say, without requiring any radical rethink of curriculum content or delivery. (The same was true of other 'multicultural developments' at the school, such as the provision of machinery for reporting racist incidents, or the use of 'third world' exemplars in science and humanities teaching.) The nature of the simplification, however, was also its major drawback: that is to say, while it recognized underlying *similarities* between languages, focusing on that which could be 'transferred', it rather ignored the existence of generic *differences* between languages (for example, different cultural-linguistic traditions favouring different forms and registers of storytelling) which, in an essentially linguistically *intolerant* social and education system, are not transferable.

In terms of what all this meant at Company Road, it could be said that CUP theory had promoted and supported the school's laudable decision to provide first-language tuition for all its Bangladeshi pupils as part of the curriculum, and that it had helped to create an atmosphere in which bilingualism was perceived by teachers as beneficial rather than as a handicap. It had also supported and encouraged the equally laudable practice of teachers encouraging newly arrived bilingual children to operate educationally in their first languages until they had developed sufficient confidence to begin to operate in a second. On the other hand, by talking sweepingly of language 'trans-ference' in terms that lumped together those skills which were readily transferable with those (generic, culture-specific skills) that were not, teachers like Mr Geddes regularly ran the risk of interpreting generic inappropriateness (as they saw it) in terms of linguistic or cognitive deficiency, or simply as 'wrongness'. Where the pressure of getting pupils through a culturally biased examination system was also strong (a system, that is, which valued and assessed expertise in certain areas of knowledge and forms of representation rather than other, equally valid ones), the irresistible temptation was often to cut through any time-consuming and potentially confusing explanations and merely to say to bilingual pupils, as Mr Geddes said to Abdul, 'What you are doing is wrong: this is what is right'.

Faced with Mr Geddes's complicated teaching brief – to correct the inaccuracies in Abdul's spelling, grammar and punctuation; to begin to teach him where he was going wrong in these areas; to extend his generic repertoire; to praise his pupil's achievements in those exten-sions; and at the same time to value, and be seen to be valuing, the generic skills Abdul already possessed – it is hard to imagine the most confident teacher not being a little daunted. The brief, however, is not altogether impossible, and, if carried out thoughtfully, is one that can bring considerable rewards for teachers as well as for pupils.

MASHUD

Another Sylheti boy who attended Company Road School at the same time as Abdul and also had Ms Montgomery as his main English teacher was Mashud. Also in common with Abdul, Mashud was in Year 10 at the school, this being his second year in England. Mashud's English class had not been allocated a support teacher, but in my work with Ms Montgomery over a period of one year I had come, both in a practical sense and in the eyes of most pupils, to fill this role. I had consequently been able to involve myself with Ms Mont-gomery on the planning of lessons, and through this planning had got to know both Ms Montgomery's teaching style and the philo-sophies and theories that underpinned it.

By the beginning of his second year at the school, at which time this study was carried out, Mashud had made steady if unremarkable progress in written English. His handwriting, like Abdul's, still bore

strong traces of the Bengali script, which made it difficult to read; he
still attempted to spell many words and combinations of words – often
misheard in the first instance – by a patchily successful strategy of
phonetics; his attempts at replicating English grammatical structures
were developing slowly; and he had only a scanty knowledge of
English punctuation. He did, however, write copiously and enthusi-
astically, if, as we shall see, not yet with any variety, and in this
respect his written work was impressive.

Quite early on, Ms Montgomery had singled out Mashud as a particularly interesting and promising pupil. In addition to his oral (L2)
reticence and copious flaws at the surface level of his writing, his
work had a particular idiosyncrasy in that whenever he was set
creative writing – or even discursive writing – assignments, he produced heavily formulaic fairystory-style moral tales which were apparently (according to information volunteered from other Sylheti pupils
in the class) translations of stories he had learned, almost by rote, in
his native tongue. This was not a unique phenomenon – many of the
other Sylheti children at Company Road often produced similar work
in response to similar assignments – but the fact that Mashud was
such a productive student, and that he never varied his approach,
threw this idiosyncrasy into particularly sharp relief.

A first attempt to account for the idiosyncrasy was formulated by
Ms Montgomery at one of our weekly planning meetings:

> Mashud seems to have a background where making up stories is
> not so highly valued . . . not nearly as much as learning moral tales.
> I suppose that must have something to do with his culture . . . if
> it's more strongly oral-based than our own . . . or even with the
> sorts of dangers in Bangladesh, which are maybe more predictable,
> and located more in the natural environment than they are here . . .
> I don't know . . . I don't know enough about it, really. . . . Here,
> on the other hand, making up your own stories and writing them
> down is a very highly valued activity.

Despite her confession 'not to know enough' about this issue, Ms
Montgomery clearly had known enough at least not to dismiss
Mashud's idiosyncrasy as a problem of cognitive–linguistic origin, or
to attribute it, as some teachers might have done, to 'unsureness' or
'insecurity'. She had asked herself questions about Mashud's cultural–
linguistic background – questions which nobody had invited her to
ask – and had come to a tenable hypothesis on which could be structured future pedagogy. That pedagogy could then itself be interrogated
as a way of evaluating the hypothesis. In effect, what Ms Montgomery
had done was to attempt to explain a phenomenon rather than merely
describe it: an attempt that had the immediate effect of opening up a

questioning, sympathetic discourse which at future formal and informal meetings would enable other related issues to be recognized, discussed and tackled in a manner far better planned and informed than had hitherto been the case. At a subsequent weekly meeting, for instance, the question of Mashud's 'essentially oral' culture resurfaced, this time finding its focus in the structure of his narratives:

AM: I wonder, you know, if you're remembering stories for repetition, if you're likely to order them in a particular way: also, to cut out . . . not adjectives as such; they could have an important function . . . but – a lot of what we would call 'background detail'.

Ms M: All that description and 'characterization' stuff. . . . Yes . . . I suppose you could be right. It would in a sense be irrelevant, wouldn't it. I mean, the moral would be the important thing . . . not what kind of day it was, less still what mood people were in. . . . None of that so-called realism or naturalism that we're so into. . . . That could all just be so much clutter. . . . It's fascinating. When you think about it, there could be the most enormous gap between what Mashud has been brought up to value in narratives and what we're telling him he should be valuing.

It has to be said that neither Ms Montgomery nor I knew enough about Bangladeshi or Sylheti story-telling traditions to be able to expound with any degree of confidence on the cause of Mashud's particular way of going about things; nor did we have access, immediately, to anyone we could ask. The key to Ms Montgomery's future pedagogy, however, and therefore to Mashud's immediate prospects in this subject, lay in Ms Montgomery's very wise recognition that 'there could be the most enormous gap between what Mashud has been brought up to value in narratives and what we're telling him he should be valuing'. That recognition effectively marked the point at which Ms Montgomery was able to distance herself from what she had been doing in the classroom, making visible procedures in our own culture that we had hitherto both taken for granted. It also resulted, inevitably, in a qualitatively different way of looking at what Mashud was writing. This involved an immediate re-identification of our task and strategy vis-à-vis Mashud and the other Bangladeshi students in the class, away from working almost exclusively on surface features and 'fine tuning' towards initiating them into the kinds of spoken and written discourse they would need expertise in if they were to be perceived of as 'successful' in English society. These initiations would, of course, have to be effected without any devaluation of the kinds of discourse the students were already proficient in (for instance, the retelling of moral tales), or suggesting that ours was the right way of doing things, theirs the wrong. Surface-feature corrections and advice would continue: however, this help would itself be perceived as qualitatively different from the other help we aimed to give.

Emergent skills that we would be looking for in Mashud's writing included creative redrafting (previously, Mashud had produced second drafts of stories at Ms Montgomery's or my request, but these had amounted to mere neat copies of teacher-corrected originals); subordination; the description of unique events; the reporting of conversations; and the introduction of characters' feelings and motives. If responded to appropriately by us, Mashud would, we hoped, come to learn something of what was valued in expressive writing in his new school, and how that was different from (though no better than) what he may have learned to value in previous ones. It was Ms Montgomery's plan to facilitate this new approach by selecting an autobiography project for the whole class to work at over a period of several weeks. This project, while being of relevance and interest to the whole class, would, she felt, be particularly useful for Mashud since it would provide an important opportunity for him to write from his own experience while at the same time incorporating moral tales into his writing in ways that seemed appropriate to him.

Having set up the project by reading a range of examples of autobiographical and pseudo-autobiographical writings with the whole class, followed by small-group discussion and the provision of optional chapter headings, the class began writing their life stories from birth up to the present day.

MASHUD'S LIFE STORY

An example of Mashud's initial approach to the project, and of Ms Montgomery's response to it, is reproduced in the following extract taken from transcripts of discussions between them after Mashud had produced a scribbled first draft of his assignment, which he had entitled 'My Life Story'. (For a fuller account of Mashud's work on this project, which raises a number of other issues, see Moore 1991.) Ms Montgomery had decided to use these sessions both to correct surface and vocabulary errors in Mashud's work and, more importantly in terms of the time given, to discuss its content with him. In particular, she wanted to encourage him to extend the length of his assignment, which was longer than anything he had previously written – a little under a thousand words – but still on the short side considering the nature of the project and the wealth of experience on which he had to draw.

Discussion between Ms Montgomery and Mashud of part of Mashud's first draft, describing being chased by a 'cow'

Ms M: Tell me about this cow.

M: Miss [laughing] cow hit me.

Ms M: It hit you?

M: Yes, Miss.

Ms M: Like this? [Raising hand and aiming an imaginary swipe.]

M: [Laughing] Miss! Like this. [Putting fingers to head like horns and using them to 'butt' the boy next to him, who, listening, also laughs.] In the lands . . .

Ms M: The lands? What are the lands?

M: Where is cow, Miss. Four cows in our lands my family.

Ms M: Lands . . . I think we would say 'fields'. So you had four cows in your field?

M: Field?

Ms M: [Writing it down on Mashud's paper] Field.

M: Four cows, Miss. [Laughing] One cow . . . bad; very, very bad.

Ms M: It chased you.

M: [Excited] Chase! Yes, Miss. I very scared. . . .

Ms M: And it hit you?

M: Yes, Miss. Bad . . . very, very bad.

Discussions like these are not held up as exemplars of good practice. Partly because of tradition, partly because of Mashud's lack of confidence and expertise in spoken English, they fall broadly into the well-documented discursive pattern of teacher initiates – pupil responds (see, for example, Barnes 1976). However, there were characteristics of these and similar conversations between Ms Montgomery and Mashud that made them qualitatively very different from those between, for example, Abdul and Mr Geddes as discussed earlier.

To begin with, Ms Montgomery did not fall into Mr Geddes's trap of questioning her pupil's reality: rather, her aim was to discover more of what that reality was, and at the same time to teach new vocabulary that would be of use to Mashud when he wished or needed to express that same reality in the future. Her questions were also *genuine* questions, designed to elicit information: not disguised statements or judgements. They focused Mashud's attention on what he was writing, and led him to consider additional, related material. While Ms Montgomery made abundant surface corrections to Mashud's work ('in spite of herself' as she was to say later), she made no effort to persuade him to add or to delete anything; merely the suggestion that 'Ramadan sounds very interesting; you must tell me about that some time'.

When Mashud had finished his second draft, using the work 'corrected' by Ms Montgomery along with some more he had added (including a section on Ramadan), he showed it again to his teacher, who first made surface-feature corrections to the added material and then offered her opinion on the work as a whole:

Ms M: Good. That's very good work, Mashud.
M: No, Miss. Short – too short.
Ms M: Well . . . Perhaps you can add a bit? What else do you think you could write about? Let's have a look at what you've got so far.

Together, Mashud and Ms Montgomery now re-examined Mashud's project, Ms Montgomery sitting beside Mashud reading while he followed:

Ms M: [Reading.]
My life Story, by Mashud.
I was born in Bangladesh in war-time. The war started in 1971, the year of my birth. Before that, Bangladesh was East Pakistan. Then they had a big war and Pakistan spread into three parts. One is in India, another Bangladesh, another Pakistan. I don't really know much about it because I was just born at that time. My mum told me about it.

Sometimes I think I can remember things I did, things I saw from the age of eleven, but I don't think I can remember things before that. My mum and dad told me they had a small house in a small village between the jungles. When the war began, everybody went to the jungle to save their lives. People took food with them and a map and a torch for light, because in those days we didn't have electricity in Bangladesh.

People who used to live at the top of a hill or between the fields had to dig a hole that they could hide inside and save their own and their children's lives. My parents said they used to live on the hillside and they dug a hole and hid in it, covering it over with some branches and leaves. My grandfather heard that we were in trouble. He used to live in another village, quite far away. He was so worried that he came looking for my parents, but he never saw anybody. He was shouting and looking for them. The Military were not far away. They heard him calling, and they came and one of them shot him. After about an hour my parents came out and someone told my dad that his dad was dead. He was shocked. It was that night that I was born.

My dad told me they had gone to look for a doctor. Also, I was lucky to be born that night because the Military had gone to another village.

When I was about ten years old we had some farms, and every family who had a farm if they couldn't look after it by themselves they got another person as a paid help, usually someone very poor.

We had four cows. One day school was closed and I was looking after the cows. Suddenly, someone came up behind me and showed a piece of red cloth to the cow. The cow started chasing me. I was running. The cow pushed me with its horns and I went rolling down the hill. I was shocked and hurt in my chest. It took me months to get well.

But in Bangladesh it's lots of fun with your friends. Every morning, we go to the swimming pool with a lot of friends. Then we go to school. School starts at ten o'clock and we have a half hour break at 12 o'clock and finish at 4. Also we have a half-day every Friday because all Muslim people go to the Mosque to pray.

Sometimes after school everyone goes home for dinner, and after that, when the sun goes down, all the boys come out into the fields to play football and other games. It's nice fun every afternoon, except Saturday – because every Saturday we have a market just beside our house. It's our own market, and we also have our own chemist and a small sweet-shop.

I have two uncles, one in Bangladesh and one in England, and I also have two brothers and a sister in Bangladesh.

Once, in my primary school, we held a competition like a wrestling match, and I was in it. I had a big guy against me. I couldn't handle him at all. He was too strong for me and so big. There were a lot of people around and I didn't know what to do, I was so shy and scared. Suddenly he jumped on my ankle and broke it! I was at home about three months. I can still remember how my ankle hurt.

In the winter time we had a big fruit garden. We grew bananas and mangoes and jackfruit, apples and lemons. Some seasons we sold them if we had a lot, or else we'd eat them.

At Ramadan my parents used to fast until 2.30 p.m. to 9.00 a.m. I used to fast some time if I could, but I couldn't very much. I got too hungry. My parents slept most of the time to use the time up. I used to get some mangoes and jackfruit for them and wash it for them. Ramadan lasts one month. After Ramadan we celebrate. The day we celebrate is called EID. On that day we get new clothes and extra food and we go to our cousins' and friends' houses and have nice fun. On that day we can do anything we want to do.

Also every year we have a big market and we call it 'Mala'.

Everybody goes. They have nice toys and music and a magic show. We enjoyed Mala a lot.

Another day, before the summer holiday, we had a sports day. We played badminton, volleyball, cricket and throwing heavy stones. There was so many people in the field. I was playing badminton. We had great fun.

This is a 'corrected' version of Mashud's work, but basically the words are his: that is to say, he put down these words in this order. Ms Montgomery's corrections at this stage had been almost exclusively cosmetic, focusing on spelling, grammar and odd points of vocabulary, though there had also been some impact on what we might call style in small, localized changes of word-order. A flavour of Mashud's original draft is given for the sake of comparison:

We had four cows. one days school close and I looking after the cows suddenle, someone come up after me and should a peece of red clouth to the cow. the cow strated chaseing me I was run the cow push me with it's horn and I when roling down the hill. I shokt and hurt pane in my chest. it tolke month to be better.

When Ms Montgomery had finished reading Mashud's new draft through with him, she returned immediately to his doubts about its length:

Ms M: Well, what else could you say?
M: [Shrugs]
Ms M: How about something more about the things you did with your friends? The wrestling match was interesting. What other things did you do?
M: Yes, Miss.
Ms M: Also, you haven't said anything about your life in England. You could write a bit about that: what it's like here for you.
M: Cold, Miss.
Ms M: [Laughs] Yes . . . Cold . . . Well, you could say that. What else could you say?
M: [Shrugs]
Ms M: Well, you think about it. Write down more bits on a separate sheet of paper and then show it to me.

Mashud appeared happy with Ms Montgomery's advice. He took a sheet of paper from the teachers' desk and spent the rest of the lesson writing busily. Next lesson, he presented Ms Montgomery with two more sections, her 'corrected' versions of which are shown below:

(i)   One time, our Sunday school was closed, and I called for some friends. We decided to go hunting, for a fox or for birds. So each one of us got a spear and we went through the jungle shouting, screaming and running. Our noise scared away all the foxes. If there was one, it would run. But suddenly one small fox just jumped out of a hole and ran away, and we all ran after it. We couldn't kill it, but it was good fun.

In the winter-time in our country, it's not very cold like in England. If we have to wear a jumper, that's winter! And in winter we do a lot of fishing in the canals. Sometimes the water is pushed into our nearest field by the canals, and we can fish in it. But it's far too dangerous to go into the water and pull nets because there are too many snakes in the water. The water is too dirty as well. But we still have a good time and enjoy ourselves in the water.

(ii) When I was about 13 years old my dad was in England. He wrote a letter to us saying that he would try to get us to England. We were so happy to come here. After about six months he came back to Bangladesh to get us.

When we came to England we felt so cold! We went to the hotel in Newbridge. Next day my dad went to the council office to apply for a house. We stayed in the hotel for two months, then we had a flat in Ferry Road. We stayed in Ferry Road for about 2½ years. Then we bought a house with a nice garden in Stoneleigh.

Ms Montgomery described her next task as 'to discuss the two new sections with Mashud and to get him thinking about how to incorporate them into the original text':

Ms M: That's really excellent, Mashud. Very good. Do you think this is long enough now?

M: Miss . . . [Tone implies 'Yes'.]

Ms M: So all you've got to do now is add these bits . . . But . . . Don't just put them on the end. In this kind of writing, it's best to put things together. . . .

M: Miss?

Ms M: Mmm . . . It's so hard to explain . . . Look . . . [Pointing to Mashud's work] Here . . . The War . . . Here . . . Your home . . . Here, you and your friends playing . . . Here, Ramadan . . . Now . . . these new bits . . . You and your friends playing . . . Put that in here. [Draws arrows on Mashud's second draft, indicating this section should go after 'a small sweetshop'.]

M: [Pointing to the second new piece] This, Miss?
Ms M: Er . . .
M: Here, Miss! [Pointing to the end of the original version.]
Ms M: Yes. Good. Put that bit at the end. It actually goes there
         quite nicely, doesn't it? Good. Well done.

Mashud returned to his work. A few days later, he had finished it.
Ms Montgomery was away from school that day, and Mashud asked
me if I would go over his completed third draft with him.

Mashud's new section (labelled (i) above), on playing with his
friends (hunting for animals, birds and fish), appeared, as Ms Montgomery had suggested, with the other references to play: tucked in
between the paragraph about playing in the fields and the paragraph
about the wrestling match. The other new material (labelled (ii) above),
about life in England, also appeared where Mashud himself had suggested: at the end of his completed script. What was of particular
interest, however, was that Mashud had independently made two
further organizational alterations. First, he had removed the short
paragraph 'I have two uncles . . . Bangladesh' from its original location
(i.e. surrounded by paragraphs dealing with recreational activities with
his peers) and replaced it at the end of the script after 'Then we
bought a house with a nice garden in Stoneleigh', where it fitted in
as a 'family detail'. Neither Ms Montgomery nor I had previously
commented on, or, I suspect, even noticed the 'inappropriate' placing
of this paragraph when the suggestion was made to insert part of
Mashud's new material here. Second, he had shifted the short paragraph that appeared at the end of his second draft – 'Another day . . .
we had great fun' – to a new position just after the paragraph about
the wrestling match, creating a new section on Bangladeshi sports.

Most of my next meeting with Ms Montgomery was spent discussing
Mashud's finished autobiography. In addition to observing a number
of techniques transferred and developed from his moral stories, such
as the ability to recount narrative in a very vivid way, we also noted
the emergence of what appeared to us to be new techniques. These
included the evaluation of experience, the adoption of a conversational
'voice', and the use of redrafting skills of a far more complex nature
than Mashud had ever shown us before. There was also evidence –
illustrated in the above examples – that Mashud had begun to re-think
the organization of his work, moving from a linear approach in which
events were organized strictly in terms of when they happened,
towards new kinds of information-clustering relating to perceptions of
similarity. This is a genre of organization more favoured, we felt, in
the dominant British cultural forms than in the forms Mashud was
already skilled in as a result of previous home and school education.

While it would prove dangerous to base sweeping claims on Ms Montgomery's lessons with Mashud, it has to be said that, just as Abdul's experiences with Mr Geddes coincided with the end of his writing career at school, so Mashud's experiences with Ms Montgomery coincided with the beginning of some remarkable developments in his. It was noticeable, for instance, that in subsequent work a number of changes occurred in his approach to writing, chief among which were: regular attempts to replicate 'new' forms or genres; inviting monolingual English peers to read and comment on drafts of his work; and substantially altering early drafts by reshaping and by making significant additions and removals. If Ms Montgomery was not entirely responsible for these developments, her approach had certainly ensured an environment in which their occurrence was not only permitted but encouraged. The indications were that Mashud was continuing to enjoy his work in English and to value himself as a writer, while at the same time developing expertise in those cultural–linguistic forms that he would need (in the first instance) to achieve a good grade in the GCSE examination for which he was entered.

AFTERTHOUGHTS: MS MONTGOMERY'S VIEW

Because of Mashud's obvious and measurable progress in English, it comes as something of a surprise, perhaps, that Ms Montgomery's own evaluation of her work with Mashud proved to be very self-critical. First, Ms Montgomery felt that she had undertaken far too much routine 'correction' of the surface features of Mashud's work, indicating that she felt 'lucky not to have put the poor lad off altogether'. Second, she became very concerned about the imposition of length limits on Mashud's work, feeling that in doing so she had effectively prevented him from deciding this matter himself. A third main area of criticism – the one that caused Ms Montgomery the greatest concern and effected the greatest challenge to her future pedagogy – related to the fact that no real explanation had been given to Mashud as to *why* his original piece might benefit from re-jigging in the way proposed.

Much has been made in this essay of the dangers of devaluing existing cultural forms while at the same time helping pupils acquire expertise in replicating new cultural forms they will need if they are to enjoy a full range of options in this society. What I have wanted to suggest is that this challenge is best met by adopting a policy of the extension of 'linguistic repertoires' (Bakhtin 1986; Volosinov 1973), rather than by treating certain cultural–linguistic forms as 'correct' and attempting to substitute these for other cultural–linguistic forms treated as 'incorrect'. With hindsight, Ms Montgomery found it impossible to say whether the changes to Mashud's work, effective though they were in terms of actual and possible academic success, were evidence of an extension of his linguistic repertoire, or whether they were simply the manifestation of a substitution process, resulting from a reasonable misunderstanding on Mashud's part that his earlier efforts had been wrong and his subsequent efforts correct.

These doubts led Ms Montgomery to think very carefully about broader issues related to cultural reproduction, and in particular to relate the anxieties inspired by her work with bilingual children to what were now, to her, emergent issues of culture and pedagogy relevant to all her pupils, regardless of whether they were bilingual or not. In interview, for example, she was to observe:

> I see now that we really need to explain things more . . . to all our bilingual kids. Showing them the right way – if you can call it the right way – is step number one. You can make some headway in that, even when the language gap is fairly wide. Step number two is to explain to them – and to explain to all children – why certain ways of doing things have come to be accepted as right and proper. For that, you actually need to be able to communicate on a far more sophisticated level because you're getting into the area of politics and sociology. If we can't be provided with bilingual teachers who have been trained in this sort of pedagogical approach, who can explain to these pupils the complicated nature of language, culture and class, there will always be a danger that we [monolingual English] teachers will end up doing the very things we're trying not to do.

While Ms Montgomery might be perceived by some as being harsh on herself, it is hard to question her wisdom in continuing to question her practice rather than rest on past achievements, or in linking her lessons with Mashud to wider issues including those of educational funding. Her concerns about Mashud's perceptions of his learning experience – and a refusal to allow herself to ignore these in the light of her own perceptions of his success – are particularly valuable in the context of this study. The juxtaposition of Mashud's experience with that of Abdul, offered as the first part of this essay, might suggest that a simple contrast is being proposed between pedagogy that is good and pedagogy that is bad. While such a contrast is intended in the broadest terms, supported by the evidence of subsequent work and development of either pupil in English lessons, the dangers of being too smug or too hasty in applauding one teacher's pedagogy as exemplary rather than as merely 'more appropriate' also need to be clearly pointed. (As has been indicated already, the two pupils' subsequent performances may have been affected by factors other than pedagogy, such as 'character' or perceptual or biographical differences.)

It is also important to contextualize Mr Geddes's and Ms Montgomery's teaching strategies within the wider education *system*. Pierre Bourdieu (Bourdieu and Passeron 1977) has written at length about what he calls 'symbolic violence': that is to say, the assertion, chiefly through educational systems, of one set of cultural forms by the powerful groups of people who own and practise them, over other sets which they perceive – and encourage *their* owners to perceive – as inferior forms. The story of Abdul and Mr Geddes could be perceived as a graphic illustration of symbolic violence at work: Abdul's existing, learned ways of telling stories are perceived by Mr Geddes – acting as the unknowing agent of a dominant culture – as incorrect, unlearned ways, and are responded to accordingly with a strategy of eliminate-and-replace. It could be argued, however, that Mashud, despite his 'success', was just as much a victim of symbolic violence himself: that he perceived his ways of organizing his work as incorrect and the school's ways, mediated through Ms Montgomery, as correct: that if he did not 'give in' in the way that Abdul appeared to do, this was because the symbolic violence perpetrated against him was simply carried out with greater subtlety. That, certainly, was Ms Montgomery's fear.

Such questions are worrying. However, teachers can worry too much about what they are not doing (much of which amounts to what they are not *able* to do given current levels of educational expenditure), and often undervalue the good work that they are doing. It is axiomatic that in an imperfect world teachers must simply do the best they can. As Paul Willis (1977: 186) has shrewdly observed:

> If we have nothing to say about what to do on Monday morning, everything is yielded to a purist structuralist immobilising reductionist tautology: nothing can be done until the basic structures of society are changed but the structures prevent us making any changes.

In the case of Ms Montgomery, it can be said that the kind of social hegemony that genuinely values linguistic and cultural diversity may still be a long way off: however, as an individual operating within and making sense of a society that does not yet value such diversity, Ms Montgomery has, through careful evaluation, been able to distance herself sufficiently from her own cultural forms to be able to achieve a level of awareness that will enable her to challenge some of the perceived truths that she has previously promulgated without question, and to adapt her own pedagogical stance accordingly. Such awareness, repeated by 'transformative' teachers across the range of subjects (see Giroux 1988), and shared on a regular, systematic basis with their clientele, can only hasten the creation of an educational climate in which the ethnocentricity of current school curricula becomes itself the focus of a concerted, intelligent and genuine challenge.

REFERENCES

Appel, R. and Muysken, P. (1987) *Language Contact and Bilingualism*, London: Arnold.

Bakhtin, M. (1986) 'The problem of speech genres' (1929), in G. S. Morson (ed.) *Bakhtin: Essays and Dialogues on His Work*, Chicago: University of Chicago Press.

Barnes, D. (1976) *From Communication to Curriculum*, Harmondsworth: Penguin.

Bourdieu, P. and Passeron, J. (1977) *Reproduction in Education, Society and Culture*, London and Beverly Hills: Sage Publications.

Cummins, J. (1979) 'Linguistic interdependence and the educational development of bilingual children', *Review of Educational Research* 49, 222–51.

Cummins, J. (1984) 'Bilingualism and special education: issues in assessment and pedagogy', *Multilingual Matters* 6.

Dalphinis, M. (1988) Keynote address to National Anti-Racist Movement in Education, annual conference.

Giroux, H. (1988) 'Critical theory and the politics of culture and voice', in R. Sherman and R. Webb (eds) *Qualitative Research in Education: Focus and Methods*, London: Falmer Press.

Moore, A. (1991) 'A whole language approach to the teaching of bilingual learners', in Y. Goodman, W. Hood and K. Goodman (eds) *Organizing for Whole Language*, Portsmouth, New Hampshire: Heinemann.

Volosinov, V. N. (1973) *Marxism and the Philosophy of Language*, Cambridge, Mass.: Harvard University Press.

Willis, P. (1977) *Learning to Labour*, London: Saxon House.

Chapter 10

School processes – an ethnographic study

Cecile Wright

Source: Edited extract from Wright, C. (1986) 'School processes – an ethnographic study', in J. Eggleston, D. Dunn, and M. Anjali (eds) *Education for Some: The Educational and Vocational Experiences of 15–18 year old Members of Minority Ethnic Groups*, Stoke-on-Trent: Trentham Books.

Editors' note: This is a chapter from a book the rest of which reports a large-scale survey of the experiences of ethnic minority students in school and work.

INTRODUCTION

Throughout this report there are many observations on how schooling may affect the progress and aspiration of ethnic minority pupils. Some of these are tentative rather than definitive: in a study involving twenty-three schools it is impossible to generate evidence to support all possible hypotheses. Schools are not alike; what may affect pupils adversely or beneficially in one school may not do so in others. The implementation of policies varies as do policies themselves: both are affected by the differing contexts in which schools exist.

We have made suggestions about attitudes and stereotypes that teachers may hold and the effect these may have on pupils. We have also suggested that the internal structures of schools and their operation sometimes have differential effects on the pupils of ethnic minority groups. To explore such suggestions, an SSRC/ERSC 'link student' attached to the project examined two schools in a Midlands authority not otherwise investigated. Acting on her own initiative but with the guidance of the research team, the researcher examined certain aspects of those schools in a manner which generated information of a kind not otherwise accessible to the project – though we have been able to attempt to replicate her evidence in other schools attended by our cohort. *It must be emphasized that the chapter describes events at the two schools under review only and is not intended to offer a picture of the state of affairs elsewhere.*

THE STUDY: TWO SCHOOLS

It was agreed that an age group one year younger than the main sample be studied to facilitate closer examination of the process of placement of pupils into sets and groupings for public examinations. Pupils in their fourth year of secondary schooling were examined through the process of classroom observation in two Midlands schools over approximately 900 hours in each school.

Formal and informal interviews were undertaken with individuals and groups of teachers, pupils and other people associated with the schools. Many interviews were tape-recorded, on the understanding that interviews would be confidential and that the identities of individuals would not be disclosed. Access was also provided in each school to confidential school records and reports.

A description of the two schools and an analysis of certain aspects of the relationships between teachers and Afro-Caribbean pupils within these schools are provided.

TWO MIDLANDS SCHOOLS: A DESCRIPTION

Schools A and B are mixed comprehensives approximately 3 miles apart. The ethnic compositions of the two schools vary considerably. The proportion of pupils of Afro-Caribbean and Asian origin in school A is approximately 25 per cent, whereas it comprises 60 per cent in school B. Despite the variation in the percentage of pupils of ethnic minority groups in the two schools, the school experiences of the Afro-Caribbean pupils in both schools appear to be not dissimilar.

School A

Originally a boys' grammar school, this school amalgamated with a boys' secondary modern in September 1975 to form a mixed comprehensive school. Although comprehensive for nine years now there is still a strong grammar school ethos amongst a section of the senior teachers. These teachers exerted considerable influence, holding positions as heads of departments or year heads. They saw themselves as wanting to get on with the teaching of their subject, but frustrated by teaching in a comprehensive and not a selective school and further frustrated by what they saw as the poor quality of the pupils. This in turn led to feelings of disillusionment. As a probationary teacher explained when she talked about the general attitude:

> Everybody just seems so disillusioned . . . everybody seems fed up . . . the staff as a whole, I mean. I came in as a young teacher, enthusiastic, full of new ideas but you soon find that the old atti-

tudes rub off on you, and so you end up thinking, 'Oh, why am I doing this? Do I want to teach after all?' and this is because of what the others say to you, the more experienced teachers. I think instead of encouraging you to try out new ideas they seem to get some kind of kick out of telling you how bad it is . . . I don't think it is a bad school.

The headmaster responded in a similar way when asked if staff exhibited attitudes conducive to teaching in 'both a comprehensive and a multiracial school'. His reply was:

In the positive sense of showing sympathy and understanding and, above all, in listening to the children talk, I am not so sure about their being a majority. . . . In a comprehensive school attitudes conveying sympathy, understanding and concern for the pupils are fundamental. This does not necessarily mean letting everyone do exactly what they want to do. . . . Nevertheless, I don't think that any child ever actually said it, but it is a story which is supposed to have been said by a child, and whether said or not, it is very true, that is, as a child once said to a teacher or is supposed to have said to a teacher, '*I can't hear what you are saying, what you are is speaking too loud.*' [underlining on the basis of emphasis by head] . . . I think that attitudes that come from people who are concerned with academic excellence and expect it to be so (remember, it wasn't a dirty word 10 years ago, it was what society expected the school to be achieving), now find themselves faced with having to turn right around and, in many cases, do feel disillusioned, very upset and bitter indeed; and honestly, the kinder the system can be in terms of early retirement . . . the better.

School B

School B was originally a girls' grammar school. It became a mixed comprehensive in September 1972 by amalgamating with two single-sex secondary modern schools. Some members of staff at the school felt that it had suffered and was still suffering from the effects of the reorganization. This comment from a senior teacher expresses a general view held by staff:

The basic problem for this school, I think you have to go back to the history of it. . . . When you have a very small, very select, very ladylike grammar school, joined with two rough and ready secondary moderns what basically happened in my view is that when they joined together the grammar school staff, or most of them, couldn't cope with the rough and ready aspect the school then came to have.

They were all in positions of Heads of Department, consequently I got the feeling that the secondary modern staff who could cope with it to a certain extent, withdrew labour. I don't mean that they went on strike, it was well, 'let them buggers do it – they're the ones in the position let them do it'. The school has never recovered from this.

The nature of the school's reorganization was also referred to in a 1979 HMI report on the school. The Inspectorate stated that 'The reorganization which came after a very late decision, produced a great preponderance of girls, many of whom were academically more able than the boys. Within a year came the raising of the school leaving age before the newly-reconstituted school had prepared courses or suitable objectives for the boys and girls who had to stay on'.

Although many of the original grammar school teachers are no longer at the school, there is still a strong academic ethos among some of the senior teachers, though it is sometimes more a sense of nostalgia than something realized in their teaching. There is also an element of nostalgia amongst the original secondary modern teachers, in the sense that, 'the staff knew where they stood within a small school, and with a reliance on a more traditional authority pattern'.

Since the reorganization 12 years ago, the ethnic minority intake has gradually increased to well over half in the first year now. This intake of children from ethnic minority groups has sometimes been associated negatively with what have been perceived as problems within the school – declining standards and discipline problems. This contention is supported by the comment of a teacher who has taught at the school for six years:

In my opinion there is a great degree of apathy, and fortunately we're just coming out of our apathy, but nevertheless the apathy was there for a long time, and the apathy eventually showed up in the kids, and the kids became apathetic. We often term this as '. . . itis' [name of the school], where you couldn't care less for anything that goes on. You get to a certain position in your job, there are a few promotional prospects, there is little back-up from the top, your job as a teacher is no longer as a teacher, you've got to start policing and so forth.

A year head who originally came from the secondary modern school at the time of reorganization had this to say on the status of the school:

This school is a low ability school because of its catchment area, which consists of a low social class and a high immigrant population. More fundamentally, it is the high proportion of immigrants in this school which is responsible for the lowering standards.

The somewhat disturbing view held by this teacher is not uncommon among members of staff. As the following comment from an HMI report states:

Many of the staff of the former grammar school for girls and the amalgamated secondary modern schools had undergone rapid changes in professional demands and were still adjusting to a changed situation which included a much higher incidence of social disadvantage than was known under the former selective system. This, together with the increasing percentage of pupils from ethnic minority groups, had been a new experience to many of the staff. Some were regarding the new demands as entirely a matter for the 'new' pastoral system and seemed reluctant to reconsider their teaching style or professional attitudes.

RELATIONSHIPS BETWEEN TEACHERS AND AFRO-CARIBBEAN PUPILS

For teachers at school A the frustration of having to teach what they considered as 'inferior' pupils is further exacerbated by having, as they perceive it, to contend with 'troublesome black pupils'. Similarly, some teachers at school B felt dissatisfied with having to teach predominantly 'immigrant' children, with their 'alien' ways, and having to put up with 'disruptive and troublesome Afro-Caribbean pupils'.

School A

It is difficult to say conclusively that there are obvious differences in the way in which teachers in the classroom interact with Afro-Caribbean pupils and that these differences are influenced by ethnicity. First, there were never more than two or three black pupils in any class, so their presence was not always obvious. Also, what takes place within a classroom context is possibly influenced by factors outside the classroom. However, the following dialogue noted during a classroom observation demonstrates how a teacher's insensitivity can result in conflict with Afro-Caribbean young people:

The teacher was talking to the class. Whilst he wrote on the blackboard, a group of four white boys sat talking to each other in an ordinary tone of voice. The teacher, being annoyed by the noise level in the room, threw a piece of chalk at an Afro-Caribbean boy who was not being particularly noisy.
Teacher: Pay attention [shouted].
Teacher: [to an Asian boy] Could you get me that piece of chalk?

Peter: [Afro-Caribbean] Why don't you use black chalk?

Teacher: [turning to the researcher] Did you hear that? Then I would be accused of being a racist, take this for example, I was down at Lower School, I had a black girl in my class, she did something or another. I said to her, if you're not careful I'll send you back to the chocolate factory. She went home and told her parents, her dad came up to school, and decided to take the matter to the Commission for Racial Equality. It was only said in good fun, nothing malicious.

Keith: [Afro-Caribbean] [aggressively] How do we know that it's a joke, in my opinion that was a disrespectful thing to say.

Teacher: [raising his voice and pointing his finger at Keith] If I wanted to say something maliciously racist, I wouldn't have to make a joke about it. I'd say it. I've often had a joke with you, haven't I?

Keith: [angrily] Those so-called jokes, were no joke, you were being cheeky. I went home and told my mum and she said that if you say it again she would come and sort you out. As for that girl, if it was my father, he wouldn't just take you to the CRE, he would also give you a good thump. My father says that a teacher should set a good example for the children, by respecting each one, whether them black or white. He says that any teacher who makes comments like that in front of a class, shouldn't be in school, that's why he said to us that if a teacher ever speaks to us like that he would come up to school and sort him out.

Harry: If it was me that you said that to, I wouldn't go home and tell my parents, I would just tell you about your colour.

Keith: Teachers shouldn't make racist jokes.

One way in which attitudes towards categorization of black pupils was fostered was through 'informal gossip among staff', as Hargreaves (1967) describes it. This is an important medium in the school, since a fair proportion of teachers do not actually teach the pupils they hear talked about. Hargreaves explains:

how in the staffroom in particular, whenever teachers discuss pupils, they import into the discussion their own interpretations and perceptions. This provides the naive teacher, that is one who has no direct contact with the child, with information which categorizes him in advance of actual interaction and defines the situation in terms of the behaviour the teacher would expect. To the naive teacher, opinions of colleagues will have the effect of acting as a provisional agent of the categorization process. In other words, one of the functions of teachers' gossip about pupils is to add to the preconceptions and expectations by which a pupil is assessed.

(Hargreaves 1967)

Such an explanation is illuminated by a white probationary teacher who expressed how she had misjudged a black pupil:

A lot of teachers jump to conclusions about pupils before they've even come into contact with them and broken through the pupil's resentment. They jump to these conclusions and these conclusions are passed round in the staffroom. You only have to sit in there and you hear the rumours and the gossip that's going around and the thing is, in the staffroom it's always the bad kids that are talked about, never the good ones, which I suppose makes sense in a way, but as a new teacher, you come in, you hear these rumours like, I used to hear rumours about Kevin [an Afro-Caribbean pupil] and I thought, 'Oh, God, I'll have to watch out for Kevin, everybody thinks he's a trouble-maker and that means he's bound to be in my class', but I mean it's not as simple as that, it really isn't. . . . There are a few white kids that are talked about but I mean that's inevitable. I think to a certain extent the West Indian kids tend to get labelled and these labels they feel they've got to live up to. I mean, you might think 'well, what goes on in the staffroom doesn't get round to the kids' but it does, it does, even if it is just through the teacher's own attitude. They can sense it, they're not stupid.

This teacher's view that the Afro-Caribbean pupils felt obliged to live up to the labels given them by the school was reiterated by other teachers. A black teacher claimed:

The West Indian pupils, especially the boys, are seen as a problem in this school because they are so 'aggressive'. You see, I am using a quote here, they are so openly aggressive and surly. . . . If it is always assumed that they are intellectually inferior, what else is there for them to do . . . every time teachers are constantly amazed by the fact that in the first year they have at the moment – there we have two or three really bright West Indian boys, and it's of constant amazement to people like Mr G . . . 'my goodness he's bright where does he get it from'. Pupils here in the 5th year are generally thought to be dross.

How might the behaviour and attitudes of the pupils be affected by the organization of the school and the teachers' attitudes and expectations? Hargreaves suggested that pupils with positive orientations towards school values largely converged on the higher streams, whereas those with negative orientations converged largely on the lower streams. He found that pupils in the lower streams were deprived of status and subsequently developed an anti-school culture which was used to gain status.

From discussions within a racially mixed group of sixty pupils, from both the fourth and fifth year, there seems to have been a consensus of opinion that the streaming system does not truly reflect ability. There was also a consensus that the streaming system works more against black pupils, as indicated in the following conversation with four white pupils:

> I think that black kids are treated rather badly in this school, for example there are less black kids in the 'A' band. In my opinion it is not because they are not capable, it's because they are not given the opportunity. Teachers generally hold a low opinion of them, for example, I'm in the 'A' band, I'm doing 'O' level English. I find that some of the 'B' band kids are doing the same syllabus, and in some cases they get the same marks or better marks than us, yet they can't do 'O' level and they're in the 'B' band.

Conversations with two black pupils further revealed dissatisfaction about the school's organization:

> We came here because our brother and sister went to this school. They got on badly, they were unhappy with the school, so they didn't try. They were also put in the 'B' band. However, they are now at [another school] in the sixth form. The headmaster would not allow them to go into the sixth form here. Anyway, they're better off there. They are both doing 'O' levels and 'A' levels. Since going there my brother has got 'O' level Grade A in maths. He never did any good here.

Further conversations with a group of sixteen black pupils reflect the general belief that the school's organization was against them. Consequently, the pupils saw very little point in trying. Further, they interpreted this perception as a *fait accompli*, an inevitable outcome of the school's attitude towards their colour. To black pupils the school seemed to be seen as a 'battle ground', a hostile environment insofar as it rejects their colour and identity. This is clear in the following discussion with a group of eight black boys talking about their feelings when teachers make derogatory comments about their skin colour in front of the class.

Michael: It's like once the man [referring to the teacher] come in the class, and ask me in front of the class, 'Why me coffee coloured', he say, 'How come Wallace dark, and Kennedy black and Kevin a bit browner? How come you that, you a half-breed?' Me say, 'No man, me no look like me half-breed'. Me say, 'just like some a una white like a chalk and another couple a una got blond hair, some have black hair, me no come ask wha that! . . . That's how he is, he just come around, crack him few sarcastic jokes about black kids.

Paul: But they're not nice at all. They're not nice. The jokes aren't nice. The jokes are disrespectful.

Kevin: They're not jokes man.

Errol: You can't call them jokes. When he cracks a joke or whatever he does in front of the class, he just turn round and laugh. You get him and the class laughing at you.

Kevin: What he is doing is running you down. He's just bringing you down like dirt. Nobody is bring me down [said with anger]. Every time I'm chuck out of [subject] completely man, because every time in [subject] he always keep calling me something about me colour and I answer back.

Errol: The teachers are forever picking on the black boys.

Michael: Like me now, them no too bother with me because them think, say me a half-breed, you know. Half the teachers in the school think say me a half-breed so they don't too bother me. Just lately they find, say me black, so they've started bothering me. Like the half-caste kids them they used to left me alone.

Kevin: They don't give half-caste kids no hassle, no hassle whatsoever. However, if the half-caste kids act black, they pick on them hassle man.

The boys were asked how they felt this so-called 'hassle' affected their academic performance. Paul summed up the views of the group:

You're not really given the opportunity to learn. Most of the time we're either sitting outside the Head's office or we are either fighting or we are arguing with them. It's just we got no time, as you sit down to work they pin something on you.

The resentment, bitterness and frustration felt by the Afro-Caribbean boys towards the school – due to the attitudes of certain teachers – is evident in these discussions. All that the boys said emphasized their perceptions of their interactions with teachers as an 'us' and 'them' situation. How then did this estranged relationship between the Afro-Caribbean pupils and their teachers affect the pupils' behaviour? As in the Hargreaves case, these pupils have developed a subcultural adolescent group within the school which is not only anti-school, but is also somewhat anti-white. This 'all-black' group is composed of both boys and girls: pupils from the third, fourth and fifth years. The thirty or more pupils move around the school together during the school breaks.

Most teachers were aware of the presence of this group but not of the reason for its development, with the notable exceptions of a teacher from South Africa and the deputy headmistress. As the teacher pointed out:

> This group is a reaction to the racism in this school, we have what can be described as a very strong 'black mafia' within the school. They feel that they belong together, so they stick together.

Further confirmation came from the deputy headmistress:

> There is certainly a race problem here at the moment. There is certainly not so much a race problem between pupils, but there is a great problem here at the moment with the congregation, shall we say, of black pupils. By the time they get to the fourth form there are very few black pupils. There are identifiable groups of black pupils as they move around the school and we have had problems this last year with a particular large group of black pupils who have set out their stalls to appear aggressive.

This group has adopted a typical 'gang behaviour' as described by Goffman (1971) in his description of 'looking cool' behaviour. The group attempts to assert its presence through both verbal and non-verbal means. As the headmaster points out:

> A number of black children, particularly boys, seem to lose interest in the school's aims (unless they are good at games, then they dissociate that from the rest) in the third year and, from then, become increasingly seen as an anti-culture . . . probably the most striking manifestation of West Indian pupils, is just that the group of large boys, and the sort of threatening physical presence, which you can see consistently around the school.

This 'gang' behaviour displayed a deliberate assertion of 'blackness' through the use of Patois – used both defensively and offensively by the group. Patois was used successfully to communicate rejection of authority. Although the teachers were aware of this 'weapon' they had great difficulty in finding anything to attack it with. This point was reiterated by the deputy headmistress:

We've got a problem at the moment, which is very nasty (I think the Headmaster was hoping to talk to you about it) where we are being faced with a barrage of Patois. It is so worrying because you see when that happens we as teachers have a choice. We either ignore it, but if it's done in public you feel threatened, or you feel that you are showing weakness if you just ignore it. You can either react equally aggressively and verbally back in Spanish, or French, which in fact is what is happening, but that is not helpful, or, as one member of staff said today, 'I came very close to clobbering him today'.

To elicit some explanation from the pupils for their behaviour, a group of sixteen was asked how they themselves perceived their behaviour in the school. In their analysis, they felt themselves to be forced into a stimulus-response situation:

Paul:	The school don't respect black pupils. We are treated badly, we are forever hassled . . . I can remember the time I was in [subject], Mr X keep saying to me 'Why you've got a tan?' – I say, 'Well I was born like this.' He say, 'Well you should go back to the chocolate factory and be remade' or something like that. . . . To me that wasn't a nice thing to say.
Keith:	We are treated unfairly because we are black. They look after their flesh not ours.
Michael:	They look after fe them white people-dem, you know what I mean, but we get dash at the back all the time.
Researcher:	You have all said that you feel that you are treated unfairly in the school. How do you feel this makes you behave?
Delroy:	Bad!
Researcher:	When you say 'bad' what exactly do you mean by this?
Paul:	It means that we turn around and make trouble for them.
Delroy:	Yeah, we try to get our own back on them. We behave ignorantly towards them, and when the teachers talk to us and tell us to do something we don't do it, because we just think about how they treated us.
Paul:	Like when you walk down the corridor, and a teacher stops you, you just ignore him. When they stop you for no reason you just irated.
Researcher:	How about you Errol?
Errol:	I try to keep out of trouble the best I can. If they

cause trouble with me I cause trouble with them it's as simple as that. If you are troublemaker, right, and you're pretty intelligent, they still keep you down. Look what they've done to Delroy, he's pretty intelligent, yet they keep him down, no wonder he causes trouble. Because I want to get on I try to keep out of trouble.

School B

As in school A, the nature of the relationship in school B between the Afro-Caribbean pupils and their teachers was frequently one of conflict. In school B the basis of this relationship may lie in the teachers' particular unease with the ethnic composition of the school: an unease at being 'swamped' and having to teach 'these alien pupils'. Many teachers try to obscure the fact that they are teaching in a multiracial school. Little attempt is made to acknowledge the ethnicity of the pupils. However, what is perceived as the belligerent, aggressive, lively, gregarious character of the Afro-Caribbean pupil, cannot be easily ignored by the teachers, and presents a constant reminder of the nature of the school. As one teacher at the school observes:

The pupils in this school come from working class and multicultural backgrounds. It seems to me that very few staff are addressing themselves to the kinds of thing (e.g. resources, teaching style, subject content, and attitudes and the hidden curriculum) that can be used to bring out the best of the pupils' cultures and backgrounds. The attitudes of teachers to West Indian and Asian cultures is at worst negative, and at best condescending and patronizing. These cultures are viewed as remote and distant, and few teachers go out into the community to learn or take part in community activities. . . . Pupils are seen as recipients, with very little to offer to the curriculum. Teachers view themselves as doing a good job by educating 'these immigrants' in the 'best education system in the world'. . . . For these 'immigrants' to start demanding having a say in the way their pupils are taught and what they are taught is viewed with great disdain. . . .

There is so much that pupils can offer to the school if there can be someone to listen and take notice. The end result is that pupils switch off any interest in the school, and how they manage to go through five years of their school lives still amazes me. They have a negative view of the school; of the West Indies, Africa and Asia and of themselves and their abilities.

Some of these views were also expressed by an Asian pupil in a social studies lesson, where the class was looking at the issue of 'Prejudices in society'. The pupil pointed out to the teacher and the class that she felt that there is pervasive racial prejudice in the school, which the teachers failed to acknowledge. As she says:

We were discussing in form period, Asian languages in this school about people who want to take it, that it would be a chance for people to learn another language, say, if non-Asian children take it they would come to respect it. The form teacher then was on about that the school is for teaching only Western ways of living, and European ways of living. She said that's what you come to school for. That opinion really shocked me, coming from my own teacher. She was trying to tell me that we're nobody. She then said that when there was a lot of Polish people in the school, they never practised any of their culture here, they went away to their own community. She also tried to tell me there wasn't any prejudice in the school. And the worst thing is she was trying to tell a coloured person that there wasn't any prejudice, and that you only come to school to learn about the European way of life. That's the thing that needs bucking up in this school. . . .

I said to her, 'I'm not willing to argue with you here because it would get me into trouble but if I ever saw you on the street I would.' Because I made a mistake once when a teacher told me that there wasn't prejudice in this school. I blew up and I tried to tell her, no you're wrong. I got myself into trouble . . . I made a mistake of doing it then in such an organized atmosphere. If I was going to . . . I should have done it out of school because in school everything is organised. The teachers are willing to back each other up. I asked another teacher, 'Well, what do you think?' she said 'You were wrong to shout back at her, full stop! Never mind what you were saying'.

The following comment from a year head indicates that the above pupil's perception of some teachers' attitudes towards certain sections of the school population was not wholly unfounded:

I find it difficult to accept the immigrant people and children that I come into contact with. I cannot change my feeling because it is part of my upbringing – I feel that the English culture is being swamped. I do not see how the Asian and West Indian pupils that I am responsible for can take on English behaviour for half a day when they are at school and change to their culture when they are at home.

To what extent then do attitudes of this nature shape the Afro-Caribbean pupil-teacher relationship? Informal discussions with Afro-

Caribbean pupils indicated that the pupils felt that certain teachers disrespect them on the basis of their ethnicity and that for these pupils the pupil–teacher relationship was based on conflict, with the pupils then attempting to play the teachers at their own 'game' in order to survive. They saw the school as condoning these teachers' attitudes. A discussion with a group of twenty Afro-Caribbean girls illustrates this:

Barbara:	The teachers here, them annoy you too much.
Researcher:	In what ways do they annoy you?
Barbara:	They irate you in the lesson, so you can't get to work.
Susan:	For example in Cookery, there were some knives and forks gone missing, right, and Mrs B goes 'Where's the knives and forks?' looking at us lot [the Afro-Caribbean pupils in the class].
Vera:	Yeah, all the blacks.
Sonia:	Seriously right, in the past most coloured children that has left school they've all said she's prejudiced.
Jean:	She's told some kids to go back to their own country.
Sonia:	Seriously right, if you go to another white teacher or somebody, and tell them that they're being prejudiced against you, they'll make out it's not, that it's another reason.
Jean:	When Mrs B told Julie to go back to her own country she went and told Mrs C [the deputy headmistress], Mrs C said that Mrs B was depressed because her husband was dying.
Sonia:	So why take it out on the black people? . . . then she's told black people to do many things, she's even called them monkey.
Sandra:	As for that Mrs C I can't explain my feelings about the woman. Because Mrs B, right she just prejudiced, she comes up to me in the Cookery lesson, tell me to clean out the dustbin, and I was so vexed I started to cry, I was so vexed by it. I didn't come to school for two weeks.
Sonia:	You see the thing is, right, they can get away with saying anything to your face, there isn't anything you can do about it.
Jean:	In Geography, this teacher dashed a book at me, and I dashed it back, and I got into trouble for it. *[group roared with laughter]*
Vera:	Most of the things that the teacher says, right, they say things that annoy you they know that you're going to answer them back, so they can get you into

	trouble. Take Mrs B, she'll walk around with a towel, and if you look at someone and smile and she thinks you're talking, she flash water in your face or she'll slap you over the head, but I've just told her that if she boxed me I'll have to hit her back. Because she's got no right to walk round doing that. If you answer her back in any way, then she'll send you down to Mrs C [deputy headmistress] then you're in trouble.
Susan:	Mrs C is prejudiced herself because, I mean, she said to Karen that she is only getting bad because she hangs around with too many black people. It's not as if [shouting in anger] as she says, black people are going to change you to bad.
Vera:	Some teachers are alright but others, you can tell that they're prejudiced by the things they do. Every time Mrs B's cooking, even if she's doing say, a boiled egg or something like that, any little simple thing you can think of, coloured people and Asian people have to cook it different. . . . Oh, well the coloured people and Asian people always cook their things different. . . .
Jean:	[with disdain] Is that what she says?
Vera:	Yeah, she's really facety you know, that's why I don't get on with her, and when I was telling me mum, me mum was going mad because she must think that we're some aliens, or something. . . . If the teachers have no respect for you, there's no way I'm going to respect them.
Researcher:	Would you say that the Afro-Caribbean boys have the same experience with the teachers as yourselves?
Vera:	The boys I know don't get the same treatment because most of the lads are quicker to box the teachers-dem than the girls, you see.

Assertions from pupils about what teachers call them may not always be believed by sceptical readers. We now quote a year head whose reference to the phrase – 'go back to your own country' supports the girls' assertions – but about a different teacher. His account also demonstrates that staff in positions of authority, if not totally condoning such utterances, do not necessarily rush to condemn them even given the pressure of a parental complaint. The year head states:

If I had one parent who sat with me in my office and said 'I have come to see you because that Mr – said to my son "If you don't like it here then go back to where you came from and where you belong'' and I was so upset at that because my son was born here and I have lived in this country for over 20 years and how *dare* [italics from year head's emphasis] he say that, because my son comes from here. I came from Jamaica over 20 years ago and I got married in this country and I have stayed here ever since and although perhaps I might want to go back to Jamaica it's not home to him.'

And that lady was quite genuine. The member of staff when I spoke to him about it afterwards – I did not call him in to speak to him about it immediately because I did not think it was either my place or my duty – I told him that she was very concerned about that being said to her son and quite frankly so was I, and really was that the sort of thing to say and he agreed it wasn't the thing to say but he said 'I was so angry at the time. The pupils had been going on at me about "You're always picking on me" ' and then finally the boy said to him that he was picking on him because he was black and he said 'That just triggered it off'. He said 'I just turned to him and said what I said. Yes, I did say that.'

I know he said it in anger but you don't even say things in anger if you don't feel them and that really bothers me a bit. But that's not the only one. I have had others who've actually said 'X doesn't like my child', but then of course X doesn't like any black child. And I think we both know who I'm referring to. . . . Black children react in a certain way because they feel they are being picked on, and because they react badly then further reaction follows.

Discussions were also held with Afro-Caribbean boys in the school, particularly with one group of fifteen pupils, who voiced similar complaints to the girls. One of the more vivid examples again illustrates conflict.

Researcher:	Do you all go around school together as a group?
All:	[defensively] Yeah, not to cause trouble.
Stephen:	At break times, we talk and have a laugh, I know she [referring to the deputy headmistress] always seem to think there is something going on.
Lee:	We normally play football together, we have known each other throughout the years.
Gary:	Friends, from long time, isn't it.
Stephen:	There is a great deal of racial prejudice in the school.
Earl:	Although some of the teachers try to hide it, but you can tell by the way they get on with you.
Stephen:	Really, it's how the teachers treat us. Because I can get on with teachers in this school, it depends on how

	they treat me. If they treat me friendly I will give them the same respect back. Some teachers, right, think just because they're teachers they're above you and they're something better, and they treat you as if you're nothing, so you think to yourself, 'well who are they to think that' . . . so you then treat them without any respect because they don't give you any, so really, it's just a two-way thing, I say.
David:	There's a few teachers who have got real interest in, if you say, black children in particular. Like various articles in the papers are saying, that we're supposed to be lacking in education and whatever, we're not exactly tip-top with the Indians and white people, you get the odd person that cares like the Asian teacher, Mr – but these other teachers don't.
Gary:	I can tell that they don't like us because we're black, it's just something about them. It's just certain teachers who are racialist.
Lee:	There are certain teachers that's true, like Mrs — and Mr — but on the whole most of the teachers are the same.
Researcher:	How do the teachers' attitudes you have described make you feel as an individual?
Gary:	Resentful.
Winston:	Hate.
Earl:	A bit small.
Stephen:	When you know that they are sort of negative and they don't really talk to you as a person, you know that they're not really bothered about what happens to you. Whether you pass an exam or not, and you think to yourself, well they're not really bothered about what you do, so that means you don't really think of it in terms of, oh well, he is really taking pride in me or her and really want me to do well, it goes beyond just teaching me, it's not something personal as well.
Researcher:	How do the teachers' attitudes affect your behaviour in school?
Stephen:	I suppose it makes me behave bad, they pick you out, on your colour anyway. They tend to say, oh well, he's black so it's to be expected, they're bound to do that, so when they give you that kind of attitude, you think oh well, blow them, if that's what they think, why not act like that.

David: It's not really as bad for me because they can't really tell that I'm half-caste (this pupil looks more white than Afro-Caribbean) like the rest of them. But I still feel it the same, but not as much as this lot.

Lee: I haven't experienced any problem in classes, but when I'm in the group hanging about the corridors I do, not really in class. Like David. I'm not really full black, I'm half-caste.

Many pupils thus see the conflict as an inevitable response to the teachers' attitudes towards their ethnicity. As one pupil succinctly put it 'you then treat them without any respect because they don't give you any, so really it's just a two-way thing'. Nevertheless, the pupils did acknowledge that not all teachers held negative attitudes towards their ethnicity.

A number of senior teachers and other staff were asked whether they acknowledge that something of an estranged relationship existed between the Afro-Caribbean pupils and teachers, and whether they attributed this to negative racial attitudes projected by teachers towards these pupils. The deputy headmistress in charge of discipline had this to say about the experience of the Afro-Caribbean pupils:

DH: The West Indians are very lively, very gregarious. They like to be together to talk. They do however feel threatened, they do feel people aren't fair to them and sometimes they're quite right.

Researcher: Why do they feel threatened?

DH: If you touch one, the reply is 'don't touch me'. I suppose it's because some people have been given a hard time. I think sometimes people are not fair, and I think they do feel it . . . they sometimes feel picked on and I can see all this when they come in here sometimes. They are very resentful and sulky and always at the back of it is that feeling that they are unfairly treated.

Researcher: Do you think that the pupils may be justified in feeling that they are unfairly treated?

DH: Not within the school no, we bend over backwards to be fair, to get to terms with the pupils, to try to get their confidence. And when you do have to grumble about something, they are always asked 'is this fair', 'did you do this' and only then do you jump. I would never punish any child who didn't agree with me that they had done something. . . .

> That's the important thing about discipline, to make them see themselves as they really are, not as they think they are.

A deputy headmaster spoke in defence of teachers:

> Because of a few children that we have, many of whom were taken in late in this school, all of which Mr [the headmaster] quite rightly said causes considerable disruption and disturbance within the school, the teachers I think if they're asked, tend to look upon this school . . . as a possible source of disturbance to them. I think that they are not comfortable enough in this school, they don't feel secure.
>
> Researcher: Why do the teachers feel insecure?
>
> Deputy head: Because we have sufficient children within this school and there are not many, a tiny minority, who have done outrageous things, who've misbehaved outrageously and who've been allowed to persist in their misbehaviour. For example, two children, Simon, a white boy, and Jane, a West Indian girl, are two children who have disturbed and disrupted this school ever since they came. Although we have tried hard with Jane, we have not succeeded . . . in keeping her calm and amenable and pleasant, as she can be. She is capable of a public display of aggression . . . I think that the actions of such children within a class, it can be within a class or publicly in corridors, is sufficient to worry teachers, and disturb them, and make them feel that within the school that is a sufficient threat to affect them psychologically, and I think that this militates against the good work of a school. It prevents teachers collectively and individually from doing their best. Such children because we have failed with them, and it's been apparent that we are not succeeding, despite massive efforts. . . . Teachers even if they don't teach them know of them, and rumours spread in school – it's not just the ordinary cynicism that you get among staff, rumours spread. I think that's worth a good study, the way in which teachers are affected by rumour.

The two comments do to an extent acknowledge the estranged relationship between teachers and certain groups of pupils. However they see this as being inherent in the pupil with the teacher as the recipient. They suggest also that categorization of pupils' behaviour, and the influence of 'informal gossip' among staff on teacher's judgements is part of the 'hidden curriculum' in this school.

Contrary to the views expressed here by the two deputy heads, conversations with other teachers suggested that the issue of 'race' was frequently the basis of the conflict between some Afro-Caribbean pupils and their teachers. An Asian teacher who had taught at the school for six years stated:

> There is a lot of racism in the school and I have often believed that a lot of multicultural talk should start with the staff before it starts with the pupils. There is little racism amongst the children . . . I, even as a friend and a colleague of the staff notice it strongly in little points of racism, all the time constantly there, it gets beyond a joke, I've lost friends in the school or I don't associate with certain members of staff purely because of the constant jibbing which eventually gets beyond a joke.

This teacher's annoyance was reiterated by a white teacher who related his experience of the school when he took up his post seven years before:

> I had kept fairly quiet while I tried to establish myself and gauge the atmosphere of the school. Even so, I had some fairly sharp differences with several members over their attitude towards the coloured pupils. There were fairly frequent serious and 'humorous' comments made in the staff room and at the dinner table that I sometimes challenged. One or two other teachers were encouraged by my willingness to argue against racial prejudice and became more vocal themselves. On reflection, racialist comments are much less common now, in my presence at least.

A teacher who had been at the school for two years added credence to the points already raised, stating that there is 'racism' amongst staff within the school:

Teacher:	Definitely I have come across incidents where I have actually seen teachers pick on children for no other reasons than the colour of their skin.
Researcher:	What evidence have you to support this?
Mr M (year head):	For example, I had a great verbal battle with him over a West Indian girl called June Green who I teach. She was a bit troublesome and still is to some teachers. She was a bit trouble-

some to me to begin with but I soon cottoned on to the fact that it wasn't her but the girl she was sitting next to in the class. When I cottoned on to that I started to encourage June, sitting her on her own, it took me a long, long time, she is a very sensitive girl.

Now I can get her to virtually do anything for me. She's great. She is still a bit shy but she's tremendous with me. Mr X wrote me a note 'would I make some notes on her, there is a possibility of her going into the unit' [withdrawal unit for disruptive pupils]. I wrote back and said no way did I think that she ought to go into the unit. He came back to me, went on about her being West Indian and all that. I said to him on what grounds did you want to put her in the unit. He said 'she's a trouble-maker.' I said to him you just don't go and put a child in the unit because she is a trouble-maker. Of course, she has not been the only case. In each case it has been a West Indian pupil rather than an Asian child.

Researcher: Well, you have only referred to one teacher.

Teacher: I have not come across such blatant attitudes amongst other members of staff but I would get that feeling, and if I can being white, feel an atmosphere like that, then the children can too, especially if their skins are black.

So far we have reported Afro-Caribbean pupils' perceptions of the attitudes held by certain teachers and how this may influence their behaviour. We need now to assess the extent to which the pupils' experience may affect their educational opportunities.

There is concern within the school about the relative underachievement of pupils – especially among the Afro-Caribbean group. This point is illustrated by the Head of the sixth form, who describes the composition of the sixth form:

Head of sixth: This year they're mostly Indians, this is the largest ethnic group of people who stay on to the sixth form, followed by the white children, then the Pakistani and West Indian in very small numbers.

Researcher: Why is the percentage of Afro-Caribbean

Head of sixth:

pupils staying on in the sixth form so low?
Now I was asked this at my interview and what was I going to do about it. I don't know. I think to try and break down the barriers that some of the West Indian children have against teachers and academic things . . . I find them all delightful in the first and second year, something happens between the second year and the fourth year, and in the fourth year they seem to have lost interest in academic things. I don't find them any less delightful, but they don't seem as interested in academic things.

This observation was supported by another teacher's statement:

There's no specific area that I can lay my finger on to explain why West Indian kids underachieve . . . what is inevitable is that a lot of West Indian children particularly the bright ones will do fairly well up to either the beginning or the middle of the fourth year, and for some peculiar reason their progress will fall off towards the end of the fifth year. There's no deterioration in intelligence or anything like that, the intelligence is there. The hard work is missing, the motivation is missing the need to get on is missing and the exam results inevitably suffer from that.

Conversations with Afro-Caribbean pupils suggest that they, like the Afro-Caribbean pupils at school A, believe that teachers held low expectations of their academic performance. However, unlike the pupils at school A, they saw the organization of the school as having little influence on their educational opportunities, with attitudes of the teachers being paramount, and concluded that the prevailing attitudes held by certain teachers would undermine the organization of any school. As one pupil commented:

Some coloured children in this school are getting bad because of the way they get treated, and they make out as if we're just doing it because we get low examination grades so we start getting bad with the teachers. They think it is because we got no sense. We're acting like that because of the way we're treated in the past throughout the school. See if you know that Mrs — and Mrs — can get away with talking about your colour and that knowing there's not a thing you can do about it because they don't believe you.

An Afro-Caribbean boy suggests that pupils can be aware that the acquisition of an adverse label in the school may influence the teacher's expectation of academic ability:

A teacher called Mrs Z she has even said it to us herself that she wants all the black people out of the school. If a black pupil comes to see her a few times she automatically labels them as troublemakers. If anything happens in a crowd their names are always shouted out, so they're labelled in front of the teachers as a bad person. So then the teachers think if he is like that he's not worth the trouble.

From such observations and discussions in both schools, it appeared that the relationship between Afro-Caribbean pupils and teachers was often one of conflict and that the issue of race was frequently central to this conflict. In school A from about the third form (as the headmaster pointed out) black pupils became aware of negative attitudes they felt that the school held towards them. Similarly in school B teachers became aware of the barriers between the pupils and the teachers from the second year onwards. The perceived attitudes of teachers seemed to convince them that the school system was 'rigged': some saw very little point in trying.

Many were still frustrated by what they saw as not 'getting on' academically. From conversations, it appeared that they were not against education *per se*; in fact a number of them had left school to go to further education. However in school their energy was not always tapped so was sometimes directed towards disrupting the school or, as one pupil said: 'to get our own back on them for the way they have treated us'. [. . .]

DISCUSSION

This chapter, based on an ethnographic case study of only two schools, has presented evidence which indicates that the low achievement of some of their ethnic minority adolescents is linked with the procedures of the schools and that these procedures may be causal or at least powerful determinants of pupil effort, performance and attitude. We emphasize again that there is no suggestion that these schools, their teachers or their pupils are representative. Similarly, there is no suggestion that they are unrepresentative. [. . .]

Evidence has been offered to suggest that within the classroom [. . .]
complex processes may be involved which can disadvantage black young people and, in this study, particularly those of Afro-Caribbean origin. These conclusions are compatible with evidence available from other sources. Tomlinson (1981), for example, in a detailed study of assignment to special schools concluded that 'The position of ethnic

minority young people in special education, particularly those of West Indian origin, is one of the clearest indications that this type of education does not exist solely to cater for the needs of individual children, but is related to the way particular groups are regarded as potentially troublesome to schools and society.'[4] [. . .]

It is tempting but over-simplified to blame teachers. We have tried to report both their difficulties and their perceptions. The educational psychologist [. . .] (who had made some serious criticisms) sought to contextualize rather than retract some previous statements:

> In retrospect I feel I said some harsh things about the situation at school B. I hope my comments will not be misunderstood, but taken in context. I was not in any way intending to blame teachers directly for the situation. Rather I was trying to present arguments from the child's point of view since teachers are able to present their own case and the children I deal with are often not articulate enough to do so.

Yet a comment by a year head in one of the study schools expresses that there is a real difficulty:

> I have also had members of staff who have actually said that perhaps some child has not been treated the same as another child because they're black. A member of staff only recently said 'If that child wasn't black he wouldn't be in trouble, he wouldn't be in the situation that he's in because the reaction of a certain member of the staff would have been different'. And when a member of staff says that, to which I could make no comment, I just said to the staff 'Well I'm sorry, if you want to take that up, you must take it up with the person concerned not me'. This is the real problem which sometimes is there and sometimes isn't.

In this case and others, possible racial disadvantage is seen as an individual matter to be handled by informal and individual means, and not within the official structure of the school. Yet if pupils face disciplinary procedures arising in part out of racial issues they are confronted by the full authority structure of the school, wherein individual teachers may be given full support by their colleagues at all levels.

We have discussed informal gossip among teachers but not similar gossip amongst pupils or communities at large. All teachers know that classroom incidents and disciplinary procedures are a major focus of conversation among schoolchildren. This knowledge is rapidly and widely spread, particularly if children have, or believe they have, been treated unfairly. If pupils discern a repeated pattern of injustice, discontent may well become general among the pupils affected and come to have a lowering effect on the whole life and work of the school.

REFERENCES

Hargreaves, D. (1967) *Social Relations in a Secondary School*, London: Routledge & Kegan Paul.

Goffman, E. (1971) *Relations in Public*, Harmondsworth: Penguin.

Tomlinson, S. (1981) *Educational Subnormality: a Study in Decision Making*, London: Routledge & Kegan Paul.

Chapter 11

Case not proven

An evaluation of a study of teacher racism

Peter Foster

Source: An edited extract of Foster, P. (1991) 'Cases not proven: an evaluation of two studies of teacher racism', *British Educational Research Journal* 16(4): 335–49.

In recent years there has been continued concern amongst educationalists and members of ethnic minority communities about the alienation and underachievement of many ethnic minority students, especially those of Afro-Caribbean origin. In explaining these phenomena increasing emphasis has been placed on the role of racism within schools. It has been suggested that many teachers have negative attitudes towards such students and low expectations of their future academic performance; that, as a result, they treat them less favourably in the classroom and in wider school processes, denying them the educational opportunities enjoyed by their white peers; and that many therefore experience alienation, low academic achievement and consequently restricted life chances.

A small number of studies conducted in the 1970s shed some light on these ideas. Following a postal survey of 510 teachers, Brittan (1976) concluded that a number had negative, stereotyped views of Afro-Caribbean students. Unfortunately her evidence, which consisted of the fact that teachers were more likely to make definite and negative responses to statements on a Likert scale about Afro-Caribbean students, and that an unspecified number of teachers made what she considered 'racist' comments on the questionnaire, was rather sketchy. Giles (1977), after researching in a number of London schools, concluded that there were 'subtle and overt forms of discrimination taking place . . . resulting from teachers' attitudes and behaviour . . . towards West Indian students' (p. 75), but failed to provide much evidence to substantiate his claims. Tomlinson (1979) interviewed thirty Birmingham headteachers and found that they tended to describe Afro-Caribbean students in negative ways. However, it was not clear from her study whether heads were describing the characteristics of Afro-Caribbean students they knew or whether they saw all such students in negative terms.[1] In an ethnographic study of an inner city secondary school Hammersley (1980) recorded a considerable amount of racism towards ethnic minority students in staffroom talk, but noted that this did not appear to result in discrimination in the classroom. Finally, Driver (1979), in his ethnographic study of a secondary school, found that many teachers responded to their Afro-Caribbean students with uncertainty and confusion, which he claims was the result of a lack of cultural awareness rather than negative or racist attitudes.

These studies provide rather inconclusive evidence on which to assess the ideas outlined above. However, over the past few years three important empirical studies have claimed to uncover more substantial evidence which appears to support them. The first was a study conducted by Peter Green (1983) which attempted to examine the relationship between teachers' racial attitudes and interaction patterns in multiethnic classrooms (amongst other things). The second was a study of 'West Indian' involvement in extracurricular sport in a northern comprehensive school by Bruce Carrington and Edward Wood (Carrington 1983; Carrington and Wood 1983). The third was a study of the experiences and progress of Afro-Caribbean students in two Midlands comprehensives conducted by Cecile Wright (Chapter 10) which was part of a wider study of the transition from school to work of ethnic minority young people conducted by Eggleston *et al.* (1986).

In this paper I intend to examine the latter study. [. . .][2] Wright's research has been widely quoted as illustrating the ways in which teacher racism and within-school processes can influence the academic performance of Afro-Caribbean students (see, for example, Carter and Williams 1987; Rex 1989; Troyna and Carrington, 1989). Carter and Williams, for example, claim that Wright's work 'demonstrated clearly and concretely' 'the role of racism and discrimination' in the schools she studied. Unfortunately, there has been a tendency to accept this study at face value rather than to examine it critically. My argument is that, on close scrutiny, it suffers from serious methodological weaknesses and biases which mean that its conclusions must be viewed with some scepticism. In my view the evidence it presents to support its conclusion that Afro-Caribbean students were significantly disadvantaged by processes occurring within the schools studied is decidedly weak. I must emphasize at the outset that I am not denying that there may be practices in some schools which disadvantage such students, but I am questioning whether this study, which claims to reveal them, has actually done so. [. . .]

CECILE WRIGHT – 'SCHOOL PROCESSES: AN ETHNOGRAPHIC STUDY'

Wright's argument is as follows:

1 In the two schools she studied teachers had negative and hostile attitudes to Afro-Caribbean students.
2 As a result they treated them in an insensitive and inferior way.
3 Because of this treatment Afro-Caribbean students developed antagonistic views of their teachers and behaved badly in school. Anti-teacher, anti-school and somewhat anti-white subcultures tended to develop amongst these students. [. . .]

First, let us look at the evidence she presents about teacher attitudes. Wright actually gives little direct evidence, from her own observations or from teacher talk, of negative or hostile attitudes to minority students or their culture. She quotes one teacher from school B who claims that a 'high proportion of immigrants is responsible for the lowering of standards' and another who feels 'English culture is being swamped', but apart from this she relies almost completely on inform-ants' accounts. These are of two types. First, she quotes a number of teachers who make generalized comments about the attitudes of other staff; and, second, she quotes comments about teachers from dis-cussions with Afro-Caribbean students.

In school A she quotes the views of one black teacher that Afro-Caribbean students are seen, by an unspecified number of other teachers, as a 'problem' and as 'intellectually inferior'; and the views of another teacher that 'West Indian kids tend to get labelled' in staffroom talk. In school B she quotes a teacher who claims that 'the attitudes of teachers to West Indian and Asian cultures is at worst negative, and at best condescending and patronizing', an Asian teacher who complained of 'a lot of racism in the school' (but who does not specify what he or she means by racism), a year head who describes a complaint from a parent about a teacher who had told her child to 'go back where you came from and where you belong', and a white teacher who complained that 'several' staff told racist jokes when he first came to the school seven years previously. She also quotes a teacher who said that he/she had observed incidents in which 'teachers pick on children for no other reason than the colour of their skin', but who, when asked to provide illustrations, presents a case which does not appear to substantiate his/her claim.[3]

Now there may be some substance to these views, but there are several problems with relying on this data. First, the informants give few actual instances to support their generalizations. Secondly, the data are from a relatively small number of teachers – two in the case of school A and five in the case of school B (and one of these – the year head – says little about teacher attitudes in general). One teacher in school B actually contradicts the views of the others quoted and claims that Afro-Caribbean students are treated fairly within the school, but Wright chooses not to treat this as an accurate judgement of the situation. Thirdly, informants' accounts are often unreliable and biased (see Dean and Whyte 1958). The evidence on which they base their conclusions may be weak, and their generalizations may be influenced by their particular values and viewpoints, and their position in the school. What they say may also be influenced by their perception of the interviewer (in this case an Afro-Caribbean woman). Wright appears to have done little to check the reliability and validity of these informants' accounts, by, for example, comparing their perceptions with those of a wider sample of teachers. She accepts their conclusions without question, perhaps because they fit in well with her overall thesis.

The second type of informants' account used by Wright is from students themselves. For both schools she quotes from a number of group discussions with Afro-Caribbean students who accuse teachers of having hostile and negative attitudes to them and treating them unfairly. Clearly *some* Afro-Caribbean students thought that teachers were hostile and treated them unfairly. But again there are problems in relying on these data to draw the conclusion that hostility and unfair treatment actually were significant features of the interaction between teachers and Afro-Caribbean students.

First, a relatively small number of students are quoted and we do not know whether their views were representative of all Afro-Caribbean students. Wright implies that they were, but does not give us any information about how she selected the students which would enable us to judge. Secondly, we do not know if the students' interpretations of hostility and unfair treatment were accurate. They may have felt badly treated, but this may not have been the case in reality. One might speculate that, given the conflictual nature of much teacher–student interaction in school and the relative powerlessness of students, there is a strong possibility that they might perceive unfair treatment which might not be seen as such by a more 'objective' observer. Moreover, even if these particular students had been unfairly treated this may not have been because they were black. One wonders if a sample of white students might have had similar views of their teachers' behaviour. Thirdly, there seems to be a tendency for the students quoted to generalize about teachers on the basis of a small number of incidents in which they felt they were treated badly. Again, we must question the validity of these generalizations. It seems a possibility that the students' generally negative attitudes to school are being expressed in terms of teacher racism (cf. Foster 1990). In other words, accusations of teacher hostility and unfair treatment are being used as a way of expressing anti-school attitudes. It must be likely that the incidence of such hostility and unfair treatment becomes exaggerated amongst such students or that what is perceived as unfair treatment, as 'being picked on', is, in fact, merely teacher response to bad behaviour which would have occurred whether the students were Afro-Caribbean or white. Indeed, I would suggest that the group interview situation that Wright used would be likely to facilitate this. Perhaps few students would want to be seen as pro-teacher or pro-school in such a situation. It is interesting also to note that in one discussion a student implies that 'on the whole' teachers are not like the two who are accused by the rest of the group of hostility and unfairness, but Wright, chairing the discussion, does not explore this idea, choosing instead to steer the students back to talking about the effect of teacher hostility and unfairness.

On the question of teacher treatment of Afro-Caribbean students in the classroom Wright again provides little direct evidence of hostility or inferior treatment. She gives one example of what she terms 'insensitivity' towards Afro-Caribbean students which consists of an argument between a white teacher and Afro-Caribbean students about whether a remark previously made by the teacher could be considered offensive. Apart from this, she relies mainly on the students' accounts discussed above. This lack of direct evidence seems to be rather surprising after '900 hours' of observation in each school where conflict and hostility between teachers and Afro-Caribbean students were supposedly common.

Wright goes on to argue that Afro-Caribbean students in the two schools developed antagonistic views (she does not say how many Afro-Caribbean students had such views) towards school *in response* to their teachers' hostility and unfair treatment – that the conflictual nature of the relationship between teachers and Afro-Caribbean students derives primarily from the teachers' negative treatment. Here, again, she relies almost totally on her student informants to substantiate this view. These accounts, as I have explained, must be interpreted with some caution. What seems to me to be equally plausible is that the anti-school attitudes of Afro-Caribbean students have their origins outside the school in the social structural situation of Afro-Caribbean communities and the poor post-school prospects of such students. Anti-school attitudes might be imported into the school situation and result in behaviour which is antagonistic to white teachers, which may, of course, serve to create the perceived counter hostility of white teachers who have to deal with such behaviour and the threat to school order that it poses (cf. Willis 1977; Weis 1985). Wright appears to have accepted uncritically the views of the students she interviewed. Indeed, she seems to have lost the detachment which is important in good ethnographic work and adopted their perspective on the school as a central part of her thesis. [. . .]

[In short], then, the data presented by Wright do not, in my judgement, give strong support for her view that 'many members of staff' in the two schools had negative and hostile attitudes to Afro-Caribbean students and that consequently there were practices in operation within the school which disadvantaged Afro-Caribbean students.

CONCLUSION

[. . .]

[This study has] been used by other writers to support the theory that within-school processes play a major part in the reproduction of racial inequalities in educational achievement. Indeed, there has been an increasing emphasis on this view in recent years. In presenting a critique of the study, I have raised a number of questions about some of the evidence which is put forward to support these ideas. In my view, teacher racism in this study is something of an artefact, and its claims should not have been as easily accepted as they have been. It would, of course, be impossible to provide evidence which established beyond all possible doubt that a significant number of teachers had negative attitudes towards Afro-Caribbean students and treated them less favourably than white students, and that such treatment was a major cause of their relative underachievement. But, in my view, we need far more convincing evidence than is provided by this study if we are to accept such ideas.

Whilst I concede that processes which occur within classrooms and schools *may* be significant factors in the reproduction of racial inequality in education, this study has failed to demonstrate that they are. Indeed, generally there is very little evidence of teacher racism and that such racism causes racial inequality in education. I think in all probability we will have to look beyond within-school processes to the economic, social and cultural disadvantages faced by many ethnic minority students, and to differences between the schools attended by them and their white peers, if we are to discover the most significant factors. Unfortunately there has been a tendency to neglect these issues in recent discussions in favour of a preference for scapegoating teachers.

In policy terms an emphasis on the importance of within-school processes in creating racial inequality in educational achievement has led many Local Education Authorities to encourage teachers (compelled in the case of some 'racism awareness' courses) to reflect on their attitudes and review their practices in order to 'confront and eradicate racism' in the words of one LEA policy statement (Manchester LEA 1985). There is nothing wrong with such reviews in themselves. Teachers should ensure that they treat students fairly and in a non-racist way. But, given that there is little evidence of teacher racism, it may be difficult for teachers to actually find practices to 'confront and eradicate', and the value of giving such reviews a high priority is questionable. Such an approach may even create hostility amongst some teachers who feel they are being falsely accused of malpractice (see Foster 1990). A concentration on within-school processes has also tended to give the impression that racial inequalities in educational achievement can be eliminated by changing teacher attitudes and practices. This seems unlikely if the source of such inequality lies outside the school gates.

ACKNOWLEDGEMENTS

I would like to thank Martyn Hammersley and Barry Troyna for their valuable comments on earlier drafts of this paper. However, Barry Troyna does not support the arguments expressed.

NOTES

1 Troyna and Carrington (1989) have questioned the ethics of some of the research methods used by Brittan and Tomlinson (and other researchers in this area) which they argue may have encouraged respondents to articulate racial and ethnic stereotypes.
2 Editors' note: in the original article Foster discusses the work of both Wright and Carrington and Wood. He also deals with some aspects of Wright's work not included in the edited version published in this volume.
3 The teacher describes a disagreement between him/herself and a year head about whether a West Indian girl should be allocated to a withdrawal unit for disruptive students. He/she implies that the year head's decision to place the girl in the unit was based on race, but gives no evidence to support this view.

REFERENCES

Brittan, E. M. (1976) 'Multi-racial education: teacher opinion on aspects of school life, part one', *Educational Research*, 18(2): 96–107.
Carrington, B. (1983) 'Sport as a side-track: an analysis of West Indian involvement in extracurricular sport', in L. Barton and S. Walker (eds) *Race, Class and Education*, Beckenham: Croom Helm.
Carrington, B. and Wood, E. (1983) 'Body talk', *Multiracial Education* 11(2): 29–38.
Carter, B. and Williams, J. (1987) 'Attacking racism in education', in B. Troyna (ed.) *Racial Inequality in Education*, London: Tavistock.

Dean, J. P. and Whyte, W. F. (1958) 'How do you know if the informant is telling the truth?', in G. J. McCall and J. L. Simmons (1969) (eds) *Issues in Participant Observation*, Reading, Mass.: Addison-Wesley.

Driver, G. (1979) 'Classroom stress and school achievement: West Indian adolescents and their teachers', in V. S. Khan (ed.) *Minority Families in Britain: Support and Stress*, London: Macmillan.

Eggleston, J., Dunn, D. and Anjali, M. (1986) *Education for Some: the Educational and Vocational Experiences of 15–18 year old Members of Minority Ethnic Groups*, Stoke-on-Trent: Trentham Books.

Foster, P. (1990) *Policy and Practice in Multicultural and Anti-racist Education: a Case Study of a Multi-ethnic Comprehensive School* London: Routledge.

Giles, R. (1977) *The West Indian Experience in British Schools: Multi-Racial Education and Social Disadvantage in London*, London: Heinemann.

Green, P. A. (1983) 'Teachers' influence on the self-concept of pupils of different ethnic origins', unpublished PhD thesis, University of Durham.

Hammersley, M. (1980) 'A peculiar world? Teaching and learning in an inner city school', unpublished PhD thesis, University of Manchester.

Manchester LEA (1985) *Policy Statement on Racism*, Manchester LEA.

Rex, J. (1989) 'Equality of opportunity, multiculturalism, anti-racism and "Education for All" ', in G. K. Verma (ed.) *Education for All: a Landmark in Pluralism*, London: Falmer Press.

Tomlinson, S. (1979) 'Decision-making in special education ESN(M): with some reference to children of immigrant parentage', unpublished PhD thesis, University of Warwick.

Troyna, B. and Carrington, B. (1989) 'Whose side are we on? Ethical dilemmas in research on "race" and education', in R. Burgess (ed.) *The Ethics of Educational Research*, Lewes: Falmer Press.

Weis, L. (1985) *Between Two Worlds: Black Students in an Urban Community College*, London: Routledge & Kegan Paul.

Willis, P. (1977) *Learning to Labour: How Working Class Kids Get Working Class Jobs*, Aldershot: Gower.

Wright, C. (1986) 'School processes: an ethnographic study', in J. Eggleston. D. Dunn and M. Anjali (eds) *Education for Some: the Educational and Vocational Experiences of 15–18 year old Members of Minority Ethnic Groups*, Stoke-on-Trent: Trentham Books.

Index

accommodation 41, 162; and resistance, by black pupils 151–4
accounts of racism in schools, unreliability of 219
Acker, S. 36
adult roles, games as a rehearsal for 19–21, 24
Afro-Caribbean culture 146, 147–8, 156, 161, 202
Afro-Caribbean pupil–teacher relationships 195–6, 199, 203–13
Afro-Carribean students 146, 148, 195, 197, 202; anti-school feeling of 147–8, 198–201, 220–1; families of 146, 158; social division of 147; teachers' attitudes to 216–17, 220; underachievement of 146–7, 158, 211–13
Aggleton, P. 162
anti-school attitudes 147–8, 198–201, 218; expressed in terms of teacher racism 220
Anyon, J. 151, 159, 161
Apple, M. 36
Arnot, M. 36
art 36, 40
Asian culture 146, 156, 161, 202, 203
Asian pupils 146, 148, 211; anti-school attitudes of 148; families of 146; friendship preferences of 131, 132, 135, 137, 143
attention-seeking 112; by boys 46, 107, 108, 120, 121
autobiography 180–7

Barker, M. 149
Barratt, D. 161

behaviour 197, 209; effect of racist attitudes on 200–2, 207, 211
Bernstein, B. 27
bilingual children, teaching of 175, 176–7, 188
black community: racism and 149; unity of 157–8
Black Sisters 151–2, 153, 154–5, 157
black students: attitude to school of 147–8, 197–8, 218; culture of 146, 147, 156–7; perceived as being responsible for declining standards 194–5; schooling of 145, 146, 159, 160; see also Afro-Caribbean students; Asian students
Bourdieu, P. 189
Bourne, J. 149
boys: attention-seeking by see attention-seeking; attitude of to girls' behaviour at school 43; attitude of to school uniform 67, 68; dominance of 37, 46, 47, 53–9, 71; domination of lessons by, in primary school 96, 97, 104, 106, 107; ethnicity and friendship choices of 135, 136; playground play of 12, 18, 23–4; quietness of 41, 42; teachers' attention and 95, 96, 97, 107, 108, 114, 119, 120; testing of teachers by 83–5
Braha, V. 131, 141
Brice-Heath, S. 29
Brittan, E. M. 140, 141, 216, 222
Brophy, J. E. 95
Bruner, J. S. 27
Burgess, R. G. 51, 85
Buswell, C. 34

Carrington, B. 217, 222
Carter, B. 217
catering 44, 45
Centuries of Childhood (Aries) 19
challenge 25–7
chi-squared tests of significance 128, 131, 136, 141
clapping games 16–17, 24, 28, 30
Clarricoates, K. 96
Cohen, P. 157
common underlying proficiency 175–7
competition between the sexes 63–4
comprehensive schools 192, 193
computer studies 37, 38, 44
conflict: between teachers and Afro-Caribbean pupils 195–6, 202, 204–8, 210, 213; between teachers and working class pupils 75, 76
Connell, R. W. 159
conservatism, in secondary schools 45
containment, of unruly pupils 86–8
conventions 167, 172–3
corrections, made to work by ethnic minority pupils 168–9, 170–1, 177, 181, 182, 184
Criswell, J. 130–1
Criswell Index 128, 131, 136, 141
cultural differences 149, 156; in story telling 169, 178; and teacher–pupil interactions 77, 79–85
cultural-linguistic diversity 178, 187, 189
cultural reproduction 188, 189
Cummins, J. 175, 176

Dale, R. 159
Dalphinis, M. 166, 173
Davey, A. G. 131, 140
Davies, B. 24, 25
Davies, L. 36, 40, 79, 80
Delamont, S. 45
discrimination 216
dominant culture 89, 186, 189, 203
Driver, G. 217
'Duggie Diggers' 86–8
Durojaiye, M. 140, 141

employment patterns 39
enginering drawing 38
Ervin-Tripp, S. 29
establishment, process of 52–3

ethnic bias in friendship choice 128, 130, 131–2, 137
ethnicity, perceived as a handicap 146
Everhart, R. 45

female gender roles, in the classroom 65–6
female peer groups, at primary school 16, 18, 26, 29–30
femininity as resistance 82–3
fieldwork, 129, 154–6
football 23–4
Forsyth, E. 132
French J. and P. 113, 114, 115, 118, 119, 120, 121, 122
friendship: ethnicity and 127–42; in primary schools 24–5, 27, 28
friendship choice, sociomatrices of 132–6
friendship patterns: observation of 136–9; quantitative analyses of 130–2

Galton, M. 95
games, in playground 12–14; *see also* clapping games; singing games
Garfinkel, H. 112
Gaskell, J. 39
gender identity 50, 68, 69, 70
gender relations: competition and 63–4; in science 61–3
gender segregation, voluntary 36–7
gender stereotyping: of abilities 36–8, 44; playground games as exploration of 22–3; of subjects 44–5
Genovese, E. 161
Giles, R. 216
Gilroy, P. 149, 162
girls: attitudes of to insults 54–6; attitude of to male teachers' sexism 91; boys ignoring of 56–7; coping with boys' sexual behaviour 57–8; ethnicity and attitude to school of 151–2, 154–5; ethnicity and friendship choices of 135–6; exploitation of weaknesses of soft teachers by 79–81; future expectations of 39; and gender roles in the classroom 65–6; participation in lessons by 115, 116, 117, 120; perception of sexuality of 59–60; playground play of 12, 13, 16–18, 19–24, 27, 29–30; quietness

of 41–2, 45–7; and school uniform 66–7; and teacher attention 114, 119; use of femininity with male teachers 82–3
Goffman, E. 200
Good, T. L. 95
Green, P. 217
Griffin, C. 53

hairstyles 69–70
Hall, S. 161
Hammersley, M. 216
Hargreaves, D. 196, 197
humour 4; and conflict of cultures 75, 91; use and meaning of 76–91

'I'm a little Dutch girl' 21
imperialism 156, 161
informal gossip: among pupils 214; among teachers 196–7, 210
institutional change, and process of establishment 52–3, 70–1
insults: used by boys to girls 54–5; used by teachers 90
interviews 51, 154, 192, 220

Jelinek, M. 140, 141
jewellery 68

Katz, L. 132
Kawwa, T. 140, 141
Kelly, A. 37, 44, 62
Kessler, S. 44, 45, 47

Lacey, C. 149, 150, 154
language 24; of games 27; of black students 152, 200–1
language skills 175, 176, 177
languages, preferred by girls 37, 40, 44, 45
Lawrence, E. 153
Lévi-Strauss, C. 92
Liebow, E. 148
linguistic diversity 169, 172–3
linguistic repertoires 187, 188
Llewellyn, M. 151

Mahoney, P. 53, 62
make-up 68–9
marriage, as an alternative to a career 39
maths 36, 44

Measor, L. 40, 61
methodological research 146, 147
Meyenn, R. J. 147, 153
mining communities 75, 78–9
Mitchell-Kernan, C. 29
Monk, M. J. 36, 40
Moore, R. 155
motherhood, girls' plays about 20
Mullin, P. N. 131, 140
multiculturalism 176, 210

nicknames 53–4

observation 51, 154; of pupils' friendship choices 129–30, 136–9, 142
Opie I. and P. 13, 16, 18, 22, 24; The Singing Game 19, 21
oral tradition 13, 14; of Asian culture 174, 178, 179

parents 45; of black children 156–9
Parker, H. J. 155
participant observer 130, 154
participation of pupils 115–19
Patois 200–1
pedagogy 169, 173, 174, 178, 188
peer group relationships 24, 29
penis size, boys' preoccupation with 59, 60
play, gender separation in 12–13
playground culture 11, 14, 16, 18–19, 27–30
playground games 13–14
plays 20
Pollard, A. 51
primary schools: ethnicity and friendship choices in 127–42; gender imbalances of teacher attention in 95–108; playground culture of 12–30
puberty, difficulties arising from 38–9
pupils, moving from single-sex to mixed schools 50, 52–3, 63, 70–1

qualitative research 145–60
quantitative analysis of friendship patterns 130–2, 136, 141
questionnaires 51, 154
quietness, of girls 3, 34, 35, 37, 40, 45–7; reasons for 41–2

race relations 146, 149

racial inequality in educational achievement 221–2

racial integration, revealed by observation 138–9

racial prejudice, pupils' perceptions of 203, 204–5, 206–7

racialism 149

racism: and class and gender 155, 159; resistance to 153, 157, 158–9; in schools 149, 150, 160, 200, 203, 210, 216

racist jokes 196, 199

racist stereotyping 150–1, 216

Rasta Heads 147–8, 152, 157

religious knowledge 38

reproduction 88, 92, 94

research 92

resistance to school 41, 56, 75–6, 79, 80, 162; and accommodation, of black students 151–4; avoidance of 85–8; and counter-resistance by staff 89–91; rhymes as 25–6; smoking as 43; use of femininity as 82–3

retaliation: fear of 56–7; language of playground games as means of 23, 25–6

rhymes 15–16; as resistance to playground power relations 25–6; rudeness of 22; see also songs, playground

Riddell, S. 53

Romaine, S. 29

Rowley, K. 140

Runciman, W. G. 92

Rutter, D. R. 131, 141

school mergers 49–50, 70–1, 192–4

school organisation, effect of on pupils' behaviour 197–8

school uniform 35, 36, 66–8

science 36, 37, 44, 45; gender relations in 61–3

second-language development 175

secondary schools: gender stereotyping in 45; mergers of 49–50, 70–1, 192–4

'self': boys and 71; girls and 71; status passages and 50; uniform and 68

self-esteem 70

sex education 61

sexism 90–1, 93, 155, 159

sexist behaviour, by boys 56–9

sexuality: flaunted by boys 58; flaunted by girls 57–8; perceptions of 59–61

singing games 20, 21, 30

single-sex schools: culture of 53; former staff of 192–3, 193–4, 195; merger of 49–50, 62, 66–7, 71, 192–4

Sivanandan, A. 149, 158

smoking 42–3

socialization, playground culture as 13, 19, 24–5

sociomatrices, of friendship choice 132–6

sociometric analysis of friendship 130–6, 139–40, 141–2

sociometric tests 128–9, 130–1; validity of 140–1

songs, playground 13, 14–15, 16–17, 31–3; gender specificity of 18

Spender, D. 95, 96, 108, 122

Stanworth, M. 40, 46, 95, 96

status passages 49, 50, 70

Steedman, C. 19, 20

Stevenson, R. L. 21

Stewart, S. 25

story writing by ethnic minority pupils 168–72, 173–4, 178, 179, 189

streaming, black pupils and 198

style, criticisms of 169, 171–4

subculture, of Afro-Caribbean students 147–8, 200–1

subjects, gender differentiation in 36–7, 39–40, 44

Sutton-Smith, B. 28

symbolic violence 189

teacher attention 114, 115, 121–2; differential distribution of 95, 107–8, 114, 119–20; measurement of 117–18

teacher-pupil interactions 52, 99–106, 111, 118; in drafting stories 168–73, 181–2, 184, 185–6; ethnicity and 150–1; gender imbalance of 96, 97, 107–8, 115, 116–17, 119, 121

teacher-researcher 50–2

teachers: attitude of to ethnic minority pupils 195–201, 202–6, 208–13, 216, 218, 220; attitudes of to pupils' sexual behaviour 58–9; attitudes of to quiet girls 40, 46;

categorised by pupils 76–7; conflict with working-class culture 85–8, 89–91; control of pupil participation 93, 104, 106; frustrations of, in comprehensive schools 192–3; gender stereotyping by 45; perceived racism of 196, 213, 216–22; perceptions of black students 148, 150–1; perceptions of ethnicity and friendship in primary schools 127–8, 139, 141; questioning of previous learning experiences of ethnic minority pupils 166, 172–3; racist attitudes of 196, 198, 203, 204–5, 207, 210–11; seeming to favour boys 96, 108; seeming to favour girls 65–6; as target of playground rhymes 15; tested by working-class pupils 75, 76, 77–8, 79, 80–6
temperamental differences, between the sexes 38–9
testing, in mining communities 77–9
Tomlinson, S. 213, 216, 222
traditional attitudes 45
Troyna, B. 222
Turner, I. 27, 28
TVEI 44

underachievement: of ethnic minority students 146–7, 158, 211–12, 213–14, 216; by girls, teacher attention and 114, 122, 122n

validity, of accounts of teachers' racism 219–20
verbal abuse 54–6
vocational needs, gender and 39

Walkerdine, V. 25, 26
Waller, W. 154
Warriors, 148, 157
Weiss, L. 159
white pupils, friendship preferences of 131, 132, 135, 137–9
Whyte, W. F. 147, 148, 155
Williams, J. 217
Willis, P. 34, 92, 93, 189
Wood, E. 217
Woods, P. 51, 76
woodwork 40, 44
working-class community 77–8; educational aspirations of 92
working-class culture 77–9, 88, 93; and school culture 75, 88–9, 92; teachers' response to 77, 79–88
Wright, C. 217, 218, 219, 220, 221

Young, M. F. D. 146